We Will Not Go to War

We Will Not Go to War

CONSCIENTIOUS OBJECTION *during* *the* WORLD WARS

Felicity Goodall

To Alan, Thomas and Stephen

First published as *A Question of Conscience* in 1997
This edition published in 2010

The History Press
The Mill, Brimscombe Port
Stroud, Gloucestershire, GL5 2QG
www.thehistorypress.co.uk

British Library Cataloguing in Publication Data.
A catalogue record for this book is available from the British Library.

ISBN 978 0 7524 5857 1

Typesetting and origination by The History Press
Printed in Great Britain

Contents

Foreword

It has been claimed that great causes inevitably need a literature, if not to initiate them, certainly to sustain them. As a Methodist I have long been convinced that Charles Wesley's hymns played as important a part in the Methodist Revival as did his brother John's sermons.

I am immediately convinced of the truth of this generalization when reading this collection of records of the stories of conscientious objectors in the First and Second World Wars.

As a pacifist I believe ever more urgently that the essential quality of the Christian Gospel is the imperative need for the recognition that conscientious objection to war lies at the heart of the spirit and teaching of Jesus. Indeed the story and example of such objectors, not all necessarily members of the Christian Church, are exponents of the living literature of the gospel of non-violence.

I welcome this publication not only as a testimony to the honesty and heroism which I witnessed when I spoke on behalf of many conscientious objectors in the Second World War. I welcome it because, in my experience, no commitment to pacifism is still so generally misunderstood if not totally derided. I welcome it even more, as over the years since the ending of the Second World War there has been a wishful longing for peace-making in many unexpected quarters. As far as my experience as an open-air preacher goes this is certainly true.

Evangelism against war and for peace today is useless unless it is rooted in the 'Way of the Cross' rather than the 'Way of the Gun'. I hope that the story of conscientious objectors will become part of the literature of hope in the total repudiation of mass violence, and that our fragile humanity can believe in general disarmament which can become increasingly possible only when we say, whatever it may cost, we will go to war no more. I welcome this book as a valuable contribution to this end.

The Revd The Lord Soper, 1997

One of a series of humourous postcards produced by the No-Conscription Fellowship.

Preface

This book is a series of snapshots from people's lives, told in their own words. It is not intended as a textbook, nor is it intended to be a history of conscientious objection in the two world wars. Instead I hope the reader will get a flavour of who these people were, and what it was like to question your conscience and decide not to participate in two world wars, wars which became the most momentous event in the lives of two generations.

Most of the information in this book has been gleaned from interviews with conscientious objectors, some has come from their unpublished memoirs, in a few cases I have quoted extracts from published letters or memoirs. The Imperial War Museum Sound Archive has been an invaluable source, especially as so many of these men and women are no longer alive. In all cases they told their stories with straightforwardness and honesty. I hope I have managed to retain this in the way I have woven their words together.

Introduction to the 2010 Edition

Since the 2003 invasion of Iraq, a handful of serving members of the armed forces have registered as conscientious objectors. Unlike the men and women in this book, these new 'conchies' are volunteers rather than conscripts, since military service was abolished in 1960.

Challenging military culture and standing up for a belief is as courageous in this century as it was in the last. But today the right to conscientious objection is recognised by the United Nations, and there is some public support – a million people marched to protest against the invasion of Iraq. In 1914 the picture was very different. War fever hit the streets as men queued to volunteer for the British army. Conscientious objection was seen as unpatriotic and cowardly, but many of those 'conchies' did serve as non-combatants in the trenches and were prepared to die. In accordance with their beliefs they were unarmed, and refused even to handle munitions. The penalty was to be shackled to the wheels of a gun carriage or 'crucified' against barbed wire. Those who went to prison, or who won exemption, were no less courageous in making a stand against the presiding culture of their day.

In 1939 a nation whose memory had been scarred by the Great War went to war with less enthusiasm, but the rise of the Third Reich threatened everything the British held dear. By the summer of 1940 Britain stood as the last bastion of western freedom, and every resource was pitched into the battle against the Nazi aggressor. Those who deviated from that overwhelming wartime spirit were regarded as highly suspect, unpatriotic, and even fifth columnists. Few could understand how men and women could deviate from the norm when Britain had its back to the wall. This new generation of conchies examined their consciences under a different light, some even put personal belief to one side. As Robert Kennedy said, 'Moral courage is a rarer commodity than bravery in battle.'

This is what makes the stance of First and Second World War conscientious objectors truly remarkable. To stand against the tide of public opinion armed only with your beliefs; to be divided from friends, family and even spouses by those beliefs; to be isolated from the defining experience of your generation. Few people have the courage not to follow the common herd.

Acknowledgements

Many people have given willingly of their time and memories in the preparation of this book and I am indebted to all of them. I am extremely grateful to Margaret Brooks and Rosemary Tudge at the Imperial War Museum Sound Archives for their help and patience during my research in the archives. I also owe a great debt to Sue Fry, who transcribed many of the interviews for me. This book would not have been possible without the help of many conscientious objectors and their relatives with whom I have been in contact. I would particularly like to mention Dr Eric Dott, Harold Holttum, Aubrey Brocklehurst, the late Edward Blishen, Leonard Bird, Frank Chadwick, the late Bernard Hicken, Tom Carlile, James Hanmer, Ronald Rice, Dennis Waters, Walter Wright, David Spreckley, Cecil Davies, Len Richardson, Olive Shaw, Meredith Edwards, Ernest Lenderyou, Gwen and Joan Bagwell, David and Margaret Jones, Joyce Millington, Maidwen Daniel, Rosalind Rusbridge, Iris Cooze, Dick Lindup, Ralph Bateman, Leslie White, Tony White, Stanley Rickman, Alan Litherland, Ted Parrish, Bill Nightingale, Frank Hoare, Tim Miles and Cedric Smith. I would also like to thank May Lovejoy, who generously lent me so many of her father's photographs and papers; Roy Blake, for giving me permission to quote from his father's memoirs; Edward Stanton, for allowing me to quote from his father's memoirs; Pleasaunce Holttum, for allowing me to quote from her father's letters; Stephen Peet, who not only lent me his parents' letters but much useful background material; Sidney Renow for giving me the pick of his enormous collection of photographs; Ken Shaw, for lending me his treasured photographs; Marjorie Wilson, for kindly lending me her husband's letters and diaries; Mrs Eaton, for permission to quote from her father-in-law's diary;

and Derek Severs, who lent me his uncle's papers. Thanks also go to Lord Soper, for his support and encouragement, Bill Hetherington at the Peace Pledge Union and to the library at Friends House. I would also like to thank Susan Roberts, my parents, and finally my husband and children who have put up with my repeated absences during the completion of this book.

Permission to quote from interviews with the following people was given by Margaret Brooks, keeper of the Imperial War Museum Sound Archives:

Dorothy Bing ref 555/9
Harold Bing ref 358/11
Fenner Brockway ref 476/4
Rachel Cadbury ref 10038/6
George Frederick Dutch ref 356/10
Alfred Evans ref 489/11
Howard Lloyd Fox ref 10173/4
Mark Hayler ref 357/28
Michael Rendel Harris ref 9325/12
John Marshall ref 10307/5
Howard Marten ref 383/6

While every effort has been made to trace all those whose stories appear in the book, if there are any omissions I can only apologize.

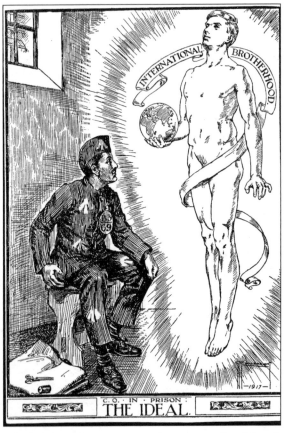

INTERNATIONAL BROTHERHOOD.

C.O. IN PRISON:
THE IDEAL.

Many COs spent years alone in prison cells with only an ideal for company.

CHAPTER 1

Individualists to the Core

On 2 March 1916, eighteen months after the onset of the First World War, British men became subject to conscription for the first time. Sixteen thousand of them chose to register as conscientious objectors and the word 'conchie' became a term of abuse. Reviled and scorned by the public, many of them were also maltreated by the military, some were even sentenced to death.

> *I remember telling somebody that if I was the only person in the world I would take this attitude. That's how I felt about it. It was a very personal thing.*
>
> *Howard Marten*

Transport yourself back to the summer of 1914, to a country largely without electricity and largely untouched by the omnipresent motor car. Every town and village is buzzing with the expectation of war and the anticipation of the glory to be won on the battlefield.

Harold Bing was a schoolboy in Croydon.

My attitude towards the war was of course critical from the start. This was very largely because I'd grown up in a pacifist home. My father as a young man had been very much influenced by his reading of Tolstoy, had become a pacifist, had opposed the Boer War and many of the friends whom he met and who came to our home were people who took that point of view. When I heard that a big anti-war demonstration was to be held in Trafalgar Square on Sunday the 2 August 1914 and Keir Hardie was to be one of the speakers, I walked from my home up to

Trafalgar Square – about eleven miles – took part in that demonstration, listened to Keir Hardie and walked home again afterwards which might have shown a certain amount of boyish enthusiasm for the anti-war cause. It was quite a thrilling meeting with about ten thousand people there and certainly very definitely anti-war. Of course at that very same time while we were demonstrating in Trafalgar Square the Cabinet was sitting at Downing Street discussing the entry of England into the war and deciding on the ultimatum which brought England into the war two days later on 4 August.

Howard Marten was another man with a pacifist pedigree – his father was a Quaker and he was brought up in a non-conformist atmosphere, like many conscientious objectors. As a schoolboy he had attended pacifist meetings during the Boer War.

I was as a boy always inclined to pacifist views. I could never side with the idea of martial violence. It didn't appeal to me at all; even as far back as the Boer War, I felt that that was inconsistent with our Christian beliefs. I was in school and enjoyed a certain amount of unpopularity even at that time, because of my pacifist views, and there was a good deal of violence in London towards what they called 'pro-Boers' – that was the epithet which was flung at pacifists. The Old Queen's Hall, which was bombed in the last war, was the scene of many meetings. That I think was my first experience of being personally involved in peace work, although my grandfather was the secretary and treasurer of a Kentish peace society, so that there was an aura of pacifism rather hanging over our family, and he did a lot of active work towards peace.

Harry Stanton was the son of a Luton blacksmith.

One had a growing sense of isolation, that one was surrounded by people who thought in different terms, who spoke, as it were, a different language. It seemed useless to discuss the war with them; their standards of conduct were depreciated, though they would refuse to acknowledge it. Yet to me the very isolation gave a strange sense of joy –

perhaps an expression of my combatant instinct! The facile taunts and innuendoes of the 'man in the street', provided daily by the leader writers of the popular press, had the effect of stiffening my resolution. And now and again as I met men and women whose convictions were leading them along the same unpopular course, came the feeling that here was something worth doing, that somehow we must hang on to this foundation of truth and sanity we had discovered, until the flood of passion and wrong thinking had subsided.

Fenner Brockway was an Independent Labour Party activist and editor of the *Labour Leader*, the organ of the ILP.

I remember the day war was declared how our heading – the banner heading – on the *Labour Leader* was 'The German Workers Are Still Our Brothers'. And we were encouraged by the fact that in Germany there were socialists who were opposed to the war just as we were.

In 1915, with the prospect of conscription, the opposition to the war took a new form. It was my wife who suggested that those of us who would refuse military service should get together. I didn't feel I could advocate this in the columns of the *Labour Leader*, although I was editor, because in a sense it was unconstitutional action and I didn't want to commit the party to that as a party. So I got my wife to write a letter to the paper and she did. And as a result of that names poured in of young men who would refuse to fight in the war. The interesting thing was that it was not only young socialists. It was young religious people; mostly young Quakers but others as well, Methodists – Primitive Methodists.

Mark Hayler was one of the first fifty members of the No-Conscription Fellowship.

The first meeting of any size was held at the Friends Meeting House at Bishopsgate, and there was a riot and the soldiers and the rest stormed the gates of the meeting house. So the chairman said, who I think was Clifford Allen, 'So as not to disturb the crowd outside' (they could hear us clapping inside) 'wave your handkerchiefs'. I've never seen that done before. This technique of crowd control reportedly worked!

So the No-Conscription Fellowship was formed with a membership of 8,000. It would become, as one conscientious objector termed it, 'the most abused institution in England'. Fenner Brockway became its secretary.

> I wouldn't say that we had any common philosophy then. We hadn't worked out all the implications of pacifism. But the statement of principles which those who joined the No-Conscription Fellowship were asked to sign spoke of the sanctity of human life and in its essence was pacifist. And we had the most remarkable unity between the young socialists and the young Quakers and the young religious people.

Howard Marten was one of those young Quakers. The Society of Friends had first adopted their peace testimony in the 1660s, laying the foundations for Quaker pacifism.

> You found the ranks of the No-Conscription Fellowship were made up of men from every conceivable walk of life. You had all sorts of religious groups, from the Salvation Army to the Seventh Day Adventists; Church of England, Roman Catholics; there was no limit. It was a sort of cross section of every type. Then you had in addition to that the more politically minded: the Independent Labour Party, and different degrees of socialists, and the ordinary political parties. Then a very curious group of what I used to call artistically minded. There were a lot of men who were not in any way organized or attached, but I should call them the aesthetic group: artists, musicians, all that. They had a terrific repugnance at war which could only express itself individually. You see artists and people of that calibre are very personally minded. They're not group minded. They're individualists to the core, so that naturally they would, almost inevitably, take a very personal attitude to that sort of thing.

Harry Stanton found his views on pacifism hotly contested by many of his friends and formed the Luton branch of the NCF on his twenty-first birthday.

> In the very first days of the war I was defending, or rather advocating, the Quaker position with regard to war

among my friends, many of whom were on the point of enlisting; though they generally acknowledged war to be an evil, they believed that in this case England must prefer the expedient course to the right one. If, however our discussions served no other purpose, they made known my attitude towards war, and prepared the way for what was to follow.

As conscription became more and more inevitable, those of us who had adopted the pacifist attitude began to consider wither our opposition would lead us. For an individual to attempt to resist the power of the state would be a tremendous venture. The number of persons prepared to make such an attempt must be very small, but they would be infinitely stronger if they could form a common plan of action.

Harold Bing and his father both joined the Croydon branch of the NCF.

The general public was not prepared to listen to propaganda at that time and while a number of meetings were held they were often broken up and speakers were thrown into ponds and otherwise maltreated. I, for example, on one occasion, was distributing literature house to house – we did a good deal of that, anti-war literature house to house – and was pursued by an infuriated householder who saw the literature, quickly came out and chased me for a long distance until he lost me in the darkness carrying with him a very heavy stick.

Unlike her Continental neighbours, Britain had drawn her fighting men from vigorous recruitment campaigns, without using the tool of conscription. But conscriptionists had been actively promoting the case for conscription since 1901, and as the war failed to be 'over by Christmas', pressure for conscription mounted. The National Registration Act of 1915 had already registered all men between the ages of sixteen and forty; it was followed by the Derby Scheme of Attestation offering inducements to those who would register as volunteers to be called on should the need arise. Chemist Harold Blake was among the thousands who were canvassed.

One of the promises given was the undertaking that no married men would be called until the supply of single ones was exhausted; while another was the right of appeal for exemption from active service from specially created tribunals. The impression was created among the public – no doubt intentionally – that all who did not attest would be conscripted before any of the groups were called up, and that only by attestation could the right of appeal be gained. The obvious result, beside the recruiting of all who sincerely meant to serve in case of need, was that the cowards took fright and flocked to attest, thinking that only thus could they obtain permission to appeal and in that manner escape military service. I myself had a canvasser visit me, who distinctly told me that if I did not attest I should be fetched among the first, and without the right of appeal. After listening to all he had to say I plainly told him that under no circumstances would I volunteer for war service. My employer also applied pressure, telling me that only by attestation could I hope to escape. I replied that if I refused to become a soldier, no power on earth could make me into one, to which uncompromising statement he replied, 'No! but they can send you to prison.' I gave him to understand that I was prepared to risk that contingency.

Yorkshireman Horace Eaton was also canvassed.

I well remember the Saturday afternoon when a gentleman called at our house for this purpose, and I had a long talk and discussion with him. I stated my willingness to join the RAMC for Red Cross service, if he could guarantee my entry into that branch, and that I should not be transferred to any other section. He said he should be able to manage that all right, but could not give any guarantee and so there the matter ended.

I was the only one on the staff of the firm by which I was employed who did not attest, and of course many were the remarks passed, and a black picture painted of what I should have to endure under conscription. My employer kindly allowed me absolute freedom in this matter and only wished to know my intentions, in order to make his plans for carrying on the business.

Quaker Howard Marten recalled the prevailing attitude to conscientious objectors.

I think people got the impression that it was only that people wouldn't fight. It was something more than that: it was an objection to having one's life directed by an outside authority.

As the First World War developed, the shortage of manpower rather indicated that there would be, at some time or other, a measure of conscription, and though I never had two minds about my personal position in the event of conscription, we did have a meeting of a limited number of friends and contacts of mine who were of similar views and we had to face, even at that stage, how far our views were consistent with an extreme attitude: that is were we prepared to adopt a pacifist position even to the point of being shot. We little realized at the time that it was going to come to that.

Mark Hayler worked in a reform school in Cheshire and objected on many grounds.

I claimed that in England there was an old tradition that a man had a right to stand on his own feet. It was a political attitude I suppose and I maintained it all the way through, although in my statement I took an ethical line, that was merely to bump up my case.

Eric Dott grew up in a comfortable middle-class home in Edinburgh.

I'm not quite so sure now but I did very much think at the time that this was the only way to help to prevent future wars, to register my protest as a CO that war was wrong and that I would take no part in it and hoping that in the future that view would prevail and perhaps future wars would be prevented by a growing number of COs until they couldn't get enough soldiers to fight.

Eric had taken on board the ideals of both his mother and father.

In the first place my mother was a very earnest Christian and my first idea as the war was going on was that this was wrong, that it was unChristian and it was utterly wrong to take life. My father was increasingly a socialist and I think the war which he hated, which he looked upon as just a scramble for territory and wealth and markets, he looked upon as just an utterly immoral thing from that international socialist point of view, and I became increasingly interested in that. So at the time I was called up I had a sort of dual feeling, I still thought war was wrong as a Christian and therefore refused to go, but I also thought the war was a wicked war from a socialist point of view.

Fenner Brockway and Clifford Allen were both on the board of the No-Conscription Fellowship. Clifford Allen lost three stone in prison and died six months before the Second World War, weakened by his years in prison. Despite his stand as a conscientious objector, Clifford Allen was honoured with a peerage in 1932 and Fenner Brockway took his seat in the House of Lords in 1964.

Both Clifford Allen and I were inclined at that time (1915) to take an absolute pacifist view and to take the view that we were not merely resisting a conscription act but that we were witnessing for peace. And that it was an action not only against the war of 1914–18, but an action against war altogether. I may remark that both of us changed our philosophy later on in our lives, but that was our view then. There was a group that took the view that this action was against the conscription act. Some of them were inclined to be philosophically anarchistic, like C.H. Norman who supported resistance to conscription because it was an authoritarian state intervention with the individual. I would say the number who took that view were small. It wasn't a matter of great debate and I don't think it was a serious division.

CHAPTER 2

Conscription

They never dreamed there would be men who would defy the
British Army. That was unthinkable; you might defy some
native army, but you'd never defy the British Army.
                                                    Mark Hayler

The Military Service Act introducing conscription took
effect on 2 March 1916. Harry Stanton remembered the
surrounding publicity, including public hoardings lavishly
spread with recruiting posters:

WILL YOU MARCH TOO
OR WAIT UNTIL MARCH 2?

Conscientious objectors felt the repercussions even before
they fell into the hands of the military. Harold Blake was
employed by a chemist in Northampton who knew his views.

> Towards the end of March 1916, my employer told me
> that he thought the military authorities would not allow
> two qualified chemists to remain in one business, and as I
> had not attested and he had, he would probably be called
> to the colours and in that event he would close down the
> business. He then asked me whether I would prefer to
> await that event or to seek another situation at once. Seeing
> that my presence was undesirable because he considered
> that it jeopardized his prospects of exemption, I intimated
> to him that I would move on at once.

With conscription in place Mark Hayler also thought about
moving on.

I thought of going on a farm but it was only releasing another man. There were odd ideas that the COs should get together and disappear. We met, the few of us who were COs in Warrington, met at the gasworks in the boiler house. There might have been eight or ten of us. How dedicated they were I don't know, if the military had come down on us some would have gone into the army, as they did. But we decided that we would go to Scotland and we would live in the woods up there, it seems crazy when you think of it now, but it seemed to be a way to meet the immediate situation, to evade the military, and we wanted to evade the military as long as ever we could. The place that was chosen was somewhere up in Scotland, on a river and it was rather deep and the idea was to put a chain across that river, which when it was put down you couldn't see, and if the military turned up we would cross the river and pull ourselves across on the chain. It seems really crazy when you think of it now. But when you'd burnt your boats as we had done it didn't matter. Of course it never materialized, I think it was seen to be not practical, it was a happy idea, we were all very young and there was a bit of adventure about it.

Under the Military Service Act tribunals were established, showing a modicum of recognition for conscientious objectors. Although the Market Bosworth tribunal gave the members of the Atherstone Hunt complete exemption on the grounds that their occupation was indispensable (as were all hunt members on orders from the War Office), only a dozen conscientious objectors were given exemption. The military was always represented on the bench and Howard Marten voices the opinion of many COs in his condemnation of them.

> The local tribunal was pretty hostile. They were men of not very great depth of vision or understanding, and although I wouldn't say that I was a complete absolutist, a do-nothing, I wasn't prepared to do anything under military direction, or to be exempted in a very restricted way.

Harold Blake, the Northampton chemist, was told at his tribunal:

'Well Mr Blake we are quite convinced that you have a genuine conscientious objection.' Here I inclined my head and quietly remarked, 'Thank you'. The clerk proceeded, 'But we think you ought to do something and we have therefore given you exemption from combatant service on the understanding that you become a dispenser in the RAMC.'

Harold was astounded. In his view combatant and non-combatant service both constituted the same thing – military service.

Therefore if I had proved conscientious objection to one, I had at the same time proved objection to the other and to give me exemption from one while denying it from the other was, IN PRACTICE, no exemption at all. Yet, it was a handsome bait, which, however, I was not tempted to swallow. It meant immediate rank as sergeant with pay and separation allowance for my wife on a comparatively liberal scale; also it meant that I should not be exposed to the dangers associated with the front line, but I would be located at a station where the duties I should have to perform would be to see that the work of dispensing was done satisfactorily and efficiently by the rank and file. All this flashed through my mind, but I stayed to hear no more, but rising from the chair I exclaimed indignantly, 'I can't accept it', and then left the room and the building in disgust.

Scotsman Eric Dott had a supportive family but was alone among his immediate circle of friends in his conscientious objection to military service. He found outside support when he went to his tribunal in 1917.

I was very young and inexperienced and I was not in the least afraid but I was awfully shy of not knowing what to say and what to do and I was much relieved to find that at that tribunal there was a lady that I didn't know in the least but I was told was there from the Society of Friends, and was there to be a friend to me during the tribunal for which I thanked her very much without having met her or known her at all. I just had to sit down and face these three officers and somehow when I look back on it now I didn't take it terribly seriously, my chief concern really was, would I know what to do and say, rather like you might if called up before a set of your teachers and you didn't quite know how to behave. It didn't strike me in the way it was meant to strike me, not frightening or intimidating, no truly it wasn't. For one thing they didn't try to frighten or intimidate you but they tried to question, which is what they were there for, to see if I really was a conscientious objector and wasn't just trying to dodge, that was their chief function because they weren't there to try me in any sense to see what my punishment would be, they were there to assess whether I was truly a CO.

Tribunal members had certain routine questions, as Eric Dott remembers.

A favourite one was, 'What would you do if your sister was threatened with rape by some German soldier?' I answered to the effect that it had nothing to do with my being a CO against the war. I think I said I didn't know what I'd do but it didn't matter in the present context in the least what I would do, the thing was this was a protest against the war because the war was wrong.

I think my main reason was my original Christian one that I thought war was morally wrong and that to take life was against the Christian ethic, I don't think I brought in the socialist ethic on that occasion.

They were very civil and very routine and they knew the kind of things I would say and were always perfectly polite, but they impressed upon me that all sorts of atrocities would happen if people did this, but I stuck to it that the war was all wrong, and that I couldn't take any part in it whatever.

They tried to make me feel guilty, they said that this was a very wrong attitude altogether. And I said it was the only true attitude a true Christian could adopt.

Alfred Evans was born into a highly political family and when war broke out was an apprentice in a piano factory.

My father was an active trade unionist, president of his branch of the United Kingdom Society of Coachmakers at a time when it was dangerous to be associated with this society, for if found out he would have been subject to instant dismissal and to be blacklisted throughout his trade. He once asked me how I regarded him as a father and I said 'good' and he replied (and it was about the time of the miners' strike in Tonypandy; Winston Churchill sent the troops down to Tonypandy and they were in danger of being shot down), 'Then if I strike for a reasonable living for you and for your father, if you become a soldier it will be your business to shoot me down.' I never forgot it.

The war came and at first I was willing on humanitarian grounds to join the RAMC (Royal Army Medical Corps). Accordingly in the early part of 1916 I appeared before a local tribunal to state my case and I was granted a certificate of exemption on condition that I joined the RAMC.

On 25 April 1916 I reported to a recruiting office in Ealing Broadway and saw a Lieutenant who asked for my exemption certificate and promptly tore it up. He then set an official document before me saying that I was to be put into the non-combatant corps and that I was to sign this paper and that I was told that I was not even to read it. I flatly refused to do this and he called the guard, two men and a corporal with fixed bayonets, and I was taken to Hounslow Barracks.

Conscientious objectors were deemed to be in the hands of the army once they were called up, and thus subject to military discipline. Therefore when they failed to respond to call-up papers the police came round to arrest them. Many COs, like Eric Dott, knew the local policeman.

He was very shy about it all because we all knew each other well and he said he was very sorry but he had come to arrest me because I hadn't gone, so I was taken then and told to report at the nearest military centre, Glencorse. I was then given my liberty, and told that as long as I reported to this military centre I could go. And rather a little inconsistently I went to the military centre and they enrolled me and told me that I would have to go to a place in Fife near Kinghorn and join the forces there and I was a little bewildered what to do, so I walked home over the Pentland Hills and spent the night at home and then did go over to Kinghorn determined that when I got the first order from the military I would disobey it. In due course we were called out on parade in Kinghorn. I said I was not going because I was a CO and the sergeant was furious and he got absolutely blue in the face with astonishment and fury. And that was when the thing really started – I'd disobeyed an order and was sent to the guardroom under arrest.

Mark Hayler worked in a reform school in Cheshire. He was sensitive to the predicament of his boss, the governor.

Now all the boys there came through police courts and my case would go through a police court and the governor said to me, 'I don't care what views you hold but don't let yourself be arrested on these premises because all the boys here come through the police courts.' So I said, 'Look here I'll promise you that they'll never arrest me here, I shall be away, I'm watching things very carefully.' Well in Newton-le-Willows the military there knew of me because I was the only CO in Newton-le-Willows. There were some in Warrington and by that time they knew there was a growing opposition and I think it got out from the school to somebody or other, probably the governor himself said 'I've got a man like that in my school'. I knew that if I went to the railway station to get a ticket I wouldn't get anywhere because they would have arrested me as soon as I got there, but I said to the governor, 'I won't allow myself to be arrested here.'

So his attitude was a very friendly one and so was the head schoolmaster, although none of them had any sympathy with my viewpoint but they knew that I would carry out what I'd decided. I disappeared that morning and cycled to Rugby, stayed the night there and then cycled onto London.

On Good Friday, which was the next day, they arrested me. I noticed a policeman came up the garden path, and of course I knew all about it. My people never worried about situations, it's curious they knew there was nothing else to do. The policeman came in and he arrested me there.

Although conscientious objectors were dubbed 'cowards and shirkers', Mark Hayler certainly did not attempt to run any further.

> My feeling was that I must not put him in a difficult position. He had his job to do and I had mine and if I was sort of caught in the act I didn't have any choice and there was no point. I said to him, 'Well let me finish this map that I'm busy on and I'll come down to the station this afternoon.' But he wasn't letting me escape, he had orders to arrest me and he couldn't do anything else.

Once they were in the hands of the army, the uniform was a potent symbol of military jurisdiction which Harold Bing put on under protest.

> I didn't think there was any point in having a physical struggle about it or anything of that kind and simply provoking the NCO unnecessarily. He was merely carrying out his orders, and so I put on the uniform under protest and of course it saved wearing out and getting my own clothes dirty.

Harold Blake took his protest somewhat further.

> I was asked the size of my boot and gave it, and was then directed to remove one of them. This I did but when required to put on an army boot, I quietly but firmly refused. Then commenced a period of rough handling when the soldiers forced on boots and other articles of army dress. Having satisfied themselves that they had effected some sort of a fit, they turned their attention to packing a kit bag with a complete soldier's kit, and I, finding myself freed from their hands, quickly reached the outside of the boots and tunic. The completion of this manoeuvre being observed, I was the recipient of another violent outburst of filthy invective which might well have made the stoutest heart quake. Two soldiers each seized an arm and held it outstretched horizontally while the heavy kit bag was hung on my back with the cord pressing hard upon my throat, and the tunic, trousers, overcoat and boots were thrown over my arms. Loaded in this manner I was

dragged and pushed back to the guardroom – a distance of about 200 yards – by the two soldiers who held my arms, and pushed from behind by a third. The pressure of the cord of the kit bag round my throat was causing suffocation, and as I felt consciousness slipping from me, I commenced involuntarily to struggle and effected the partial release of one arm, which was quickly utilized in the direction of removing the obstruction to my respiration, by inserting a finger under the cord. But in doing this I stumbled and fell, and while on the ground I was treated to a volley of kicking from heavy army boots aimed at whatever part of my anatomy presented the best target, the practical assault being reinforced by the inevitable storm of foul abuse.

An hour later Harold Blake was forcibly dressed again.

They rapidly stripped me of all clothing, and then commenced to replace it by army dress. The actions were accompanied by voluminous abuse, and from their manner, I formed the opinion that they strongly disliked the task which had been assigned to them. One of these sergeants had been sent home from the war front being wounded in the hand, and during the dressing comedy he showed me his badly battered hand and remarked, 'I've nearly lost my hand fighting for you, and now you won't do your bit.' In reply to this I said 'No! not for me. I neither ask nor accept such a service from any man.'

While putting on Blake's trousers the two sergeants discovered they had been trying to force two legs into one trouser leg and the ice broke.

The rest of the dressing process was carried out without further abuse, but to the accompaniment of quite a friendly conversation, and when, after the two sergeants had finished their task upon me, I asked them if they would shake hands as a sign of the absence of animosity, they complied with a right good will.

Blake was subsequently court martialled and sentenced to six months hard labour.

George Frederick Dutch, a Quaker, also refused to put on a uniform.

The Major was very unpleasant, hectoring. He said, 'Well all I can say is that in my opinion conscientious objection is just another name for arrant cowardice.' He said, 'Take him away. Don't put a rag on him, he's got to dress himself.' And of course the NCOs did as they were told. I was taken back and they stripped me of my own clothing and put the uniform down beside me and said, 'Now you've got to put it on.' I said, 'Well I will not put it on.' They said, 'All right you've got to sit there.'

George was then left alone in his tent.

I sat there for a day or two and the whole camp was interested. Everybody knew what was going on. Soldiers used to come and say, 'Go on, stick it boy, stick it if it kills you.' The Major was very much disliked and I can understand that. I can see what type of person he was. Not only the officers, but the men, didn't like him, and he must have noticed it because after a day or two suddenly my tent was taken up and taken right up on top of the cliff overlooking the sea. This was in November and it was pretty cold, misty weather. And I was taken up there and my uniform put beside me again by the tent pole and just to make things worse they rolled the tent walls up so that the wind came right into the tent, all round and I could sit there and freeze. Which I did. And the orders were that nobody was to come near me. The Major noticed the other men coming in, you see and the orders were that nobody was to go near me until I dressed and came down. Well I didn't dress and I didn't go down and I stayed there and I'm not quite sure how long it was, but I think it must have been at least ten days and nights in just my singlet and pants and socks. Just sitting like that in the tent, and before I'd been there many hours I was frozen right through with exposure, so that I didn't feel a lot, I was just insensitive. I could be an ordinary soldier by the Major's order if I would put on the uniform and go down, which I would not do and the order was that nobody was to go near me – and they didn't go near me, even NCOs didn't come again. I just sat there, day and night, just set my teeth to stick whatever came.

Finally the doctor intervened and he was taken inside.

Many conscientious objectors who applied to tribunals for exemption from military service were offered non-combatant duties, and there were 3,300 conscientious objectors who served in the NCC during the First World War. Horace Eaton was one of them. After the war he compiled his memoirs from a diary kept at the time.

The question often recurred to my mind as to whether I could not do something for the wounded and suffering. So I took up a course of training in the St John's Ambulance and attempted to join the RAMC through the recruiting office at Bradford, but without success – seeing I had not passed an examination. Before the session was over, conscription became law, and I was bound to make a decision one way or another. It was the greatest crisis in my life, and only those called upon to face a similar issue or problem can realize the terrible weight of responsibility one felt, and above all the anxiety to do that which was Right.

It was at this point that there appeared to be something lacking in the church where I had been taught the ideals to which I was seeking to remain true. We had no organization to help us in our stand against war and conscription, and this was an experience of disappointment and trial. One could not even claim that in our tenets as a church we were against all war. Thus what should have been some support to us was missing – and I believe only the Society of Friends are clear upon this matter as a body. So many in the Christian Church supported the war and in fact some ministers and members were very good recruiting agents.

Horace went before a tribunal in March 1916 and was given exemption from combatant duties. He appealed against the decision and asked to be allowed to join the Friends Ambulance Unit, but this was turned down.

A non-combatant corps had been formed by the military authorities for conscientious objectors – and it was understood at first their duties would be to bury the dead on the battlefields and other unpleasant tasks in the trenches. So here was another big problem! Should I refuse all service to the country in which I had been brought up and thus be sent to prison – or should I undertake non-combatant duties?

For over a fortnight I pondered on the matter, but could not definitely decide which was the right path for me to take. Much of my time was spent out of doors – chiefly in Horton Park – as I was liable to arrest any day, as I was an absentee. Here I also met other COs in a similar position – and we shall not easily forget those days during our present lifetime.

However, I seemed to be led to the conclusion that the right way was to undertake any service I could conscientiously perform – which would not take the life or assist to take the life of another. So accordingly I called at the Bradford Recruiting Office on Friday 16 June.

Horace was sent to Richmond Castle with the Non-Combatant Corps.

Many conscientious objectors were sent to Richmond who refused to do anything, or to put on khaki. Although I had not quite the attitude as these young fellows, yet I admired their courageous stand, and attitude against the bullying methods of militarism. The methods adopted to try and make these young fellows into non-combatants or soldiers often made one's blood boil with indignation. We hear talk of Prussian militarism and all its inhuman treatment – but it appeared to me that all militarism was pretty much the same. One young fellow who refused to put on khaki was stripped and left on the parade ground with only a shirt on, for a good while. Two NCC chaps took off their caps to him as a sign of their admiration – and one said, 'Stick it lad'. A captain overheard the remark and ordered his arrest under DORA (Defence of the Realm Act) and he was put in prison for fourteen days. I have seen several of them kicked about – pushed along and kicked on the heels to try and make them march. One fine looking fellow was brought in on Tuesday 26 June by two soldiers handcuffed, and a very heavy kit bag containing all his things – and heavy boots were fastened about his neck – nearly choking him. He was pushed about and finally put in the cold cells where he nearly collapsed.

In the autumn of 1916 Horace Eaton recorded the fate of another CO.

We were very sorry to learn that one S. Cooper of Leeds who had been a member of our corps, had gone insane. At Richmond he refused to do anything and I understand was rather badly treated. His case was brought up in the House of Commons and I remember one of the officers being rather upset about the matter. This young fellow broke down with rheumatic fever and as he was pulling round again, he was sent on to us, into such rough conditions, and just as the winter was settling in. He seemed to improve a little – but always hobbled about with a stick and to us he appeared a physical wreck. Later he was sent on to Sheffield Hospital for medical examination – and they pronounced him fit for general service. What a ridiculous decision! He was probably a marked man – seeing his case was so much well known. After this he appeared somewhat strange in manner – and on the Friday as he was going on leave for the weekend – he said goodbye to some of our fellows and remarked he would not see them again. On the Saturday afternoon a telegram came to hand from his father – that the son had gone insane.

Thirty-one conscientious objectors are known to have gone insane as a result of their treatment.

While Horace Eaton's life in the NCC was punctuated by these dramatic incidents, the men's day-to-day work was to perform menial tasks in support of the combatant forces. They built an aerodrome and helped the Royal Engineers to build some stables at Darlington.

We had various duties to perform – sometimes assisting to build the stables and other times cleaning out various places in the town for soldiers' billets. One day a part of our company were sent to the railway station to unload a railway van for another company of soldiers. They moved almost everything except some rifles and ammunition and these they refused to handle. Regular soldiers had to be called upon to finish the work. We expected trouble – but heard nothing further, so probably the captain had smoothed over the affair.

News of similar protests reached him through the grapevine.

A large number of an NCC at Newhaven on 21 January 1917 refused to load munitions and were court martialled. Thirty-eight were sentenced to six months imprisonment with hard labour. In our own company we often had trouble because of the NCOs trying to bully – but the result generally was a warning by the officer to the NCOs against such methods. Just about this time a part of our company were put upon certain work and they soon discovered it was to be a rifle range – so they refused to proceed further. The usual warnings were given about the penalties for disobedience, so part of No. 4 company were allotted the task – they too refused, but the officers got over the difficulty by ordering the members who were Plymouth Brethren to do it, and they complied as it appears to be a part of their belief to do as ordered – and those who give the order are held responsible to God.

There are Primitives, Wesleyans, Congregationalists, Baptists, Roman Catholics, United Methodists, Seventh Day Adventists, International Bible Students, Jews, Church of England, Socialists and Atheists. These attend their respective meeting places and thus we become fairly well known, and who can estimate our influence upon others.

The relative freedom of men in the Non-Combatant Corps gave them the opportunity to spread their views and opinions to a wider public – although the public didn't always welcome the exchange.

During railway journeys we had always ample opportunity for stating our views on the war – explaining our stand as COs. Thus we were generally enlightening others – as we usually were given a fair hearing and our statements were fairly well-supported.

One of our fellows went on leave recently and travelling in the same railway carriage was a young lady who enquired what regiment he was in. He stated that he was a member of the Non-Combatant Corps, and she had many uncomplimentary remarks to pass concerning us. However, this young fellow is a local preacher. He explained his position and also placed before her the Christ life and ideal. He was still engaged in this conversation when reaching his destination, so he obtained the young lady's address, wrote her a letter enclosing a gospel leaflet. She replied thanking him – but said she was pleased to note the pamphlet was written by a soldier – and how she admired *real* soldiers. Her letter concluded that if heaven was inhabited by conscientious objectors she had no wish to go there.

On the night of 9 August two of us went down to another village named Riveton Park – about 3 miles away. This is another busy colliery place same as all the other places around, and we found some supporters of our position. Rather an encouraging change this – as we usually found a good share of scorn and hostility. Some people invited us in to supper at one house – where we had a very interesting time – talking over COs.

A few women who were definitely hostile (of the rougher class) would gather at the camp and call us all kinds of names in not very choice language and threatened to do all kinds of things against us. Wherever we go, at first we are looked upon as some special, suspicious kind of beings but in due time when people know us we are generally respected and in some cases admired. We are certainly bearing testimony to our beliefs and we hope seed will fall upon good ground and bring forth fruit in other lives that will be determined to stand for peace – and against bloodshed and war.

CHAPTER 3

The 'Frenchmen'

*I think that there was a very definite movement, that they
would break our resistance by sending us to France. If they
could get us into the firing-line then they could pass the
death sentence and that was that.*

Howard Marten

In May 1916, on whose orders it is unclear, the army sent
some fifty conscientious objectors to France. Londoner Alfred
Evans was one of the 'Frenchmen', as they were nicknamed.

We were all in Harwich Redoubt a fortress built inside
a hill – it had been built to house French prisoners in
the Napoleonic wars and was a vile place in which severe
punishment was given out. For example, Corney Barrett
and Rendall Wyatt were strapped up in strait-jackets and
stood against the wall in the hot sun of the May of that
year and the vindictiveness of the military prison staff saw
to it that the strait-jackets were strapped too tightly. I and
Harry Stanton and Bernard Bonner were later put into the
cells, completely dark, dripping with water and overrun
with rats, for three days without food.

For Harry Stanton the low temperature in the cells was one
of the worst features of solitary confinement.

It seemed impossible to keep warm. The three punishment
cells were built end to end, into the hill, and the only
light which reached the second cell came through a filthy
window in the dividing wall between it and number one.
The third cell depended solely on a similar window in

the wall of number two. At no time during the day could one see to read in number three; moisture trickled down the walls, and the floor was rotten and broken through here and there. Number two cell was rather better – not so damp; not quite so many holes in the floor – and by standing on tip toe under the window it was possible to read for a short time each day. Number one, in comparison, was quite a desirable apartment; still dampish, but much lighter. I had been put into the middle cell, and I found it almost impossible to sleep, so bitter was the cold. I welcomed the dim light which marked the coming of daylight outside, and the prospect of change.

On Saturday, 6 May, we had just finished dinner when we were suddenly taken before Colonel Croft. We were taken in separately, and it was clear from the faces of the men who preceded me that something serious had happened. When my turn came I found the Colonel surrounded by a large group of officers of lesser rank.

'I am sorry to tell you,' he said slowly, 'that I am instructed by the War Office to cancel the order for your district court martial, and to send you to France with the 2nd Company of the Eastern Non-Combatant Corps.'

The news came as a shock, though the decision was not entirely unexpected. Our guards had repeatedly told us that we should 'soon be pushing the daisies up!'

The spirits of the 'Frenchmen' appear to have been undimmed, as Alfred Evans remembered.

An officer told us we were to be taken in irons to France where we would be under active service conditions and if we persisted in our line of conduct we would be shot. We were asked to take our pay and make our wills in a space provided in the army pay book and this we all seventeen of us refused to do.

The men were moved from Harwich in the middle of the night and taken via a circuitous route across London and down to a boat at Southampton. Meanwhile another group of conscientious objectors in Richmond Castle was also destined for France. John Brocklesby was one of these sixteen conscientious objectors sent to join the

Non-Combatant Corps who refused to obey orders. He
wrote later in his memoirs:

> The resistors at Richmond were in two parties, eight
> being in the guardroom and eight being in the cells. As
> the guard went to turn out the men in the guardroom, our
> chaps offered resistance by clinging to tables, chairs or
> doorframes, and they got some rough handling from the
> guard. I asked to see the captain and begged him to let
> me speak to the guardroom lads, saying I hoped I could
> persuade them to give no more trouble. He looked very
> surprised but gave me permission and came to hear what I
> should say.
>
> I said, 'Look here chaps it's no good offering resistance
> to those orders. If you use force to resist, I can tell you
> the army knows all about force and you don't stand any
> chance. We must rely on spiritual forces. For my part,
> they can take me where they will, even into the front line
> trenches, but they will never get me to raise my hand
> against my fellow man.'
>
> There was no further trouble of that kind all the time we
> were in the hands of the military. Later on at Southampton
> we met the group from Seaford who carried marks of
> rough treatment. I remember Stuart Beavis had his glasses
> broken. I felt led to give them the same advice, and there
> were no more manhandlings.

None of these conscientious objectors had been allowed
to warn their friends and families, as Howard Marten,
one of the Harwich men smuggled across London by
train, remembered.

> Somebody in the train crossing London threw a note
> which landed on the platform and got to somebody whom
> he knew, and that was the first word that got round
> that we were on our way to France. And it enabled the
> No-Conscription-Fellowship and a number of people to
> realize our whereabouts.

By the time the No-Conscription Fellowship was aware
of what was happening the Harwich group had arrived at
Cinder City Camp, Le Havre. They were sent out on parade.

Alfred Evans takes up the story.

On the vast parade ground before a line of some thirty officers, were paraded about 1,000 men and one of us was placed with each battalion or whatever the number was and the parade was then ordered to 'shun, right turn, quick march. Not one of us moved.

There was a lot of shouting, movement amongst the officers and the NCOs as the mass of the men nearly reached the edge of the parade ground and small parties were sent back and we were dragged off. But for a short time it must have been an amazing sight to see this small group of us scattered motionless over the huge parade ground. I'm sure that none of us who were present at that event will ever forget that sight. We were held fast by the collecting parties and marched off to the army service stores, I went to an engineering shop eventually and was told to feed an automatic saw; I didn't stand to attention before the officer giving the orders and had my ankles kicked together but not hard. I didn't feed the saw and for all I had known, the steel rods may still be on the turntable there. One of the Camerons came over to me and said, 'I don't agree with you laddy but I admire your pluck' and gave me a drink of tea. There were stormy scenes when the officer came in and saw that I had done nothing and once again I was kicked to a position of attention and this wasn't done so that it hurt but to make a show of discipline before the rest of the men.

Later, however, I was kicked again and this time made to feel it. That afternoon we were all split up and put to various jobs. I and another of our chaps, it was Howard Marten, we were put into a foundry which was casting railway chairs, the things that hold railway lines to the sleepers. Since the men were obviously hard pressed we decided to give a hand and after about half an hour someone spread the report that we had given in and the officers came back to see us. Immediately we stopped work. In the foundry one is given oatmeal water to drink – I was ordered to drink this water, I refused to do that and an infuriated sergeant gave me a punch and poured the stuff over me. I left him to clean it up. At the end of the day none of us had given in, and that night we were in the guardroom awaiting events. About that time a soldier sent up his dinner to me with his compliments. I was completely taken aback, sending my thanks and appreciation by one of the guards. I never saw him or even found out who he was – I only hope he fared well and survived the war. Three or four days later we were paraded in front of the guardroom and told that we were to be sent up the line, where if we persisted in our course of action we should certainly be shot.

Howard Marten remembers how the army used psychology in a bid to bring the conscientious objector into line.

We were forever being threatened with the death sentence. Over and over again we'd be marched up and read out a notice – some man being sentenced to death through disobedience at the front. Whether they were true cases or not I don't know. It was all done with the idea of intimidating us.

The military authorities didn't know quite how to react. It was something quite outside their experience. And it became clear that we weren't people that could be bullied into it.

Despite the bullying, not all the soldiers they encountered were unsympathetic and there were many incidents of small kindnesses like this one remembered by Alfred Evans.

At about 7.30 the sergeant of the guard, Irish guards, looked in – he was a tall gaunt man, wiry and tough but a jovial soul – he asked us, 'Have you boys got any money?' And we said we had a bit but not much. 'Give it to me, there's nobody about they've all gone into 'town' tonight, those officers and men, and I thought you boys would like a bit of a "do", you've a tough time before you.' He was a grand lad and did us proud. He either went himself or sent down to the canteen and brought back a load of stuff which our own money could never have paid for.

Three or four of the men, including Harry Stanton, were moved to a Field Punishment Unit at Harfleur to serve twenty-eight days.

Soon we were called out for our first experience of field
punishment. Provision was made for this by means of a
wooden framework, consisting of uprights 4 or 5 yards
apart with connecting beams at a height of about 5 feet.
We were placed with our backs to the posts, and arms
outstretched. Our ankles were then tied together and our
arms tied tightly at the wrists to the cross beams. We were
to remain in this position for two hours. For those of us
who were of average height the strain upon our arms was
just bearable, though our wrists quickly became numbed,
but for those who were shorter, the punishment was
painful in the extreme, since they were forced to stand
entirely on their toes in order to relieve their arms of the
dead weight of the body.

Finding they had no tent boards to separate them from the
mud, Stanton and another CO, Brewster, took advantage of a
pile stacked nearby and made themselves more comfortable.
When their actions were discovered they were rewarded with
a rather more vicious version of field punishment.

Brewster and I found ourselves being taken off to quite
another part of the camp. The prison was surrounded,
not by a wall, but by a double barbed-wire fence,
through which one could see, and be seen by everyone
passing. We two were on this occasion placed with our
faces to the wire of the inner fence, and tied in the usual
manner at the wrists and ankles. As the ropes with which
we were fastened were tied around barbed wire instead
of the usual thick wooden posts, it was possible to tie
them much more tightly, and I found myself drawn so
closely into the fence that when I wished to turn my head
I had to do so very slowly and cautiously to avoid my
face being torn by the barbs. To make matters worse it
came on to rain, and a cold wind blew straight across the
top of the hill.

I did not feel however that we had any special
grounds for complaint – we were exceptional cases,
and militarism was making an effort to break down our
resistance. What did seem to me shameful was that any
voluntary soldier, who was offering his life in what he
believed to be his country's service, was liable to such a

punishment for quite a trivial offence, or at the instance
of a prejudiced superior.

The group's stay at Harfleur was brought to a sudden end,
and they were marched off under armed guard. One of the
soldiers told Stanton:

'You are going to Boulogne, and from there to the "front
line" so that you can be shot if you still disobey orders.' He
seemed very indignant, 'I would sooner shoot the officer
who gave me the order,' he said fiercely, 'than shoot one of
your fellows! I came out here to fight the Germans not to
murder Englishmen.'

They were not sent to the front line but a disused fish market
in Boulogne – another field punishment barracks. Although
they had been manacled to the poles of their tent at the camp
in Harfleur, the conditions at Boulogne, recalled by Alfred
Evans, were far worse.

We were handcuffed with our hands behind our backs and
seventeen of us were put into a dark underground cage
about 12 feet square, certainly not more than that because
we paced it out. The cage was made of heavy timber
mounting with inch thick planks and 1 inch space between
each plank which allowed a little light from the opening of
the passage to filter through.

With us was one latrine bucket – no lid – for seventeen
men. When any man needed to use the latrine one of us
undid his trousers which was simple enough but pulling
them up again and fastening them was very difficult.
A man could with difficulty clean himself from his
rear excretion but being handcuffed to the rear could
not possibly fasten his trousers at the front. The antics
resulting, so that this job could be accomplished, were
sometimes very funny. We protested to the assistant
provost marshall about this and we got it stopped after
about three days.

The food was limited to four hard biscuits and 8 ounces
of bully beef – that's corned beef – per day with heavily
chlorinated water. At the end of a month I went down
with dysentery and was taken to Number 13 Stationary

Hospital, Boulogne. There a very nasty thing occurred – I was very weak by this time and they set down a wounded man and tipped him up and before I had a chance to pick him up the RAMC picked him up and said, 'There's the bloody man who wouldn't help a wounded soldier.'

Howard Marten and three others regarded as the ringleaders were taken before the base commandant at Boulogne.

Well it was all water off a duck's back. I hardly knew what they were talking about most of the time. And of course, what must have galled them was that while we were reasonably civil, we were never prepared to do things in a military way. We never saluted anybody; we never stood to attention. Well, of course, that was a frightful crime in the eyes of the military authorities. Interviewing an officer I'd think nothing of putting a hand on his desk, in a very friendly casual sort of way, and of course that was disgraceful. It didn't even occur to me. I treated them as I'd treat any normal person.

Soldiers were issued with a regulation postcard to send home from the front. On it was a series of standard sentences. John Brocklesby, from the Richmond Group, had managed randomly to alter one of these postcards so that it read:

'I'm being sent to B ou long.' (*sic*)

Thus the men's whereabouts were confirmed. Questions were raised in Parliament by sympathetic MPs, and the Reverend F.B. Meyer and Quaker journalist Hubert Peet were allowed over to France to bring back a report on the men. Stanton and the others were interviewed by Meyer.

He told me that at the request of Lord Kitchener, he had come to France to interview us, in order to find out the truth about our attitude towards the Military Service Act. Lord Kitchener had been anxious, said Mr Meyer, that we should be fairly treated, and had wanted to know whether we would be prepared to serve the country in some way other than military service. I replied that while there was certain service which I was very willing to do for my country, I could not agree to do anything which would facilitate the prosecution of the war. It was possible that under certain conditions, I should be prepared to do work under the civil authority, but I could give no promise to do so. Some of the officers sitting by listened very impatiently and restrained themselves with difficulty from interrupting.

It may be imagined that we were immensely encouraged by this sign of the devotion and resource of our friends in England.

The visitors were taken for a tour of inspection through the prison, but were not brought to see our quarters. We were amused afterwards to hear that Hubert Peet had described the barracks as a clean and airy place, which if applied to the punishment cells, would have been, to say the least, inept. The description may, however, have served to relieve the anxiety of many at home, whose imagination had doubtless painted into the picture even darker hues than were warranted.

The other groups of COs from Richmond and Seaford joined up with them at Henriville Camp. On Saturday 10, Monday 12 and Tuesday 13 June 1916 the men were all tried by Field General Court Martial – which had the ultimate punishment at its disposal – the death penalty. Evans was among those court martialled on 12 June.

On the Monday I was taken before the court martial in Boulogne, which consisted of a Colonel and two captains, and was a Field General Court Martial. A FGCM has life and death powers. At the invitation of the President I made my own statement saying that I was opposed to war on religious and political grounds.

A day or two before the trial a captain came to see me and said, 'I've just left the company office looking over your papers – they're marked "death" in red at the top. Do you intend to go on with this?' I said 'Yes, you see sir, men are dying in agony in the trenches for the things that they believe in and I wouldn't be less than them.' To my utter astonishment he stepped back a couple of paces and saluted me and then came forward extending his hand which I then shook heartily. I never saw him before nor since.

On Thursday 15 June the men who were regarded as the four ringleaders, including Howard Marten, were the first to be taken out on to the parade ground to hear their sentences.

There was a big concourse of men, mostly of the Non-Combatant Corps and the labour battalions, lined up in an immense square. We were taken to one side of it, and then under escort taken out one by one to the middle of the square. I was the first of them and until my verdict was known, nobody knew exactly what was going to happen. Then an officer in charge of the proceedings read out the various crimes and misdemeanours; refusing to obey a lawful command, disobedience at Boulogne and so on and so forth, and then, 'The sentence of the court is to suffer death by being shot.' Then there was a suitable pause. And one thought 'Well that's that.' And then, . . . now the second thing, 'Confirmed by the Commander in Chief.' That's double sealed it now. Then another long pause, 'But subsequently commuted to penal servitude for ten years.' And that was that. And the thing that interested me and the others particularly was that penal servitude meant your return to England, and would get us into the hands of the civil authorities at a civil prison. You see as long as we were in the hands of the military authorities we were subject to military punishments. We could only go on offending.

CHAPTER 4
Prison

Some could rise above it. To some prison was hell; it was really impossible for them. It wasn't for me. It worried some and to such an extent they just about went off their heads.

Mark Hayler

More than 6,000 conscientious objectors were refused exemption from military service, court martialled, and sent to military prisons. In 1916 Mark Hayler was sentenced to 112 days hard labour and sent to Wandsworth Prison. He arrived just before midnight and insisted on seeing the governor.

And I told him, 'I'm a CO. I've just come from Aldershot and I am a civilian, this is a military prison', because Wandsworth at that time was a military prison. 'Oh,' he said, 'I can't help that', or something like that, just pushed it aside. He said, 'I've got men like you in irons down there.' I wasn't frightened.

Eric Dott served his 112 days hard labour in Wormwood Scrubs.

I didn't feel it a punishment, it never struck me in that way though it was meant to be. The labour wasn't hard, they called it hard labour but I was sewing mailbags most of the time, stitching mailbags with hemp we were given, that was my hard labour.

We were in solitary confinement and you were allowed out for I think an hour for exercise and then back to your cell again, and the exercise was strictly supervised so that you couldn't speak to anyone else. You were pounced on at once by the warders if you tried to talk to any other person. You went round in a circle in this exercise yard and then back to your cell again. If the warder talked to you, you could talk to him but couldn't initiate any conversation at all. He wandered round the place and peeped in at the peephole to see that you were all right, or if he had occasion to tell you this or that he would open your cell, otherwise you saw nothing of him at all, you were just alone.

During that first period of solitary confinement we got no letters but after that month was up I was allowed to write home and tell them I was fine. The first month, it was very boring, but being young and with a good memory of all the things I knew I didn't find it too bad, but some of the men found it awfully hard that first month. You were quite alone, had the Bible, which was a great asset because for those who liked reading it was a very good thing to have. And then after a month there was less strictness. They came round with a tray full of books from the library and you could pick your book, and have reading then of your own choosing to some extent, which was a great help. And I remember I got *Nicholas Nickleby* and read the whole of it with great attention and interest.

Harold Bing spent a total of three years in prison.

One's power of concentration tends to decrease after long months of imprisonment. You find yourself turning over a page and then waking up and saying, 'Well what have I just read?' Your eyes had sort of passed over the letters but the contents hadn't entered your brain at all; it hadn't been memorized. And so one had to make quite an effort to concentrate and one's power of concentration certainly declined.

The cell was about 6 feet by 13 feet with one small window above one's head so that you couldn't see out of it except by standing on your stool – for which of course you might be punished if you were found doing it. In the door there was a little spyhole with a cover on the outside so that the warder could come along and open the spyhole and spy on you at any time to see what you were up to. So that you had the sense of being watched the whole time – which gave you a very uncomfortable feeling at first until in time you grew indifferent to it.

In the cell, there was a plank bed which stood up against the wall during the day, put down at night with a mattress. For the first month you were not allowed that mattress, slept on the bare plank boards. At the end of a month you were given a mattress. In addition you had two or three blankets and a rough pillow. There was also a small table and stool, the chamber pot, the can for water and a metal bowl in which to wash, a little shelf on which one kept one's knife, spoon and fork, a pot of salt and any photographs which one was allowed to have in. One was normally permitted not to have more than two or three photographs and they must be of members of one's family or close relatives.

Scotsman Eric Dott was far from home and family.

There was a very high window that you couldn't reach and gave quite good light in to the cell. You couldn't see from it even if you stood on the little stool that you had. I used to crane up and try and see out of it and I could just see the line of the underground railway at some distance and you could see the sky.

My thoughts just rolled, I thought of what I read and what they were doing at home. I was in no problem about why I was doing it, as I had thought of it all pretty much before, but some of the other men they were much less easily placed. Many of them weren't readers, many of them had people at home who were very underpaid and perhaps ill and they had all these worries that I hardly knew because I came from a happy home, quite well off with no worries or dependants and it was so different for those who had dependants who were badly off, or were ill.

Quaker journalist Hubert Peet had three small children when he went to prison in 1916, and kept their photographs in his cell. Throughout his three years in prison he sent his children pencilled self-portraits and descriptions of his surroundings.

Now I want to tell you about the little room in prison in which I have been living. It is about as big as the scullery

at Peak Hill with a iron door with no handle on the inside
and a little window with iron bars on it high up in the wall.
All it has is a little table, a stool, a few pots and a wooden
bed without any legs. This is put up against the wall during
the day with the bed clothes over it. I have a spoon to eat
with, a funny tin knife, a tin plate and a mug which I wash
up myself after every meal. For breakfast and supper I just
have porridge and brown bread and that's all. No butter or
jam or cake. Then for dinner I get bread and potatoes and
sometimes suet pudding, sometimes soup and sometimes a
little bit of meat.

The limited prison diet posed added problems for vegetarian
COs like Harold Bing.

When I first went into prison one simply ate the rest of the
food and left the meat and the meat went back in the food
tin to the kitchen. In Winchester I found it was possible –
a sort of smuggling arrangement – to exchange my meat
for potatoes with the prisoner in the next cell and I did
this for a time. When inquiries were made, as the result
of letters from the Home Office, about the position of
vegetarians, the prison doctor examined me and weighed
me and expressed his surprise that I was maintaining my
weight although according to my statement I was not
eating the meat. So I confessed to the doctor that I was
in fact exchanging it with another prisoner. After a fairly
long struggle we did manage to get the recognition of a
vegetarian diet and an arrangement was made by which
instead of meat, vegetarians were supplied with a piece of
cheese, sometimes a little extra vegetable. There was also
an arrangement by which those who did extra work to the
quota allotted to them could get a mug of cocoa before they
went to bed at night and some did that.
    As the war went on, and the diet became more restricted,
many prisoners felt that the vegetarian diet was rather
preferable to the ordinary diet and quite a number of
prisoners who'd not been vegetarians applied for vegetarian
diet. The first few who applied were granted and then the
prison authorities came to the conclusion that this was not
something with which they should comply and so no one
was allowed to change his diet during a sentence.

Of course this meant that when they started their next sentence many men did apply for a vegetarian diet.

At the end of their sentence, conscientious objectors were released, returned to barracks where they would disobey an order and be court martialled once again and returned to prison. It was a strategy used against the suffragettes – what was termed the 'Cat and Mouse' treatment. At the very least, it enabled the COs to snatch a glimpse of loved ones during the brief interlude between prison and the guardroom back at barracks. Sympathetic soldiers escorting them would sometimes allow them to exchange a few words with their loved ones or to buy a decent meal *en route*. Once back in the guardroom awaiting their next court martial, they had the freedom to send more letters home. In reality these were tiny flashes of light soon forgotten once the next prison sentence began. Mark Hayler sank into depression at one point in the war.

I remember having a spell of thinking, 'I'm never getting out of here – if the war goes on then I shall be here for years.' That kind of condition that produces thoughts like that is really, astoundingly, disrupting of one's character.

Then there's no one to talk to, it's no good talking to the chaplain, maybe one in a thousand who wants to be bothered, and of course there's nobody else, that's why you talk out of the window sometimes to the man next door. How conditions affected some I never knew, you didn't know what was happening in the cell next door. Men would shout out in the night, yell anything out to break the monotony. And when things went on month after month and went into years, it seemed as though there would never be an end to it you see.

Some people can't bear their own company. It's too much. Probably people who exaggerate situations, same as a person who can't bear the dark, they're longing for the morning, it's a claustrophobic condition I suppose. Day to some people never ends and nights never end. Well, that's all very well to some people and its unbelievable what it can do to you and if you work yourself up into a state you bang your head against the wall – anything to change the conditions, and there were some who suffered tremendously. You could condition yourself but these were people who couldn't, I mean if a man suffered from asthma and there was no means of getting any help. People weren't all like me who had good health and some were easily sent off balance physically, they were easily thrown off and those that had cares, home ties and so on. I had none of that kind of thing, I was fortunate, but these people were several and were living the lives of several people and being able to do nothing whatever, those are the conditions that begin to be amplified.

Eric Dott's sunny personality carried him through his sentence at Wormwood Scrubs.

We had our humour, even there in Wormwood Scrubs because there were quite a number of Scottish prisoners there and they started whistling Scottish tunes to each other, and sort of replying with them you see. And this infuriated the warders who tried to stop them but they couldn't, and it really was the most amusing episode how they would whistle the 'Bonny Banks of Loch Lomond' and that kind of thing and someone else would reply with some other Scottish tune and they even got a little bit of conversation through it by replying with some appropriateness – they sort of sent messages.

We were allowed visitors after the first month and I used to receive a little indirect news that way. I had an aunt in London and she was very much against me being a CO, but she came to see me and talked and gave me a little news – one of my cousins had lost his life in the war and she told me about that, not real war news as to how the war was going, we only got that when we got to Dartmoor.

Ironically, the 'Cat and Mouse' treatment allowed news to filter through when Harold Bing was in prison.

It's extraordinary how much news did come through because there was the fact you see that so many of the men were on short sentences – six months, nine months, twelve months – and therefore continually there were COs going out to camp, generally being tried in the neighbourhood and nearby camp or barracks and coming back again. And while they were out of course they got newspapers and they were visited by their friends and collected all the news. So that whenever a CO came back for a second or third or fourth time everybody was anxious to get news and it soon spread round. So that we were kept fairly well-informed as to what was going on not only with regard to political events and the war but also with regard to politics of the CO movement. I remember there was great excitement when the news of the Russian revolution came through. People thought this would make a great difference to the war.

The prison chaplain, not usually sympathetic to conscientious objectors, did give some war news during the weekly service. Harold Blake recalls one example.

Somewhere around the middle of August 1917, the chaplain made the astounding statement in his war news, that the efforts for peace being carried out in this country – including the resistance to military service on the part of conscientious objectors – were subsidized by German gold. Whether he believed that or not, I do not feel competent to say but the lie so incensed many of us that we individually decided to forego the 'privilege' of attending chapel. To carry this resolution to effect it was necessary that we ask to see the chaplain and obtain his permission to be absent. Even had he not granted that permission I think it would have made no difference to our attendance, or non-attendance.

Most prison warders could not comprehend the stand taken by conscientious objectors. Some were downright hostile. Harold Bing, who became a teacher after the war, was friendly with two or three warders while in Winchester Prison.

I was working with one of them particularly who became very friendly and his daughter was attending the secondary school at Winchester and was having considerable difficulty with her maths and occasionally, when he opened up the cells early in the morning at 6 o'clock, he would push into my cell surreptitiously, his daughter's homework and ask me to check it for her, correct it if it were incorrect, or indicate, give her what help I could. And then when he came round to distribute the breakfast at 7 o'clock he would take back the corrected work and when he went home to breakfast himself – take it to his daughter. This went on for some time. After that warder's death, which occurred I think very shortly after we were released from prison, a number of us who'd been in that prison raised a fund to enable his daughter to continue at the secondary school which otherwise her mother could not have afforded to have done. And in fact one CO who had been in Winchester Prison and who had a number of shops in the London area found work for that girl and her mother a little later. So that we did try to repay the kindness which that warder had shown to us.

Many conscientious objectors were philosophical about the hardships they had to put up with. Eric Dott was in the peak of health.

There weren't rats, there were cockroaches, but I think that was the only kind of plague that you could say. Sometimes they got in and it was difficult to keep them out of the food. Most of the time you were in your cell and locked up. In Wormwood Scrubs it wasn't cold, the place was adequately heated. I was there in summer, so I'm not the best judge of that but I don't remember anybody complaining it was cold.

I often think how different it was for me. There I was young and fit and many of them couldn't face it the same way as I could because I was young and fit.

Fenner Brockway and some of the other leading lights in the No-Conscription Fellowship actively defied the prison system.

We found the prison system was absolutely inhuman and denying human rights. We were not even allowed to speak to each other. Of course we did but we always had the sense of doing something which was prohibited and which if we were found doing it would lead to punishment – bread and water, solitary confinement.

But a point came when many of us felt that it was undignified and humiliating to accept the system itself and we decided openly to resist it. For ten glorious days sixty of us ran our own hall in prison. Speaking openly on the exercise ground instead of marching five steps behind each other and not saying a word – round and round. We took arms, we played games, we organized concerts every night. We were shut in our cells but at a window – we had lots of Welsh boys who could sing beautifully – they would sing at the window and everyone down the side would hear. But the effect became disastrous in Walton Prison, Liverpool, because not only did our own boys hear but the ordinary prisoners heard as well. And so the five leaders were isolated and then we were transferred to other prisons. I was transferred to Lincoln Prison. I had eight months solitary confinement at Lincoln Prison. Three months bread and water treatment until the doctor wouldn't allow more. And yet one had a sense of freedom which I can't describe. I mean the Governor would summon me into his presence, but instead of going in and standing at attention and everything else, I'd say, 'Good morning Governor. Nice morning isn't it.' One had an extraordinary sense of personal liberty, personal freedom.

While he was there Fenner Brockway found some infamous allies.

The Sinn Fein leaders were detained in that prison at the same time – De Valera and the others and they got to know I was there. I was in a cell alone – twenty-three hours and twenty minutes out of twenty-four shut in the cell; forty minutes exercising alone. Anyhow they got to know I was there. And one day I heard a step outside my cell. Got up on my stool and looked outside and there was a red band man – a red band man is a prisoner who's allowed to go about with warders – and he signalled to me to get down and through the open panel came a message from the Sinn Feiners: 'Just heard you're here. We can do anything except get you out. Let us know what you want'. I ordered daily newspapers. And they used to supply me with these papers every day. The red band man had the job of cleaning out their latrines in their yard. He used to put them in a drain, I'd put them in my trousers; changed them every day and the warders never troubled to search my cell because I was so absolutely isolated and they didn't think it possible. And I think the Sinn Feiners saved my mind in that long period of solitary confinement.

Talking was forbidden between prisoners and the men were only allowed to speak to a warder when spoken to, but conscientious objectors adapted to their conditions and devised ways of communicating with each other, usually using Morse code. Harold Blake didn't know Morse until his third sentence.

> During the greater part of my third sentence the cell next to mine was occupied by a young Scottish telegraphist, who taught me the Morse code, so that we could converse together – or play draughts. The commencement of this was accomplished by him 'in writing' the code on his cell slate, and then we exchanged slates.

Young active minds devised all sorts of cunning ways to improve their lives as Harold Bing recalls.

> The only writing facility in a cell was a slate and the slate pencil and therefore if you filled your slate you had to rub it all out again. There was no writing material except periodically when you were allowed to have the notepaper in your cell and a pen and ink to write your monthly or fortnightly letter. But here again a little ingenuity was used and some prisoners managed to make little ink wells by taking a block of cobblers wax – which was used for waxing the thread for making mailbags and so on – making a hole in it, sinking a thimble into the wax and then covering it up with another piece of wax. So that what appeared to be a block of wax was in fact a block of wax with a lid and when you lifted the lid there was a thimble sunk into the wax. And that thimble you filled with ink when you had your fortnightly or monthly ink for writing your letter. With ink pots of that kind there was produced in Winchester Prison a periodical called the *Winchester Whisperer*. It was written on the small brown sheets of toilet paper with which we were supplied – different people writing little essays or poems or humorous remarks, sometimes little cartoons or sketches. And all these bits of paper were passed surreptitiously from hand to hand and reached the editor who bound them together with a bit of mailbag

canvas, used for repairing, for a cover, and this issue of the *Winchester Whisperer* was then passed round secretly hidden under people's waistcoats or up their sleeves. And as it happened, despite many searches, no copy of the *Winchester Whisperer* was ever captured by the warders, though I think some of them suspected its existence. And all the copies were finally smuggled out and placed in some depository in London, in some library. Most prisons where there were COs managed to do something similar. Canterbury Prison ran a little surreptitious magazine called the *Canterbury Clinker* and others with, again, similar names in other prisons.

I used as a pen a needle, writing with the hollow end – dipping the hollow end into the ink. This meant of course one had to be always dipping the needle into the ink for almost every word. But it did produce thin writing so that you could get a good deal on one small sheet of toilet paper.

The *Winchester Whisperer* was a handy pocket size, about 5 inches square, and was bound with mailbag hessian with the title embroidered on the front. It was one of several 'conchie' prison newspapers. Harold Blake recalls the 'editor' of the Wandsworth periodical.

He was, in build and feature, almost the double of Mr Lloyd George. This man undertook the publishing of a news sheet which he designated the *Old Lags Hansard*. This periodical was written by hand in block characters on sheets of toilet paper, and sewn together with thread; and on account of the labour involved, only one copy of each issue was published. However, it went the rounds passing from hand to hand, and finally when it had fulfilled its intended purpose, it was contrived that it should fall into the hands of Mr Walker, the Chief Warder. The vastly amusing part about the whole business was that the last page always contained the announcement, 'Look out for the next number, to be published on . . . [date]' and in spite of all the efforts of the authorities to trace its origin, we were not disappointed. Once indeed it was a day late, as they made the declared date a search day; but the editor presented his apologies in his editorial to the effect that he was a day late in publishing 'owing to an official raid on our offices'.

As well as spending long hours sewing mailbags alone in their cells, COs mixed with other prisoners in the various prison workshops. During his third sentence Harold Blake became aware that, although he and other COs had specified that they would not take part in work that was of a military nature, prisoners had been stuffing canvas with cork to make fenders for naval ships and were making foot racks for army use. Therefore he refused to work.

> I asked to see the governor and then acquainted him with my decision, explaining that I no longer trusted the authorities to respect my scruples in connection with war work, and I was determined that I would not participate in war in any capacity, the only means by which I could be sure of remaining unentangled in such service was to refuse to do any work whatsoever so long as I was kept in prison.

As a result Harold was kept in solitary for eight months and deprived of books apart from five religious books. He was allowed one educational library book per month.

> On three separate occasions during this period of solitary confinement, which lasted eight months, I was unfortunate enough to have inflicted upon me, *A Short History of Our Own Times*. This book might be described as the political history of the reign of Queen Victoria, and I cordially detested it; three months irritation with that book was almost enough to drive me to distraction, and I was strongly tempted to push the abominable thing out of the window.

Bearing in mind that it was reading material of any nature which helped to keep many COs sane, he must have been desperate indeed. Another diversion was needed. In the next cell was another CO, Stanley Hodgson.

> During my solitary confinement at Hodgson's request, I wrote out, on toilet paper, a complete series of lectures on elementary human physiology, and delivered them to him one by one, as they were completed.

Harold Blake also did a series of lectures on the working of the motor car – for the same 'client' – but in October 1917 he was beginning to feel the effects of his imprisonment.

I began to get apprehensive lest my memory should fail altogether, for I became aware that that facility in me was not anything like so acute as heretofore. Therefore I borrowed, in the evenings at supper times, from Stanley Hodgson, a copy of Shakespeare's plays, which he got from the library for my especial benefit. I returned it to him at breakfast time each morning, so that it was never found in my cell. From this I committed to memory whole scenes, which I recited in my cell with the utmost enthusiasm. The memorizing was hard work at first, but I found that as I persisted in my efforts, my memory regained its wonted activity.

It was towards the autumn of 1917 that my internal organs were becoming deranged, I suffered from spasms of extremely severe pain across my middle as though I were being screwed up in a vice. At first these spasms were separated by fairly long intervals of time, but gradually they became more and more frequent. The attack culminated in a violent turn of vomiting, and altogether feeling used up, I was then better until the next attack. I recognized the symptoms as those of a congested liver due to an unsuitable diet; the diet in fact containing far too much starch for my particular case, and throwing on the liver more work than it could cope with.

A year later the attacks had become more frequent, and Harold was suffering from loss of appetite.

I remember that at one time during this period, I existed for four days on one potato. I simply could not swallow the food, and naturally it was only to be expected that my strength should fail.

He collapsed and was taken to the prison hospital, this time for several months.

My second despatch to hospital constituted a great surprise to me. Although I was aware that I was in a very weak and emaciated condition, I did not for a moment imagine that

I was the subject of a disorder serious enough to warrant removal. It was true that the slightest exertion beyond the most slow and leisurely movements occasioned me considerable discomfort and caused me to gasp for breath; but I concluded that to be the result of extreme weakness only. I was in fact so weak that I had not the strength to carry myself upright but stood and walked with drooping head and bowed shoulders.

Harold Blake did survive to write his memoirs and to see another war – his health restored. But, as Harold Bing remembers, not all were so lucky.

Some died in prison; some went mad; some broke down in health completely and never really recovered; some were discharged because they were on the point of death; some suffered terribly from insomnia – it was almost unbearable for them. This depended partly on one's physical constitution I think. It depended very much upon one's temperament. I mean those whose temperament was such that their life depended on social activity and contact with other people – the very sociable type – found solitary confinement almost unbearable and almost a strain under which they broke. Those who had, shall I say, more resources within themselves or had the more monastic temperament, adapted to it very easily. And the greater the mental and spiritual resources an individual has the more he can stand those conditions.

It was always said of the ordinary criminal in England, that when the International Commission on the Penal Systems met in Geneva early in this century and assessed the prison systems of the different countries they reported that they considered that among the civilised countries the English prison system was the most severe because of the silence rule and the solitary confinement – because this is particularly hard to bear for people who haven't got much education or much internal resources. And therefore for many people it was extremely hard.

According to No-Conscription Fellowship records, ten conscientious objectors died in prison.

CHAPTER 5

The Home Office Scheme

Many of them were really sad men as it were who couldn't see the holiday camp atmosphere that a young happy man like myself could do.

Eric Dott

In 1916 the government established centres where COs could be sent to do work of national importance under what was termed the Home Office Scheme. Harold Blake along with other COs received a letter in his cell at Wormwood Scrubs in September 1916.

The first paragraph of the letter seemed to point to the conclusion that the army was desirous of ridding itself of the embarrassment of conscientious objectors in its ranks, and was beginning to realize that it could hope to achieve nothing by a continuance of a policy of attempted coercion against firm conviction. And that was the only piece of satisfaction to be drawn from the document. Yet such is the indomitable woodenness of the military mind that the last two paragraphs (the major portion of the letter) abound with threats of further coercive measures. A further piece of almost incomprehensible imbecility is brought to light by the statement which declared that in any event the conscientious objector's name would still be included in the list of the army reserve. Were these people totally incapable of grasping the fact that we resolutely refused to be branded as the property of Caesar? – to be stamped with his image and superscription? That one blunder alone was responsible for opening the eyes of many to the traps and pitfalls with which the Home Office Scheme abounded.

Evidently the authorities had no doubts but that we should eagerly embrace this proffered opportunity of escaping prison life, for without even asking if we agreed, a warder commenced to measure us for fitting the clothes (or should one say – the uniform), of section W of the Army Reserve to be supplied to those who accepted. But again there was blundering in estimating the inflexible mental and moral timbre of many of the men with whom they had to deal. I believe that I am correct in saying that I was the first to refuse acceptance of this insulting attempt at subversion, and when the officer essayed to put a tape round me, I told him that he was merely wasting his time, as I should not for a moment dream of agreeing to such obnoxious terms.

To accept ANY condition of exemption from military service is to me equivalent to entering into a bargain with the government that, provided I am not required to do the killing, they can carry on with the war and kill as long and as hard as they like; and I am not prepared to make such a bargain.

As his sentence in Wandsworth ground on and on, Blake was assayed with doubts about his decision.

But when the feeling of despair had descended upon me, the lust of the flesh for ease and comfort began to tempt, and to war, with the spirit. Why should I remain in the cheerless prison when by merely signing an unimportant paper I could end my lonely isolation in comfortless confinement? I need have nothing to do with the war, and surely I could not do more for God and the cause of peace, while I enjoyed a measure of liberty. How could such a small body of men as we were, hope to accomplish anything by offering ourselves against the might of the most powerful empire the world has known? Was I not kicking against the pricks and wasting my life in futile attempts? And what of those whom I had left outside? Was not my first duty to them?

For men in prison the degree of freedom offered by what were really workcamps was a great temptation. Despite his opposition, Harold Blake recognized this.

No one, save he who has been confined for months in the prison cell, can have the faintest realization of the fierceness of such a temptation to lower the standard. In the innermost recesses of my soul I knew that the smallest compromise with the forces of evil would be wrong, and would in the end secure the victory for evil, but should I not be justified by virtue of the greater amount of activity which I should acquire outside?

I struggled against these flesh-pleasing and alluring suggestions and sophistries for hours, my distress of mind becoming greater and greater as the minutes slowly dragged by. At length I felt that my mind must become unhinged, and reason give way under the strain, and at the thought of insanity my overwrought nerves produced an irresistible impulse to laugh. I realized with horror that I was hovering on the borders of hysteria, and remembered that the best antidote was a good shaking . . . and springing from my stool I threw myself violently against the cell wall.

He was rescued from his despair by a dream in which his sister appeared as part of a heavenly choir.

Many others were prepared to 'make such a bargain', among them Eric Dott, who accepted the scheme in 1917 when it was well established.

When we'd done our 112 days hard labour at Wormwood Scrubs we were offered a choice of going to a place where we could do work of what was called 'national importance' and have a certain amount of liberty there as long as we stayed in one of these centres like Dartmoor or Wakefield where they had made special arrangements for that, but there were a certain number of COs who refused to accept that. They said that this was collaborating with a wicked government who was running an immoral war and they became known as the absolutists and they were sent back to prison again and had a very hard time of it.

Whether by design or not, the scheme split the ranks of conscientious objectors, as Harold Bing, one of the 'absolutists', reflected later.

Although some were inclined to think 'Well they've let us down a bit', I don't think there was any really hostile feeling towards them. There was a recognition of course that we were all in the same boat and for some men, shall we say, with family responsibilities or whose wives were unsympathetic, it was always a terrific pressure on them to get out in order that they could communicate, keep in touch with their wives instead of being completely isolated from them. It was in some cases a necessity to save a marriage and therefore we were not critical, although we felt – those of us who were absolutist – that was the right position and wished that everybody would take it. But I don't think we felt censorious towards those who felt unable to take that position, either for practical reasons, or because they couldn't see the principle involved, as we saw it.

Howard Marten, one of the 'Frenchmen', and an active member of the No-Conscription Fellowship, felt the split was inevitable.

You couldn't get away from it. Conscientious objectors were some of the most argumentative people. You found so many different points of view; it seemed inherent among pacifists. You see, the very thing that brings them to that point; they're men of strong individuality, and when you get that clash of personality coming along you almost inevitably strike strong differences of opinion.

Harold Bing, who was an ardent pacifist all his life, chose to remain in prison.

A considerable number of men accepted this scheme and went down to work at Dartmoor and later at Wakefield Prison under this Home Office scheme. But a considerable number of us refused to accept this scheme because it involved accepting a position in the army reserve with of course the possibility of call-up later on and because it was accepting, acknowledging, the system of military conscription. And we said that we were opposed to conscription, not merely the conscription of ourselves but the conscription of other people as well. Not only were we opposed to war, we were also opposed to conscription and therefore could not accept any service under a conscription act.

Howard Marten did accept the scheme.

We hoped it might be in the national interest. You see, many of us felt that with all its imperfections, it might open the way to a more enlightened treatment of the penal system, as you might say a by-product. Anyone who had an interest in penal reform felt that the Home Office Scheme could possibly provide the nucleus for a more enlightened method of dealing with ordinary prisoners. But unfortunately, you see, you had a category of man who wouldn't work the Home Office Scheme. They didn't want the scheme to work and they weren't prepared to work it. Well you can do very little with men like that; and there was that element present which was most difficult for us, who were trying to work things.

Harry Stanton refused to accept any service under a conscription act when offered the Home Office Scheme, but was nevertheless sent to Dyce Work Camp near Aberdeen in September 1916. In his memoirs he remembered how his departure from Wormwood Scrubs was delayed by twenty-four hours.

I examined my garments with some curiosity. The reason for the delay in our departure was now clear. The agents of the Home Office must have spent the previous day ransacking the stalls and barrows of Petticoat Lane. The underwear was new but shoddy, the boots second-hand, heavy and too large, but how otherwise could the prison commissioners be sure of my getting them on? For trousers, I had the choice between a pair of golden brown corduroys, and a pair of purple hue, but equally odorous and capacious enough for two normal people. A new, very new waistcoat of the same safe proportions, embellished with fancy buttons of coloured glass. I could not imagine for what kind of person it had been designed. Of jackets I had the choice of two; the more notable one of ample proportions and Victorian design in the seafaring tradition, but both giving evidence of long and hard wear. The crowning point was a

tiny cotton cap made in the college style. There was no sign
of collar and tie.

We were all clothed with some degree of similarity,
with a tinge of seafarer-cum-coster. The handsome
waistcoats with their fancy buttons were a source of
mutual congratulation – save for common envy of a man
whose buttons portrayed horses' heads. The tiny caps set
over the pale unshaven faces gave a ludicrous turn to the
otherwise rather solemn outfit.

When Eric Dott arrived at Dartmoor Convict Settlement, a
year later in 1917, the 'uniform' had evidently improved. The
day after his arrival he wrote to his sister Kathleen.

Last Friday I was fitted out with the 'Home Office'
clothes – a tweed jacket and waistcoat, corduroy trousers,
a good overcoat, warm flannel drawers and vests and
shirts, warm socks, strong boots, cloth cap and muffler and
leather leggings, all good, well made clothes! On Monday
afternoon I and about thirty others got notice to pack
up next morning – and Tuesday at 10.30 found us all in
Paddington station with our own clothes and our change
suit of Home Office clothes in big bundles under our arms.

It was a delicious journey – and for a time I could do
nothing but gaze in admiration at the abundance of trees,
and green fields and delicious country. It was a refreshing
sight after the dusty brickwork of Wormwood Scrubs.

We were a very jolly party and the day passed quickly
enough – we arrived at Princetown, quite a small village up
in Dartmoor, about 6 o'clock and about 10 minutes walk
took us to the huge convict prison where we are settled.

There were about a thousand COs at Dartmoor, a quarter of
them religious objectors and the remainder socialist and political
objectors. Mark Hayler came from a Quaker background but
deemed his objection to war to be on moral grounds.

Well of course there was the religious group. Even
within that group there must have been quite a number
of variations, from Plymouth Brethren down to anything
from Salvation Army, Christian Scientists, and of course
Methodist and Congregationalists, all the denominations,

not so very many Church of England, for the reason that that was the establishment – I think there were some only they weren't so noticeable as some of the others. There were only small groups out of each lot but they were quite distinct. It's interesting at Dartmoor they wouldn't allow us to use the church. The Bishop of Exeter refused the conscientious objectors use of the church in the prison. If we'd been murderers we'd have had a free hand, and we could have sung 'God Save The King'.

Eric Dott was a socialist and a Christian and found it a congenial place.

At first I was a little surprised to find it was a proper prison where we were to stay – but I was soon put all right about that – I picked up with a very nice young man almost at once (they appear all very nice men here) and he undertook to show me all around. In the first place we went to my cell, which we prefer to call a 'room', and I found that all the doors have their locks screwed up and that there is nothing to keep us in our rooms. In the course of conversation with my new friend, I learned that there are only two or three warders in the whole place, that it is practically 'run' by the COs themselves, that nothing is ever locked except the big outside door at night, and that after working hours are over at 6 p.m. we can wander anywhere within about 5 miles round, so long as we are inside the prison by 9.30 p.m.! Some prison! More like a well-arranged holiday camp.

The food is in abundance and we have meals all together. There is a good big library here, though I have not been able to inspect it yet, and they have a reading room and a common room where all kinds of games go on (ping-pong among them!) and, I was told, a good deal of gambling too, which they have had to suppress. Then there is a concert room, and a gymnasium!

All this after the solitary seclusion and severe restrictions of Wormwood Scrubs is indeed enough to carry us off our legs a bit – and so far as I saw last night there seems to be a good deal of wasted time in the evenings – excited talking and playing at games constantly – I can't be sure how others find it, but I feel that I will need to take great care

to get some good sound reading done and to substitute self
discipline for prison discipline.

Eric Dott's descriptions of Dartmoor in his letters home are
tinted with the optimism of a youth glowing with health and
enthusiasm for a cause. But conditions at Dartmoor were
undeniably better than the notorious Dyce Work Camp a
mile and a half from Aberdeen. It lasted for only a few weeks
in the late summer and early autumn of 1916. Harry Stanton
was one of the 200 men sent there.

In the sunshine the camp seemed pleasant enough; but
it looked as though only a moderate rainfall would turn
it into a bog. The tents we were told, were leaky and had
been condemned long ago. Sanitary arrangements were
primitive. We were a curiously assorted company ranging
from Anarchists to International Bible Students, and
Quakers were sometimes able to keep the peace among the
more extreme pacifists, for in the camp discussions there
were many occasions of dissension.
  In the morning following our arrival we started work on
'the quarry'. I found the work very hard and exhausting
and was thankful when the first spell of two and a half
hours came to an end. My hands were sore and badly
blistered; my back had apparently stiffened in a curve – I
wished never to see a wheelbarrow again.

Similar traditional convict's work was also done at Dartmoor.
It was not a job enjoyed by the usually ebullient Eric Dott.

Stone breaking is the task for wet days. Though it needs to
be pouring before we are kept in from Mis Tor. The stone
sheds are long low buildings with side quite open – simply
a wall at the back, a roof and two ends. There are several
of them, and the outdoor parties have to crowd into them
and sit behind a long stone bench, with a little hammer in
one hand and an iron hoop on the end of a handle in the
other, and break stones. You put your iron ring round a
few stones (which are, roughly, a little bigger than a golf
ball) and you smash them into gravel with your hammer.
All the time you are cramped for room. The wooden
plank you sit on is too near the stone bench, and there

are men crushed up against you on either side. You are very cold and desperately fed up. The men play draughts with the stones, or keep a book beneath the bench to read at convenient intervals, like school boys reading 'Tit-bits' underneath the desk.

But here is a bit of good news. I was only on that work one day, when the doctor said that men who wore glasses were not to do stone breaking. So when the others are sitting cramped and shivering, I and a few others are in our own cells sewing mailbags.

Men on the Home Office Scheme produced the *News Sheet*, which circulated between the various camps. In one edition was an account of the work at Broxburn camp.

Here a number of conscientious objectors sent from Wakefield are employed. The work consists in making manure from carcasses of animals and bones with the addition of chemicals. The work is naturally very disagreeable. The raw material is pulled to pieces with the pick and shovel and then placed in barrows and taken to the mill for refining. Two men then catch the dust in bags and weigh it, when it is then ready for farmers. A very nasty smell pervades the place, and clouds of dust affect the men's bronchial tubes to such an extent that a large number of them have been affected and bronchial troubles are prevalent. The men are bothered with much coughing, and spit up a considerable amount of green matter.

Normally this work was done by casual labourers passing through the town who wouldn't do it for longer than a day but among the men employed on this was the Medical Officer for Health for Argyllshire, Dr J.C. McCallum – just one example of the highly qualified men among COs. The newsletter also reported cases of smallholders and farmers who were employed as navvies on the scheme leaving their land untended, at a time when the government was trying to encourage the nation to grow more food.

Despite the privations COs on the scheme did have relative freedom to go out and enjoy themselves, going fishing, painting and walking. A group of men from Dyce even went to see the *Mikado* in Aberdeen, but more commonly they made their own entertainment. In a letter home, Eric Dott delighted in the intellectual stimulation he discovered all around him at Dartmoor.

Lately there have been a great number of classes started: English, French, Shorthand, Logic and many others. All these reveal the energy that there is in our settlement, for most of the men have done a hard nine hours work before their classes. The shorthand class is elementary and no use to me, but there is an attempt afoot to get up a 'speed' class which would be an immense help to me and to many others.

One thing I notice about the men here is that they discuss and debate on every subject imaginable – they can't help arguing – whenever the kind of work permits it, they gather into groups and talk and talk. A very constant theme of dispute is supplied by the differences of the religious and the political objectors. The men who believe in the literal inspiration of the Bible and in the story of the creation, etc., come in for a good deal of chaffing – and I admire the way they take it – I have never yet seen any one angry here.

Even in the grim tented camp at Dyce the COs started putting on entertainments which obviously endeared them to some of the locals. Harry Stanton recounted some of the highlights of life at Dyce in his memoirs.

Our concerts were often attended by some of the farmers and their families, and very soon the 'artistes' began to receive and to entertain rather more select though less critical audiences in neighbouring farmhouses. There were many signs of friendliness from the natives. We found that the minister of the Free Kirk was a member of the Fellowship of Reconciliation and many COs began to attend his services. The Aberdeen newspapers discussed us and our relations with the Home Office and we were agreeably surprised to find the Aberdeen Free Press taking up the cudgels on our behalf.

One Sunday a number of Friends (Quakers) came over from Aberdeen, and we held a meeting within an ancient stone circle not far from the camp. We sat there quietly with little thought of the strange rites in which the great stones had played a part thousands of years before.

For the men at Dyce these were the highlights of an otherwise harsh existence characterized by insufficient food, and demands from the Home Office for working hours at the quarry to be doubled from five to ten hours a day. The COs petitioned against the change, threatening to strike, but for Harry Stanton and his comrades day-to-day survival was to be of greater concern.

We soon found that our living conditions were none too healthy. Several men were suffering from chills; and there was no provision for nursing them. Some of them lay on the ground in the draughty bell tents, with a black Scotch wind howling outside, others had been moved to a cowstall at a neighbouring farm. As the weather worsened many of us moved our beds to the farm buildings; a few managed to find lodgings in the village. This was against the strict injunction of the agent, who repeatedly issued orders that all must return to the camp, but to no purpose. The situation was clearly growing serious. The only medical attendance was that of a doctor of irregular habits, who came over from Aberdeen at irregular intervals. His attention was called to a CO named Roberts who was lying ill in the stable. On his next visit he pronounced him dangerously ill and had him removed to the camp where a corner of the recreation tent was partitioned off as a ward. But in such conditions there was no hope of recovery and Roberts died within a few hours.

The camp committee renewed its demand for some facilities for nursing and improved medical attention. As a result, the authorities gave orders for a ruined cottage to be partially roofed over, to serve as a dispensary and emergency hospital and to be staffed by COs. The doctor was replaced by a more reliable one.

After the death of twenty-year-old Walter Roberts, the first conscientious objector to die, Dyce Work Camp was closed and the men dispersed. Harry Stanton was sent to Wakefield.

Looking back over those weeks at Dyce I saw that we had done nothing to further the cause of pacifism. We had been a nuisance to the Home Office Committee; and had convinced some people of our inherent laziness. The few we had left behind in prison were doing more to establish the rights of conscience than was accomplished by all our efforts to tire the authorities into granting concessions. Surely to 'work the scheme' was to abandon our opposition to conscription.

Men on the Home Office Scheme were brought into greater contact with the general public and several groups were attacked in other parts of the country, where some did agricultural work under the auspices of the scheme. Harry Stanton was transferred to Wakefield Work Centre and he and others became suspicious that COs who were being hired out to private employers were inadvertently sending other men off to the war. Stanton and others refused to work and were returned to prison. Alfred Evans, one of the 'Frenchmen', was on the Home Office Scheme for a few months but returned to Winchester Prison and was released from there on 12 April 1919.

I was on the Home Office Scheme and I went down to South Wales to work on the waterworks and it was a slave driving job and they put professional slave drivers over us, people who had been slave drivers over African natives. Anyhow, we found out that the government were paying the employers the trade union rate of wages, while they were paying us halfpence a day, so I called our boys together and said what about it, they said 'Go, go and tell them we're not having that, we don't mind working for the halfpence a day but we're not putting money into employers' pockets, not a bit of it'. So in twenty-four hours we were on strike. I went back to prison. I saw that it was futile.

At Dartmoor little attempt was made to disguise the pointlessness of the labouring jobs given to Eric Dott and his fellow COs.

We were all put on to what they called work of national importance, which was just a farce because they just found digging for us to do. We were supposed to be laying a pipe line or something and it was of no importance. We never got it done anyway, but as long as we were there and doing this job and didn't try to go away we'd considerable liberty there at Dartmoor.

I was in a group that was called the Mis Tor group; the Mis Tor was one of the high peaks in the Dartmoor surroundings and it was because our place of work was out in the direction of this hill that we were called that. And we had two wardens who stood over us and saw that we dug the trench, and nobody took it very seriously at all and we'd dig slowly and the wardens were very friendly and as long as they saw we were doing some shovelling they didn't take any other interest in us, and we'd break off at intervals at lunchtime and then we'd have meetings there and have learned discussions on philosophy and socialism and religion and all that kind of thing. Lively meetings that we exchanged views in.

The building was a bit grim, but our life wasn't very grim there really, or perhaps I shouldn't say that, if you were young and fit as I was you could relatively enjoy the time there. But there were many older men and men with worries at home for whom it was very hard. That was one of the really hard parts of it for people in poor circumstances, their families got a small pittance, I can't tell you how much it was, less than what the soldiers got for their families and that made it very hard. And those who were not so strong and fit found it very hard, because conditions were very rough; you slept on boards with a thin mattress between you and hard boards, and altogether you had to be fairly fit to stand it. I think of several of those that I met with, one of them was a young man, Peter Brown, who had active tuberculosis, who got no sort of treatment for it whatever and whose family at home were very hard up and he died not long after he got back home. And there were others in similar difficulties. There was a man whom I didn't know personally, who had diabetes and they knew nothing about the treatment of diabetes and one of our leading men among the COs, C.H. Norman, who became a leading leftist politician afterwards, he struggled hard to get that man with diabetes better looked after and to some extent he did.

Like he should have been on a proper diet, I don't know
whether he needed insulin or not, but he wasn't getting
any treatment, and it was a great struggle to get the
authorities to meet that kind of problem.

By the time they reached Dartmoor all the men had served
prison terms, some quite lengthy, and their health was worn
down. In February 1918 Mark Hayler nursed Henry Firth,
the only CO to die at Dartmoor.

I was working in the hospital at the time I attended him. I
was a sort of orderly you know, he was only a boy, twenty-
one, and he was a local preacher with the Methodists, and
his wife came down from Yorkshire, and I can see her now
sitting not in the cell but on a chair outside the door.
   He had pneumonia. He'd been badly treated at
Dartmoor, he should never have been sent out on the
moor in bad weather. He should have had an indoor job
and he got this cold and he got pneumonia. Anyway, I
stayed with him all the night and brought him through
to the morning and when I went off duty at 8 o'clock or
whatever it was he was still alive, but he wasn't alive at
8 o'clock the next morning. It was the only funeral from
Dartmoor and the whole of the men attended the funeral,
they insisted, they couldn't have prevented them and they
followed behind the coffin down to the railway and it
was put on the little train at Princetown and taken down
to Plymouth, that's the little railway that winds, single
line along the moor, you can see it for miles on its way to
Plymouth which is about 10 miles away.
   And we went to the station and it was all arranged by
our own people, we didn't allow the prison authority to
do anything except what they had to do, and some of the
COs got hold of some fog signals and they put them on
the line here and there. As the train went out of the little
station at Princeton these went off, a sort of farewell. And
I remember nearly a thousand men sang a hymn, 'Abide
With Me'.

The No-Conscription Fellowship recorded that seventy-
three conscientious objectors died as a result of their
treatment at the hands of the authorities.

CHAPTER 6

Those at Home

I am very well now and do enjoy this sunshine. At least as much as I can without you to share it with me. I do wonder how you stand the heat. How I long for you to be free in the sunshine. The air is full of the scent of the roses and the pinks. Do you remember what the wild roses smell like!

Edith Peet, 13 June 1917

While conscientious objectors struggled to oppose conscription their wives fought their own battle. In July 1918 Edith Peet was living on the Isle of Wight with her three children. She wrote to her husband Hubert in prison.

I go green with envy when I see all the jolly holiday makers on the sands here now. Daddies with their families, and honeymoon couples everywhere. Then I realize that probably all the men about are enjoying a short holiday before they begin 'killing' again (for the men go into 'mufti' as soon as they go on leave) and I feel thankful that things are as they are – in a way. I hope that if 'concessions' come along you will take them, if only for the sake of others, and for others who are coming on afterwards. I know on the other hand that it will only make it harder for the public to realize that the only and right course is 'unconditional' release. So few understand. I really thought Mother did for one, but we had a *very* painful talk about it the other day and I find that she does not at all understand the *real* point. Father does better than she does and says his opinion is that it ought to be unconditional release or no release at all. How I ache at the thought of it going on and on for you but may God give you the strength to go on for it is the only way. You know that I stand with you and, in all I can do outside here, back you up. How I wish I could do *more*. If only I could do a little to help these children of ours to be more ready and fitted to fill their place in the world as worthily as their father is filling his I shall be thankful. It will be a great help for them in the future Hubert, this out and out stand which you have taken. . . .

As well as emotional difficulties, Edith and other women struggled financially. Through his involvement with the No-Conscription Fellowship before he went into prison, Mark Hayler encountered the problems of those at home.

My mother used to go with my sister and sometimes with my father to pay in money. We had a maintenance fund, we couldn't give very much, perhaps about one or two shillings a week and my mother and my sister they used to go to certain houses and pay this money.

And you would have a man maintaining his mother, but there were critical situations because they would have had to go into the army and if they didn't there was no money coming in you see. We kept a fund going and lots of other things were done to keep the homes together, and that side of the work was quite an interesting piece of work, real social work it was. I remember going up to Upper Norwood and discussing with a man there and he said, 'How can I, I'm all with the conscientious objectors, but I've got a family and if I go I'm the mainstay of the family'. And I said if we could help you somehow would you, and he said, 'Yes I would' and he did, and I sometimes meet his wife now even after all these years and she says, 'We never regretted it, although we lived on nearly nothing, but the Fellowship and the whole set up was such a glorious piece of work, we made new friends and all sorts'. It meant a great deal to some of these men. I used to write home and my letters were read at the weekly meeting at the Friends Meeting House in Croydon and always kept in touch, and the NCF visited us in prison and went to the tribunals. They did all sorts of things and were very active.

Harold Bing, another Croydon man, had a sympathetic family behind him. His sisters Dorothy and Phyllis were also active peace campaigners. Dorothy Bing remembers the NCF meetings.

> They had reports of any of our members who were due for trial. We had letters read – they were allowed a letter once a month from prison and they were brought by various wives and so on and we read the letters out and discussed them. We arranged social gatherings. We took the children out because we felt the kids might be missing their daddies and so on. Took them on visits to fire stations and places of interest.

There were cases where marriages broke down because the wife was unable to accept her husband's position. The Home Office Scheme was a temptation because it gave men more access to their families through more frequent letters and visits.

While Hubert Peet was in prison his father died but he was not allowed to go to the funeral. For his own children, their father's long absence due to imprisonment was difficult to understand. Hubert Peet was very aware of this and with characteristic skill simplified his predicament beautifully when he wrote to them from the guardroom at Hounslow Barracks after his first court martial.

> I expect it is difficult for you to understand why I am not at home with you all, I would be if I could, but I am not allowed to. Someday you will understand all about it, but I will try and tell you something now. The English People and the German People have got angry with each other like two children who want the same toys, and hundreds of men are now trying to kill each other. Now Daddy and Mummy and lots of other people think it is wrong even if another person gets angry with you, for you to get angry with them. The only thing to do, even if they try to hurt you is to love them and love them all the more. That is what God does if we are naughty, as we sometimes are when we forget. We hope that the other people will, because we are still kind to them, see what God is like and will then feel sorry.
>
> This is why your Daddy says he cannot be a soldier and go and try and kill the daddies of little German boys and girls. Most people think he ought to go and because he will

not and he thinks it is wrong, they are shutting him up in prison this afternoon. There are a lot of other men there who think like Daddy that it is wrong to fight, and I believe that people outside will come to see that's why it is that we won't get angry with the Germans, because we believe that even if they began the quarrel this time it is better to go on loving them than trying to hurt them, and that they will then stop being soldiers and fighting and we shall come out of prison.

Edith Peet wrote back soon afterwards.

The girls talk of you continually and of all they are going to do and tell you when you come back. They are being so very good and I very seldom have any tears or bother. The letter you sent them before you went *right* away was so dear. We read it often, they like to hear it and I think they have quite grasped what it means. Mary stands up for you very much but I heard Joan say to her the other day, 'I think Daddy ought to have gone to have been a soldier when they wanted him to go, Mary'.

'I don't' said Mary very promptly.

Because the Society of Friends was the only religious organization which, as a body, made a stand against the war, Quakers like the Peets had a supportive network of friends which certainly helped to sustain Edith for the three years Hubert was in prison. But the chance of encountering the wives of other COs was fairly slim in rural areas like the Isle of Wight where she and her children spent part of the war.

I think I told you that I had heard of a CO's wife at Ventnor. I have been over to see her and find we have many things in common. The greatest, being that her husband, P. Bagwell, was taken to Scrubs the day you were and came out of Wandsworth after his 112 days the day you did. Since then he has been in Wandsworth and is looking for his fourth CM in April 1919. Mrs B is such a nice woman – rather older than I am and is keeping a stationery business in Ventnor. They have been married eight years and have three children – Joan, seven, Gwen, five and a half, and Philip, four. I found them out just in time to invite them to Mary's birthday picnic. I am so thankful to have come across others of our thinking as near as Ventnor. There is also a NCF branch as Sandown but it is very weak at present and meetings have dropped for a time. Several Sandown COs have returned to work on farms etc but are not considered genuine by the inhabitants because they have taken alternative work.

Harold Blake's adored wife Amy was not so lucky and felt under pressure from some of those around her. While he was in the guardroom at Mill Hill Barracks Harold received a letter from her which so upset him that he destroyed it. His reply survives.

My poor wife,

I received your letter last night and have had rather a restless night over it.

Yesterday I felt that I was doing right, but now I am not sure. Perhaps my first consideration should have been to you my darling, and if that is so, I have made a ghastly and awful mistake. But it is too late to alter things now. Too late! If it were not too late I would give in and take my place in the RAMC yet I am convinced that that action would be wrong.

You forget dear, that I have not been given the opportunity of doing work of National Importance. Even if I had, I should consider it quite as wrong as the RAMC and of the two I should prefer the latter. Oh! my darling, you can never understand the terrible fierceness of the temptation you hold out, when you ask 'for my sake'. I am beginning to understand something of Adam's feelings when Eve tempted him. Yes, 'for your sake' I would sell my soul now if it were possible.

I do not know how you are going to live either, but I had faith in the promise Jehovah jirah (The Lord will provide). Now everything is dark and I cannot see the way out. Oh! darling, forgive me if I have appeared to desert you, but you know I have acted from the highest motives. Just think! if this act were to remain in force, how would you like your children dragged from you and broken on the wheel of militarism? Yet that is what would happen, and for the sake of the unborn we must break the fetters, whatever the cost. You yourself have a great sacrifice to undertake for this great end. Probably your part is harder to play than mine, but let me be proud of my wife, and able to say to her children, 'Your mother bore her part bravely in the fight for your freedom'.

And now dear, I go to take the consequences of my action, but my confidence is shaken, and I pass from the outer world with vain regret, and a feeling of utter loneliness. Do not think hardly of me.

Yours in anguish, Harold.

Relatives received a standard letter informing them which establishment a prisoner was in, and were allowed to exchange one letter a month in the early stages of the war. Later rules were relaxed and they were allowed two. But visits were infrequent and difficult for loved ones who often lived far from the prison. Eric Dott's family was in Scotland but he had an aunt who visited him during his sentence in Wormwood Scrubs.

I knew my aunt who came to visit me would disapprove of what I'd done, but it was very kind of her to come and visit me and she didn't press that point at all, and she told me that my cousin Alastair Geddes had lost his life in the war, but she didn't, as it were, blame me in that. I think that she thought I was a genuine CO and thought that this was my thing to do but she was very sorry I'd done it.

Harold Bing was another CO too far from home for regular visits.

I only had one visit and that was at Wormwood Scrubs because Winchester was too far from home. And there is a sort of narrow corridor with a warder walking up and down. Either side little cubicles, the prisoner on one side of this little corridor and the visitor on the other. So there's a space between and there's a wire grille in front of the visitor, in front of the prisoner. And so you're about 2 feet apart and can just talk through this space and a warder walking up and down the whole time listening to everything that's said. So you get very little but family news. An attempt to communicate anything which the warder would regard as political or having to do with prison or planning an escape, the visit would immediately be stopped. Later on, certainly in Winchester, they had a more, shall I say, a more humane arrangement by which the visitor and the prisoner were brought into a room and sat either side of a table with a warder usually sitting at a little distance. If he was hostile he'd probably have tried to overhear every word. If he was a friendly warder he made it obvious that he wasn't listening.

His sister Dorothy had a vivid memory of the same occasion.

We were let in with a big key and the door was locked behind us and we were taken into a small room and then he was brought out behind a sort of grille and there was a warder standing within a few yards of you. But some of them were very decent; they sort of walked a few paces away so that you could talk personally. And of course some of them were hard because they'd got boys at the front, naturally, and when my cousin was killed it was the governor – or a warder – who came in and said – just blurted out you see – 'Anyway your cousin's been killed in France; that's where you ought to be' – you see that type of thing. Terrible shock for Harold because he was so fond of Tom. We all were. A very fine lad.

Harry Stanton remembers one visit at Winchester Prison.

He ushered me into a small room fitted with two parallel counters, a yard apart and with fine wire barriers. Beyond the second barrier was my mother. At first I could find little to say to her, and she was too anxious about my health and circumstances to talk freely before a stranger. But when the warder broke into our conversation to express his views 'as a Christian man on the righteousness of war', my mother firmly reminded him that he had no right to take up so much of the time which was all too short. This had the desired effect, and we talked without further interruption till with a triumphant 'Time's Up!' my guardian hustled me out of the room.

Edith Peet managed to keep her husband informed about the whereabouts of other COs and gave him news from the *Tribunal* – the newspaper printed clandestinely by the Central Board for Conscientious Objectors. She visited Hubert sometimes travelling from the Isle of Wight, and even took her eldest daughter on occasion.

> It's so good to think that I can really write to you at last but I find it difficult to know how to begin. But when I look back the time seems very short since I last saw your dear face. I never can be thankful enough that I did have that chance of seeing you, for the memory of the peaceful happy look you had has been with me ever since and I *knew* that whatever came, you would have a quiet mind and feel absolutely certain that the way you had gone was the only way.

Gwen Bagwell, playmate of the Peet children, remembers visiting her father.

> One of the things I think I vaguely remember is going to see my father in prison, and it was a great talk on the telephone box thing and very dark and black, I couldn't see, and there was a grille which he looked through to mother and to me and I was down there standing and mother had to lift me up before he could see me and I'm told that I said, 'Look Daddy, I've got a new vest'.

Growing up in a pacifist household surprisingly had meant few brickbats from the neighbours, although what hostility there was sticks in Gwen's memory.

> I think perhaps we were aware of it when Joan and I went round to our friends at school, round to their houses to get them to sign a petition to get father out of prison because of course the COs stayed in prison until March or April of the following year (after the war ended), and we asked for them to be out and we had some experiences then, didn't we? 'No, we won't sign it, you let him sink there,' that kind of thing, which was a bit hard to take.
>
> We went to a party at Christmas time and the host had lost her husband in the war and they gave presents to the children, they gave a gun to my brother and he wouldn't take it and then, I can't remember the remarks, but it was a lot of tears over that.

Having a CO in the family inevitably left its mark on Harold Blake's mother.

> She still persisted in her faith that nobody could do aught but recognize my sincerity and act accordingly and my heart sank as I realized the crushing weight of sorrow that was in store for her. Crushing indeed it was, and its effect upon her when I again saw her after many months of incarceration – not withstanding that I had previously been warned of the great change in her – rendered me speechless and staggered me so greatly, in the weak condition in which I then was, that I was compelled to sit down in order to avoid falling in a state of collapse. The treatment to which I had been subjected by a Christian community – the superscription by the hand of Caesar – left its mark indelibly impressed upon the delicate tissues of her mind so that even while unconscious upon her deathbed she constantly called for her 'prison boy'.

Harold Blake's mother did not die before her 'prison boy' was released in 1919, but those three years of his imprisonment had had a terrible impact on her as Harold saw for himself when he returned home.

> When I reached the house I entered slowly and wearily, and proceeded into the room where my mother sat. I had been told that I should find a great change in her, but was nevertheless totally unprepared for the sight which met my eyes. When she saw me coming in, she rose to come to meet me, and I observed that her frame – but particularly her arms and hands – shook, with an agitated nervous jerky movement and that she tottered in her gait. She came forward one or two uncertain steps, and then came to a stop clinging to the table for support. The shock was so great to me, that it order to prevent myself from falling in a heap on the floor, I hastily sank on the nearest chair, and with a cry of 'Mother' I buried my face in my hands. My mother renewed her efforts to come to me and placing her trembling hand on my bowed head, she said, 'Don't cry my boy, you're home now'.

When Harold found his beloved Amy waiting for him in an adjoining room he cried out her name.

All the pent up longing of slow drawn out years of heart-breaking separation were compressed into the utterance of that one loved name. I stood rooted to the spot, gazing in delight at the fascinating sight before me; afraid to stir lest the slightest movement of a finger should break some magic spell and cause the entrancing vision to dissolve into nothingness before my eyes. . . . Then with a few rapid strides I crossed the room to take possession of the hands held out to welcome me, and gently drew my wife to me. I had left her a young man in the full vigour of health and youthful energy; I returned a broken, aged and grey-haired old man. But the affection between us burned with the undiminished warmth of an unchanged devotion.

Although their feelings were undimmed, with the war behind her, Amy rarely referred to her husband's conscientious objection in later life, and never went into a church again. It took Harold some time to adjust to life outside prison.

I experienced some difficulty and strangeness in returning to my normal mode of life. One of the things which troubled me greatly was a stiff collar – that absurdity of modern life. My rest was broken and disturbed – frequently destroyed – by horrible and nerve-wracking dreams. I was always awake and restless long before the household stirred, and at times I dressed and stole out for long walks before the others were up.

The No-Conscription Fellowship continued to care for COs and their dear ones and arranged a second honeymoon for Harold and Amy at the farm of a Quaker near Bromsgrove – even sending £3 for their expenses.

CHAPTER 7

Friends Ambulance Unit

Passing an aid post with an over-loaded car on one occasion an orderly rushed out saying: 'For God's Sake, stop; I have not had a car for two hours!' and behind, stretched on the plain in the moonlight, were 400 wounded Canadians.

Corder Catchpool, April 1915

A witness for peace has been part of Quaker belief since the seventeenth century and during the First World War 1,200 conscientious objectors served with the Friends Ambulance Unit. Set up in the early days of war, it was at first a band of volunteers, trained in first aid at a camp at a Quaker hostel called Jordans in Buckinghamshire. Once conscription was introduced some men were able to get exemption on condition they served with the FAU.

Howard Lloyd Fox had a Quaker mother while his father was a member of the Plymouth Brethren. He was twenty when war broke out.

As soon as war was declared, I wrote to the war office and offered my services with my Douglas motorbike as a despatch rider. I had a sort of boyish idea that I could get to France and do something in the war without having to go through the trouble of being drilled and disciplined. I had always avoided, partly at my mother's request, partly my own feeling, joining an OTC corps, it was not compulsory at school and I didn't join. My mother was very strong on peace. The War Office were rather slow at accepting my offer of myself and my motorbike. Sometime, I think about November, they wrote and said they would be glad if I would report somewhere,

by that time I had already joined the FAU, so that put paid
to that.

I knew Philip Baker, vaguely, who was largely responsible
for it, and as soon as I heard the unit was being formed
– I wasn't in time for the first draft. I think I joined the
FAU about September 1914, I remember being interviewed
by Sir George Newman who was Head of the Education
Department and he asked me for my service in the unit.

At the tented camp at Jordans the volunteers did physical
training and took a first aid course. Before they left for France
they were also inoculated against typhoid. Howard Lloyd Fox
went to the London Hospital for part of his training.

We went to see operations being done, the idea being you
must get used to seeing blood if you wanted to go into the
ambulance service. I don't know whether I was extra blood
thirsty but it simply amused and interested me very much
to see people being operated on. I was put in charge of
squads who went down to London Hospital because they
knew I wasn't going to faint when I saw blood and could
help anybody who felt that way inclined, and we worked
in the outpatients' department, doing all sorts of jobs, very
primitive business by modern standards. London Hospital
was down in the East End, near the docks serving a very
poverty stricken area of London. We used to go for route
marches, with all sorts of army recruits, up the Edgware
Road, round Hampstead Heath, several hundred of us, the
FAU only provided a small squad and there were a large
number of other recruits.

Members of what was initially called the 1st Anglo-Belgian
Field Ambulance Unit wore khaki like the rest of the
troops – a uniform they had to pay for themselves. Corder
Catchpool was away on holiday on the Continent when war
was declared. He joined the FAU on his return and landed
at Dunkirk in November 1914. His letters home give a vivid
picture of what he found.

As soon as we got alongside they asked for immediate
volunteer dressers; hundreds of wounded at the station,
and no one to attend to them. I shall never in my life

forget the sights and sounds that met us. Figure two huge goods sheds, semi-dark every inch of floor space – quais, rails, everywhere covered with flimsy French stretchers, so that in places you had to step on them to get about – and on each stretcher a wounded man – desperately wounded, nearly every one. The air heavy with the stench of putrid flesh, and thick with groans and cries. Four-hundred of these wounded, and one French medical student to attend to them – an English staff officer and an English naval officer helping voluntarily. Half dead as we were with fatigue, we flung ourselves into this work throughout the night, the need was so great. Consider this man, both thighs broken, and he has travelled 20 kilometres, sitting on the seat of a crowded railway carriage. Or this one, with his arm hanging by a shred of biceps – or this, with bits of bone floating in a pool of pus that fills up a great hole in his flesh, laughing bitterly when I turn away to vomit, overcome by the stench of sepsis – he may well laugh bitterly – he has lain eight days on the filthy floor in an outhouse of some farm near the front.

The priests touch more than we, hurrying through the solemn rite – they need to, men are dying on all sides.

Once they'd dressed the wounded, Corder and his fellow volunteers loaded them on to hospital ships and they were shipped round the coast to other French ports.

We never get more than a few hours sleep at a time, our work is to redress the wounds; most have been several days with only the first field dressing – filthy at that – and are frightfully septic. The priests glide about in the semi-darkness; they always 'administer' in cases of doubt, to be on the safe side – so that the man shall be I mean – after which the chances are he turns over and dies – bad psychology.

Half these cases will lose a limb; perhaps the blinded men are the saddest, if one excepts those who have gone mad. If one could grasp it, or stopped to think, one would be in danger one's self – the work is one's safeguard, and the need of help so urgent that I have never tasted purer happiness than during the past week.

Our ideal as a voluntary unit is to fit in where the pressure comes on overworked or inadequate staffs. The poor men are so grateful for the little service one can render – sometimes it is merely to make them more comfortable to die, or the even humbler service of making them a little cleaner; thou can imagine the joy of seeing clean white bandages replace filthy rags, and knowing that underneath wound or flesh has been bathed clean with antiseptic lotion.

Besides various scissors, forceps, lint, bandages, surgeon's gloves, eau oxygenee, tinture d'iode, and other medical necessaries, my little haversack goes down crammed with chocolate and cigarettes – especially the latter. See the *piou-piou's* face light up at the sight of a 'cigarette Anglaise'.

Corder Catchpool's patients were mostly French, with an occasional Briton, but there were also quite a number of Germans. Although these men were 'the enemy', members of the FAU made no such distinction, in either their feelings about them or their treatment of them.

One has to help the latter mostly by stealth, but it is lovely to be able to do so now and then. They are, of course, prisoners of war, and we are not free to do as we like. The French are apt to be very jealous. Their wounds are the most frightful of all – sometimes they have lain a week without any attention at all. They are very brave and do not expect any kindness or attention. They suspect the drink one offers them, and often need a lot of persuading before one can touch their wounds.

The unit established a base hospital at Dunkirk with dressing stations at Ypres and elsewhere along the front. The FAU ambulances travelled along appalling roads into the danger zone to bring back wounded and dying men. While working in Ypres in January 1915 Corder wrote:

One thinks, just that thin line of weary men in the trenches with their rifles, between us and the powerful enemy ever watchful to burst through at a moment of weakness. But when I hear our guns booming, and the burst of the shell after, 'Poor Germans,' say I to myself involuntarily, 'I hope no one was hurt by that one'. Or when I see them firing with rifles and shrapnel upon a Taube, as they did this morning from our courtyard, I shudder to see him brought down. I ought to be wild with joy, you know; but then I am a poor soldier, and a special brand of patriot, it's admitted.

It is grand the way men give all – their comfort, their lives, gladly to serve their country, in a cause they believe to be right. But when I look out of my window at night, as I do now and see the starlit sky prostituted by those blood red patches of flame, I turn away sick at heart and go to bed and think that they with all the sublimity of their sacrifice are dupes; we, dupes; all the world, dupes of the handfuls of charlatans who make wars, exploiting, trading upon, those nobler traits of human nature. 'Your country needs you,' cry armament manufacturer, Junker, Chauvinist, well-knowing that at that cry millions of hearts that beat true and honest will begin to beat proudly and courageously, and millions of men will march out to slay their brothers. Thank God from the bottom of my heart for the inestimable privilege of being allowed to try and patch up the results of this ghastly mistake. But oh! the infinitesimal effect of the patching. The awful smallness of one's self amidst these vast forces. I was chatting to a lad in the wards this afternoon; both arms amputated, and he was trying to compose a letter to his fiancée about it.

During the summer of 1915 Corder Catchpool was made Adjutant and spent much of his time at headquarters dealing with administration. Some men from his unit joined the army and Corder began to express the view that he was no longer sharing 'all the dangers and hardships of a fighting soldier.'

I feel more and more that we who have been spared are only justified in going on living if our future lives manifest, at every point and at all times, a heroism AT LEAST equal to that of the soldier who is killed in battle.

Corder became increasingly discontented and after the introduction of conscription in March 1916, he voiced a disquiet shared by many FAU men that their presence was forcing other conscripts, who might have done medical duties, into the front line. He was also concerned for other conscientious objectors.

> A good many of my boys are getting restless, being afraid that COs will be forced either into the NCC or into prison, and that if so they must resign the FAU and take their share of the hardships.

Corder and others did resign, and the absolute exemption which FAU members had been given was withdrawn. He spent the rest of the war in and out of prison – but a great deal happier and more fulfilled than during the quiet days in FAU headquarters in France.

Howard Lloyd Fox had become chief accountant at FAU headquarters in London until in February 1917 he managed to get a replacement at HQ. He had the opportunity of joining a hospital ship in the Mediterranean, a hospital train or hospital barge in France, or a hospital at Dunkirk.

> So I started driving an ambulance for what became the Dunkirk Ambulance Service, serviced entirely by the FAU. I was rather nominally head of a convoy of six cars doing the work in the Dunkirk area, which was just the sort of job I wanted. It involved taking the Colonel and medical officer round the army medical depots in Dunkirk. Dunkirk when I first got there was a very big centre for munitions supplied to the British army. It was brought in to the Dunkirk docks and stored there, presumably, and distributed by road and even by canal over Northern France to the Ypres sector. That made it very vulnerable to night attack by airplanes, every time there was a full moon or near full moon, we had a hectic time at night. Six months of bombing and long range shelling from a large naval gun, a 21 incher, used to drop shells at intervals into the Dunkirk area, right into the middle of our hospital complex, without killing anybody.

There were also women serving with the FAU. Rachel Cadbury served as a nurse in France from October 1917 until 1 January 1919. She too recalled the heavy bombardment of 1917.

Bombs the whole night, bombs and shells. Under fire from air, land and sea, because we had a bombardment from the sea at one period. Sometimes people say, 'Were you frightened?', I said, 'Oh of course not, I was doing my job, I wasn't frightened'. But the bombardment from the sea was a bit shattering because it was so noisy, so sudden, it came unexpectedly. Word came round to each ward, you're not to take your men to the dugout – you must stay in your ward with the men. The men were terrified. I wasn't but the men were. I'd only two hands, I couldn't hold more than two. It was frightening, it only lasted for about twenty minutes or something like that. I wasn't worried, really, I was worried for the men.

Both Rachel Cadbury and her future husband Paul served in the Friends Ambulance Unit. He was a driver and spent several months working on an ambulance train. She remembers some of the men's injuries.

We had a lot of head wounds. There was a lot of shelling out in the port and a monitor was hit and we had a lot of head wounds.

A lot of flying men came in, very untrained, you had to start the plane by whisking its propeller around and if you weren't careful you got hit by the propeller, and we had a lot of those.

We had a lot of things like pneumonia, chills on the kidneys, bladder troubles – from the trenches. We had a lot of eye cases because it was very dusty, drivers of various kinds.

Finally at 11 a.m. on 11 November 1918 the Armistice brought the First World War to a close. Rachel Cadbury remembers.

I was on night duty – the buildings which we'd taken over as a hospital had a big conservatory and we could get onto the top of this by a little ladder. We knew that the armistice was coming and so when we were off duty in the middle of the night, we went up there and to our delight it was all quiet on the western front, there were no flashes, no shells, nothing. A little light but no shells.

Some men who joined the FAU did not enter the medical unit but went to work on the land under the auspices of the FAU. Harold Holttum had a Quaker background and had been to the Friends School at Saffron Walden. In 1916 he was granted exemption to work in the unit's agricultural division.

I did know one or two COs who had been sent to prison, but there were exceptions. In some cases it might have been that the tribunal was more rigorous than mine was. I was known locally, but in a big town all the young fellows who came up before them were strangers. I went down for a few days to the Quaker's centre at old Jordans near Beaconsfield. We were encamped there for about a week and the FAU agricultural division had inquiries out all over the country and applications were coming in from farmers for help. I went to a village called Bourton, near Southall where the racecourse was. I worked for a farmer named George Norwood, he was a Wesleyan local preacher. I worked there for two years until he was turned out by his landlord who wanted the farm for his son – as we all supposed to keep the son out of the army because he didn't want to go in – and then I was sent to another farm near Beccles in Suffolk and then to another one in East Sussex which was a complete washout. I was the only chap on the farm who knew anything about farm work, it was run by a community calling themselves, Women Co-operative Farmers Ltd – all smallholdings, the farm divided up, with a little house here and a little house there and the central farm does all your horse work for you; it was a complete mess. But I was only there a few weeks and then the armistice came and I was told I was free to go where I liked. There was another CO lodging with me and we both worked for the same farmer. Farmers were urged in many cases to plough up their grassland and grow corn. There was quite as much encouragement by the government for farmers to grow more corn and meat, particularly after 1916 – when the sub warfare became more intense it was every bit as urgent then.

Harold Holttum was isolated from other conscientious objectors during the war, and rarely encountered any antagonism.

I was confirmed that all war was wrong, that was obvious to me, increasingly the only question that could have arisen in my mind was, 'Is it right that all these poor blokes are going out there and you're doing nothing to help them?' But I was doing something to help them, I was looking after the mother of one of them – I was paying for her lodgings, she was looking after me I admit. I was producing food for the people in the town who couldn't grow their own bread and quite honestly I was too busy to think much.

I had no problem with the farmers or the people working on the farms, on one occasion I went into the little town of Southwell for a haircut and the man in charge of the shop said, 'I have a conscientious objection to cutting your hair.' I said, 'Very well sir, goodbye'. I don't say we parted good friends but there were no more words. I never had any other real trouble.

Some of the papers were rather bitter about it but I didn't bother to take them. The conservative papers were more forthright on this matter; the liberal papers, that is the *Daily News* and *Westminster Gazette*, were a little bit more considerate, they didn't approve always but they weren't so damnatory you might say.

CHAPTER 8
Aftermath

I think it left most of us with the sense that it would have been better if it hadn't been so.

Mark Hayler

When the First World War ended the conscripts who had fought for their country did not immediately return. Most of the men who had fought for the right to have a conscience were not released from prison until April 1919 and were disenfranchised for ten years. The most immediate problem for COs was to get a job, as Harold Bing found out.

At that time if you looked through the advertisement pages of shall we say, *The Times Educational Supplement*, very frequently at the head of the advert was 'No CO need apply.' Advert after advert had that. And sometimes if you did apply, well, you got turned down as soon as they knew you were a pacifist.

Harold Bing found a teaching job in Cheltenham, at a school with a sympathetic head. Alfred Evans, one of the 'Frenchmen', had been apprenticed in a London piano factory before the war, he also had trouble getting a job.

I was drummed out of London. Nobody would give me a job in London. I went to see Wolfenden – under whom I'd been apprenticed and I went there to dinner with him on one occasion and he said, 'That's all right don't worry about it', he said, 'I'll write a letter or two for you. I shall have no influence in London, I shan't be able to, if you want to work in London I shan't be able to do anything for you, but if you want to work in the provinces I think you'll be able to get a job without too much difficulty', because there was a shortage of tuners you see. It was purely economic, they wanted a tuner and so I got a job.

Another of the 'Frenchmen', John Brocklesby, lost his first job after a week, and recorded in his memoirs his surprise at the strength of public feeling against COs.

I was surprised to find how bitter local feeling was against me; it seemed much worse than in 1916. I had thought that having proved myself sincere they would give me credit for it. But no, they had suffered the poisoning effects of nearly three more years of war. Possibly they had thought that the British army, the only God that many of them trusted, would certainly break such resistance. But we had beaten the military and they hated us for it. I could feel it as I walked in the streets, and I saw it in the faces of people who at one time pretended to be friends. One fact was very plain – former friends who had lost near relatives in the war welcomed me back into the old relationship at once.

First World War conscientious objectors had stuck doggedly to their convictions despite the unpopularity of those views. The experience left psychological scars on men like Mark Hayler.

It's dogged me all my life. Even when I became a director of the building society years afterwards, I was asked to go on the television, and the directors of the building society saw it in *Radio Times* and they never knew what my views were of course. I said, 'You won't want to be friends with me after you know what my story is.' So they said, 'No it won't make any difference.' So I said, 'You have no idea, I'm a regular criminal you see.' Of course they just laughed, but I was surprised what the reaction was, very friendly but it was still there, they would have preferred if I had resigned from the board.

When the whole war was over I got many jobs and then I was interviewed by committees and the last question was always, 'What did you do in the Great War?' I knew that was the end. I remember getting one very good job somewhere, and the secretary came to me and said, 'The whole committee's very sorry about it, but we couldn't possibly employ you with a record like that.' They couldn't get past it you see, no one would be responsible for employing a man who had been in prison.

It still continues among the more ignorant lot, but among others they would prefer that it hadn't been so and in some senses I would prefer that it hadn't been so because one doesn't like to leave a trail of that kind behind you. You've been tainted, and I can quite understand to people who are not in movements like I've been it doesn't carry any worth or value at all, you've just spoiled your life you see.

Conscientious objectors in the First World War achieved more than even their idealistic young minds could have dreamed possible. Their accounts of prison conditions led to reforms shortly after the war, and they laid the foundations for an acceptance of conscientious objection to military service, which benefited those men and women who questioned their consciences in the Second World War.

Alfred Evans had no doubts about his stand, but questioned what it achieved.

Now looking back on it I wonder about it all and thinking in the present set up was it worth it, but I think it was. Then you hark your mind back to another thing, do you know how the gladiatorial fights were put an end to in Rome? There was a monk and he jumped down among the lions and went before the Praetorium where Caesar was sitting and told him off and then went and got chewed up by the lions. And that put an end to it. There were no more gladiatorial fights after that and you see if there is any progress in this world at all it is of the heterodox and not the orthodox. I'm satisfied that I did my modest bit and I don't regret a single thing of it.

There were sixty thousand conscientious objectors in the Second World War. The increased numbers were evidence of a burgeoning peace movement among the generation growing up in the shadow of the First World War. They were no more popular than the First World War 'conchies', and many lost their jobs, but on the whole society was a great deal more tolerant.

CHAPTER 9

The Interwar Years

I was brought up a Wesleyan Methodist and we were encouraged to be soldiers of Christ, and I thought this was a dreadful thing for civilized Christian nations to be at each others' throats and trying to disembowel each other.

Aubrey Brocklehurst

In the aftermath of the First World War, as the true horror emerged, the peace movement blossomed. In *Peace News* a photograph from 1924 shows conscientious objector Harold Bing, who became a lifelong peace campaigner, and his sisters Dorothy and Phyllis, dressed in white, shining exultantly under the banner of the No More War Movement.

Nearly all the Absolutists of the First World War did become active either in the No More War Movement or the Independent Labour Party or the Quakers, if they were Quakers, in the interwar period.

Of course there was a much greater number of COs in the Second World War. No doubt this was partly the effect of the stand of the First World War COs and partly of course, I think, the kind of experience and education of the interwar period. Whereas in the First World War, in 1914, war took us by surprise, and was something which we felt was inevitable and everybody's duty to take part in it, there was a much more critical attitude towards war which had developed during the interwar period in the labour movement, the socialist movement. At one period in the 1920s you got not only the ILP but the Labour Party and the Trades Union Congress passing definitely anti-war resolutions. And although of course these were no doubt ephemeral, they did indicate a changing attitude towards war. Of course the war came less suddenly too, because from 1933, when Hitler came to power, one could see the war clouds gathering and people had time to think about it and make up their minds. It didn't just take them by surprise as in 1914. And in 1914 there was a tremendous enthusiasm for the war – war was a glorious thing, it was a crusade and so on – those who went to the Second World War went there with a feeling, well this is an unpleasant necessity. But there was no glorification of war, no enthusiasm for it.

Eric Dott had trained and set up in practice as a doctor in the interwar period.

A lot of time had passed when the Second World War came round. By that time I was a doctor and could have taken part as a doctor in the war, although, as it happened, they ordered me to stay at home as they were short of doctors in the sick children's hospital.

In the second war I still felt that the war was wrong, and I would say so, but I didn't feel that it was wrong for the men to go and fight in it if they believed that was the right thing to go and do. I felt more that the general consensus of national opinion overruled private and individual opinion in a way that I didn't think in the First World War. There I thought that the individual's opinion was absolutely the ruling point for him to follow, in the second, I felt that the overwhelming national opinion was a bigger thing than one's private view.

Many First World War COs considered Fascism, and its arch exponent Adolf Hitler, to be a greater evil than war itself. Fenner Brockway was one of them.

In the Second World War though I was not a pacifist and though I was tremendously anti-Hitler and couldn't oppose the Second World War as I did the first, I remained chairman of the Central Board of Conscientious Objectors because I believed in the liberty of conscience so much.

Eric Dott also saw Hitler in a different light from the Kaiser.

> I do think that did play a part because the Second World
> War did have very different causes. The First World War
> at the time I thought was utterly wrong and was a scramble
> among the nations for trade and colonies, but the second I
> recognized was very different indeed and socialist Russia
> was fighting against Hitler, and the war was more justified
> in national opinion. I still would have been very unwilling
> to play a shooting part in the Second World War. I hardly
> know what I would have done if I hadn't been a doctor and
> had been called up, but I think I would have been a CO
> and tried to join an ambulance unit or something like that,
> I wouldn't even then have been prepared to go out and
> shoot a man I couldn't see.

Harold Holttum had been granted exemption in the First
World War provided he worked on the land under the
auspices of the Friends Ambulance Unit. He was nearly
forty-three when the Second World War started.

> In middle life I suppose you have time to stop and think
> and alter your ideas a bit. When Churchill implied we
> should form a local defence volunteers force, I thought
> that's the best thing I can do. It was after Dunkirk and
> he [Hitler] was going in through Poland, he'd first allied
> himself with Russia and then declared war on them, and
> then Norway and the rest of them, and I thought, well this
> bloke's got to be stopped. . . and the only way to stop him
> was by taking arms, I didn't like it, but it was the only way.
> I joined the Home Guard and I had a rifle, an American
> rifle. Then they gave me a Lewis gun and made me a lance
> corporal and gave me squads of four to teach how to use it.

A new generation of conscripts was growing up in the shadow
of the First World War. Edward Blishen was a pacifist cuckoo
in a military nest.

> My father was a very military person, came from a very
> military family, not an important military family, but
> they'd all been privates or NCOs throughout the nineteenth
> century. My grandfather, my great uncles and so on, they all,

as part of their existence, served in the regular army and then did something else afterwards. So my father had been in the First World War as a bombardier.

He was in the Territorial Army and was in camp at the outbreak of war itself on 4 August 1914, so he went straight into training and very quickly into the trenches.

Anyone who went through the First World War as he did in the trenches in France must have been incredibly damaged by it really, extraordinarily damaged by it. He was wounded in 1917 and was sent home. But he was not sympathetic to pacifists at all, no in fact he had a rather dour outlook on things and believed what had happened to him should jolly well happen to you because that was part of the justice of things, so he rather felt that if he had fought a war perhaps I ought to fight a war as well.

Edward was born in 1920 in New Barnet, Hertfordshire.

My earliest memory of my father is of a man sitting in the corner of the kitchen weeping, I must have been about four or five at the time. He had a breakdown, delayed shell shock, couldn't go to work, couldn't get into a bus, couldn't get into a tube. He went to the doctor who in the way of a doctor at the time said, 'There's nothing I can do for you, go and dig the garden,' which didn't help my father at all. But he actually cured himself by taking a penny bus ride one day and then walking back, and doing that until he could take a two penny bus ride and he did that until he could get all the way to Whitehall, because he was a minor civil servant. He didn't speak much about the war, one or two anecdotes, that's all.

I read novels like Remarque's *All Quiet on the Western Front* and I read Sassoon of course and Graves and it began to seem to me that the work of these men was an immense protest at what had happened and one ought to take the protest seriously and what the protest amounted to was a protest against the whole business of going to war and I felt I mustn't not get involved in this however strong the inducements to do so, however strongly the need to join in was. I think the most decisive thing to me was seeing in Charing Cross Road, when I was about sixteen, outside a second hand bookshop, a book which consisted almost entirely of photos of men without faces, they were men who had survived the First World War but without faces, everyone of them with the hideous remains of a face. I remember standing and reading and making myself look through this book and thinking I can't be at the other end of this, I can't be someone who does that to somebody, but it was that sort of thing that very strongly moved me. I was moved by such things and when the war actually came in I was about nineteen and I wouldn't budge on it.

John Marshall, a young journalist at the beginning of the war, was also a great reader. In his boyhood he had catholic tastes.

Half of me was entirely conventional macho reading *The Wizard* and *The Rover* and idolizing tough men who would slaughter hundreds of other men you know. But also rather horribly fascinated by all these stories of the murder and destruction. There were numerous anti-war films at that time and they had a great influence on me. I read the novels of both *Journey's End* and *All Quiet on the Western Front*.

And when several of us got together we found we were anti-war and it was partly in my case a revolt against having been compulsorily in the Officer Training Corps. You didn't have to go in the thing but there was enormous pressure from one's friends to go in the thing. Although I didn't do too badly from it – I actually won the shooting prize on the main range. I could use a Lee Enfield rifle even before I became a pacifist.

Born into the Church of England, John became a Methodist, but was heavily influenced by an older Quaker friend. Reading Aldous Huxley was the turning point.

There's an essay which was written by Huxley as a consequence of the Peace Ballot of 1934 . . . and it's called 'What are you going to do about it?' And it's an immensely persuasively argued advocacy of pacifism stage by stage. Done in a rationalistic not a religious way you see and it was that set me going. And looking at it now I can see that it would influence almost anybody who was of a particularly receptive frame of mind. . . .

And remember that Huxley was arguing that wars are of their very nature purely largely destructive and they generate the seeds of further wars. . . . The part of this Huxley essay that actually appealed to me was where he knocks down these patriotic arguments one after the other like 'war is a law of nature', he makes fun of it and destroys it by all kinds of counter examples such as 'animals for example do not make war on their own species', 'Lions don't eat lions'. 'They always make war on something else.'

Aubrey Brocklehurst's father had been too old to fight in the First World War, but the experiences of his teachers left an indelible mark on his impressionable teenage mind.

I began to hear some pretty horrific stories of what had happened and I remember hearing about the Somme and that wasn't the only occasion where men were slaughtered in the thousands. And so I thought this was no way for Christians to behave or civilized people and if war came along again I resolved that I was going to refuse to take part.

It was a Methodist household and we went to church twice on Sundays and Sunday school as well and this all seemed to me to be completely inconsistent with Christian civilized countries behaving like this and ordinary honest working-class people in different countries being goaded by the politicians into hating the other side and they trotted out these atrocity stories in order to inflame your hatreds and so on. I mean at the beginning of 1914 before August, people had been visiting Germany, Germans had been coming to this country, everybody getting on quite well together and suddenly these situations flared up and everybody is told that it's not just a patriotic thing but a matter of survival that you go and kill the other side as fast as you can. This seemed to me to be no way for Christians to behave.

Len Bird was working in a Yorkshire solicitors' office.

In my early years I lived in the hero worship of a father who'd gone off to war to fight for his country and been very badly wounded. So my recollections certainly up to my early twenties were of the usual patriotic idea of fighting for your king and country.

It would be probably about 1933 and the chief in the office who was a brigadier came to me one morning and asked me to type out for him some notes that he had. When I looked at it, it was the story of what he'd experienced in the First World War at Passchendaele when the group that he was with, the battalion from Leeds that he was serving with, had been ordered to attack this strongly held German position and many of the men that he knew had been killed or maimed or were dying and so forth and they'd been three or maybe more times, ordered to attack this hill and been repulsed with these heavy losses and he was asked to relate his personal experiences of that occasion to enable someone who was writing a book to have the details.

And I know this had quite a serious effect on me. I remember telling him that I thought it was a terrible thing and I suppose it was really so bad that he wouldn't have any of the girls in the office typing it.

Frank Chadwick's father had also served in the First World War, in the Dardanelles and Gallipoli.

My parents were supportive, my father had had a rough time in the First World War, but what had sort of hit him and sort of destroyed his faith in God, was the fact that on 28 October, which was just before Armistice Day, his youngest, and presumably beloved, brother was killed in action in Italy, and of course I presume that the family wouldn't get to know about it, due to the slowness of communications until after the Armistice so there'd be all the euphoria of the Armistice, everybody very happy that the war was over of course and then there would come the bombshell that he was killed in action after the Armistice had been fixed. And I think, that, as we say in Yorkshire, 'Killed his pig', and he lost his faith in God and everything else, and brought me up as an atheist even though as a young boy I had access to the family Bible on my mother's side. My mother's side of the family was middle class, my father's was, what is described as the labouring classes. I was brought up to be against war in that sense but specifically to be an atheist.

Others, like Bernard Hicken, were affected by the medium of cinema.

I think my aversion to war was helped by seeing a film when I was quite a young boy called *All Quiet on the Western Front*. Whereas very often films and stories idealized it, and made it a glorious thing, this didn't. It showed war in its most awful form and how bestial it was. I can remember one soldier being hit in the stomach and screaming and I knew I just couldn't be at the other end of the gun that caused that situation.

Stephen Peet was the youngest of four children. His brother and two sisters had seen little of their father Hubert as he had spent three years in prison as a First World War CO.

I was born in 1920 after the war when father had been released from prison. I was born into it and therefore I absorbed it and it became a way of thinking without very strong conviction behind it, so that I was aware that my father had been in prison for his beliefs a few years before and that he was a religious journalist.

I didn't have guns and toy soldiers and when I was quite small some of my happiest times was with the boy at no. 6 who had toy soldiers and playing on the grass with him was wonderful. It wasn't thought right at home so I had great pleasure playing elsewhere as a result. Most of our friends were Quaker families so there was quite a lot of similar thinking.

I seem to remember vaguely when about ten or eleven going to school and I happened to mention that we were voting Labour and by chance two or three boys I was talking to considered it a monstrous thing, so I was aware that it was better to keep quiet than to argue about things I didn't really understand.

I'm very much conscious of the fact that my parents thought things through and joined Quakers from a strong feeling, conviction is the right word. I just accepted it as a norm, rightly or wrongly.

Tom Carlile's father had joined the army as a regular soldier in 1902 and had described the grim details of war to his son. Tom was a pacifist in the making when the Spanish Civil War broke out in 1936.

Had I been old enough, because there were some of my friends who went to Spain, I think I might have well gone. But during the course of the war I realized that it wasn't quite so simple as being the goods and the bads fighting one another. For instance, while I was not Roman Catholic I had some sympathy for Roman Catholicism, and when the stories came out about nuns and priests – whether they were true or not is besides the point – being massacred by the Republican forces. It's not black and white. Anyway a close friend of mine went to Spain and came back in a short space of time, because he was involved in some explosion and he was shell-shocked, and I spent some time with him and he told me of the experiences that he had had and the issues that were involved. I was already aware of the political factions within Britain within that time and here again it was being repeated and being repeated with some terrible effects; they were literally murdering one another. Munich happened at the end of 1938, and I realized that there was going to be a war and at that time I joined the Peace Pledge Union and was relatively active from then, and some may say getting ready to oppose the war which I felt then was fairly inevitable.

James Hanmer's father had also been a professional soldier, lost his arm in the Boxer Rebellion in China, and during the First World War was a recruiting sergeant, but it was his mother who was the major influence.

I think I got a lot from my mother, she was peaceable. Anything to avoid trouble. I remember in 1919 after the war was over we still had the blockade against Germany; it went on for another six months and lots of people were shocked and horrified to think it should go on after the war when a lot of Germans were very hungry. I can see her now in Derby marketplace crossing the road to sign a petition wanting the government to end the blockade. That's something I've never forgotten. I suppose I was influenced by my mother. I remember when I went to the grammar school in 1920, in the first form, our form master was head of the OTC (Officer Training Corps) and I remember speaking in a debate in the first form – should the OTC be compulsory, and I was dead against it so that's my background you see.

I remember making my mind up to be a pacifist in 1929, and in the 1930s I joined the League of Nations Union and took part in the Peace Ballot. The Peace Ballot was run by the League of Nations Union, and it was a nationwide petition, we called at every house urging people to support the League of Nations as it was called then, the United Nations now. I joined the Methodist Peace Fellowship which was formed in 1933; I was Secretary of the Branch of the Methodist Peace Fellowship in Derby and I talked everywhere. I know it was mainly adolescent pacifism, obviously I hadn't thought it through wholeheartedly.

I suppose I was twenty-one when I joined the Fellowship of Reconciliation in 1931. I remember vividly the rise of Hitler in the 1930s and I used to talk to any group that would have me.

Aeronautical engineer, Ronald Rice, was fascinated by military planes like the Hawker Hart and the Hawker Fury and was a member of the design team for a new bomber.

At about the same time a great aunt of mine introduced me to a church I hadn't been to before. This church had become very lively under the influence of a curate. The vicar had been on the stage, he'd been in the police, he was in the Fleet Air Arm in the Mediterranean when he started to revise his Latin and Greek to go into the ministry. The curate was a very muscular looking man and he was a former heavyweight champion of the London police and fire brigades. The vicar in his sermon told us that it might be right for us to give up the idea of war, that pacifism might be right and it was at the same time that Dick Sheppard wrote his well known book *We Say No*. I read this and I heard the sermon and I saw straight away it's obviously right, I haven't had my eyes opened to the wrongness of the military method and so I set about worrying about what I should do when I had a job in an aircraft factory, designing.

I changed my job into a helicopter job and I think if I'd known that helicopters were going to be such a great success in rescuing people I think I would have stayed, but in those days the altitude record for a helicopter was about 20 feet inside a hanger strapped with chains to prevent it overturning; nobody had thought of putting the little propeller on the tail which Sikorski did later and solved the problem and made the helicopter a viable concern. So the helicopter job didn't satisfy me because I felt it had no future, and I felt I wanted to do something for ordinary people. Aviation seemed to me then to be for luxury, because in those days there weren't many aeroplanes about, and I wanted to help ORDINARY people. So in one way and another I changed my profession from bombers to bodies as you might say. I changed from the profession with potential destructive power to the profession of healing, a mechanical profession where I could use my mechanical ideas and so I became a chiropractor.

Gwen Bagwell and her sister Joan were the offspring of a First World War CO who had spent three years in prison. In their twenties they formed peace camps and travelled round the country preaching and entertaining people with peace plays.

As students and early teachers there was a group of six of us who went peace camping from 1935, for four or five years we went and camped with the backing of the Friends Peace Committee and held meetings in villages, one a night. My brother would speak about the economics of it, and held up a one pound note and said, 'What did this get spent on?' Sometimes we would give the woman's point of view and everybody spoke on some peace topic, like that.

One of our camps was on Salisbury Plain and we had soldiers in the audience. The local Methodist preacher was one of our very few supporters, who said, 'I'm sorry you haven't had so many people tonight but if you'd like to come along to my church and take over the service you can do.' So we did that on two separate Sundays. We also did peace plays in the villages on the Isle of Wight where we lived. We had no artificial amplifiers or anything. Very often we were in noisy places – I remember at Winchester we were isolated on an island in the centre of a highway and we had to shout across to people on the pavement with traffic coming in between.

I don't think we converted many people, perhaps strengthened people. I think it made people think, the fact that we were students and giving up our holidays to do this meant something.

A major boost to the interwar peace movement came when Canon Dick Sheppard wrote a letter to *The Times* suggesting that young men and women sign a pledge renouncing all war. Thus in 1934 the Peace Pledge Union was formed with thousands of members pledging, 'I renounce war and will not support or sanction another.' The response was overwhelming. Dick Sheppard was rung up by the Post Office to say they'd got four sacks of mail for him. By the time war broke out there were 100,000 members of the PPU. Dennis Waters was among them.

I came from a very normal background. I had an elder brother, older sister and younger brother, and I was the only one who was the oddball. I was just a normal member of the C of E but I'd always had this strong feeling about the rights of the individual conscience. I'd always admired people like Thomas Moore, but when you put your finger on it, it is difficult to say exactly why. During the '30s I found myself joining the PPU and listening to people like Donald Soper and Bertrand Russell, Fenner Brockway, George Lansbury – all the big names, and I went to some of their meetings, and of course I came to meet people with similar views, including my wife – she was a pacifist before I was.

I think it was above all the fact that the state did not have the right to coerce the individual into doing something which he believed in his innermost conscience was wrong. And I've always held that view and I still do. And it's always those in literature who stand up for that particular principle that I warm to, take Arthur Miller's *The Crucible*. Now John Proctor is no hero, but he finds his salvation at the end by saying that he has finally made up his mind, that he will not give the pinch of incense, that the state has not the power to do him down, and there he finds his manhood. Now characters like that I admire very much.

The Peace Pledge Union produced a newsletter, *Peace News*. Michael Rendel Harris came from an upper-middle-class Quaker family in Devon. He was not a member of the PPU, but his mother was.

> She used to – which caused the family acute embarrassment – buy the *Peace News*. She was a JP, and she'd sort of leave copies in a court, or on the top of a tram or she'd go out somewhere immensely respectable and she'd bring the copy out, to our utter embarrassment. She'd say, 'I would like you to read this.' She had a very large handbag and she used to bring these out and scatter them all round at very unsuitable places.

Walter Wright, born two months before the outbreak of the First World War, searched his conscience throughout the 1930s before deciding to become a CO.

> I remember as late as 1935 when Mussolini invaded Abyssinia, I can remember then feeling that I would willingly go and fight for freedom and all that sort of thing, so I was by no means pacifist at that time, although I think I had tended towards it. I just wasn't sufficiently convinced not to be influenced towards war when I felt that the League of Nations was a cause to be supported. But I think it was by the next year, 1936 I think, I had become much more convinced then I joined the Fellowship of Reconciliation, again I think I was influenced by some people of roughly my own age whom I met through church membership. Also I was very much influenced by Donald Soper, because the office where I worked in London was not far from Tower Hill and when Dr Soper used to speak on Tower Hill, I often went along and listened to him. I think that was a fairly powerful influence on me, and from then on I became more and more convinced and even in 1938 I think I must have had my doubts because I remember at the time of the Munich crisis when Chamberlain came back with his 'Peace in Our Time' message, I remember going to church in the evening. Prayers of thanks were offered for peace having been secured, and I felt very much torn, I felt really disgusted that we were expressing thanks for

peace when it was peace, as I saw it, at the expense of the inhabitants of Czechoslovakia. I felt even then, that if war had broken out, I would object, I would be a CO. And I've never really been able to reconcile logically the feeling that I would have to object to war and the feeling of disgust at giving thanks for peace.

Joyce Allen was already a pacifist when she encountered the Peace Pledge Union.

I think it must have been the summer of '36 when I was fifteen, one Sunday evening after church I walked down the Woodgrange Road, and in those days on a fine Sunday evening there would be people on soapboxes at the corners of all the roads. Just by the station there were the blackshirts – a huge gathering of Oswald Moseley's blackshirts. I was just sort of idly listening to them all, just interested, and there was the PPU and somebody standing on a soapbox talking about pacifism and of course I joined there and then. Of course after that I was in touch with the PPU all the way through.

David Spreckley joined the Peace Pledge Union in 1936 working full-time in its London office. Coming from the landed gentry his background was very different from most PPU members.

I suppose the focal points were lower middle class, artisan worker, those sort, and not many right from the bottom, about where the centre was. But you see the PPU members or pacifists, you had the two extremes. On one extreme you had people who were concerned only with saving their souls, on the other extreme you had idealist, starry-eyed activists like me, who were concerned with saving the world, and in between every sort of mixture you can imagine. I almost disliked a lot of the very religious ones who were there literally for their self. When I went through this farce of a CO board I had to sit and listen to them, and I got really disgusted with them. They'd bring their vicar or their Methodist group preacher with them and say what a silver-white-lily soul they had and how they should be saved. So you had that type, simply saving their souls, and they on one side were as bad as the people who wanted to support the war and sat on their backside in some cushy job. And there were those of us – totally unreligious background, common sense politics – although I didn't know it was politics then.

With his background as a former cavalry officer who'd converted to pacifism, David Spreckley got widespread coverage in the press when he spoke at PPU meetings all over the country.

At that time the PPU was forming at least five groups a week and so I'd be going off to them, telling them how to start. I was only twenty-one, so God knows what the hell I was doing. We did some public meetings outside and we got heckled there. These were mostly PPU meetings so they invited the press but there weren't any potential hecklers so they went round heckling. I've faced plenty of hecklers in my time, having spent a lot of my time on a Hyde Park platform with Donald Soper.

David Spreckley was based at PPU headquarters at no. 6 Endsleigh Street, Euston.

Well first of all there was Dick (Sheppard), a lovely person but very naive – that was the problem with the PPU, it was much too naive, for one thing it arrived much too late on the scene to do anything much, and secondly it was very negative just this process of signing the postcard and just normal things after that, demonstrations with placards and things – there wasn't enough political content. Many years later, I was a member of the CND executive for about three years in the '80s. Now CND have managed to have a much bigger impact (with the same number at its peak) on world politics than the PPU ever did.

Dick was surrounded mostly by university intellectuals, Alex Wood and Wilfred Wellock, an ex-Labour MP and a Quaker, he was a brilliant speaker and about the only one who talked politics all the time. There were several Labour MPs, Jimmy Hudson, a teetotaller, then there was Donald Soper of course. The younger staff were very much like me, I think, very idealistic and fairly young and madly keen, but not one of us very politically aware.

David Spreckley left London to work with children in Hong Kong for a while.

I went back to the PPU, and at that time, I was in charge of trying to get Jewish refugees out of Germany. It was very hard work because for every single individual coming out you had to get a British subject with a bank balance to sign up that if that person became any burden against the state that they would pay. So most people managed to sign up for one or two and the bank had to endorse it.

We had to find people who had money but the funny thing was I had still got my account with the bank in Pall Mall – I don't know what it's called now – called Cox and Kings, which is the bank only for cavalry and guards officers, nobody else. So I didn't have to go in with a form, I think I just sent it in or something, and they endorsed either ten or twelve, because they had never seen the things before. They hadn't the faintest clue what they were doing and actually I shouldn't have been allowed to sign up more than one, so I managed to sign up twelve before they found out, and they called me in and told me to take my account away.

I should think personally I was responsible for about thirty. When the Germans marched into Czechoslovakia I took part in a Christmas thing trying to show the people that we were concerned with them. We took sweets and chocolates for the children, all very piddling really but just an effort over that Christmas.

As more refugees were fleeing from the Continent David Spreckley came up with a publicity stunt to encourage the government to open its doors to them.

We wanted to show that the unemployed in this country weren't against bringing in refugees, because the government line, of course, was that they are, because we're protecting the unemployed, the usual thing – we've got the same thing today. So we organized a lunch at the Ritz Hotel, there were six refugees and six unemployed.

We got taken for a ride because to find the unemployed we went to a Communist-run organization, which was called the Organization of Unemployed, or something like that. They marched down Piccadilly with their banners, got all the publicity for themselves, so our story never got across at all.

Cecil Davies was an early signatory of the Peace Pledge and actively campaigned for peace in his home town of Penzance.

When air raid precautions were introduced – late '38 or early '39 – the PPU issued a single page leaflet called 'Air raid precautions – a message to every householder', which argued rightly or wrongly that air raid precautions are really a softening up operation in preparation for war. And I distributed these house to house in Penzance quite a lot and as a result the chief constable summoned me to go and see him, Mr Kenyon he was called. He was very nice and all that, told me I oughtn't to be doing it; I didn't stop doing it, in fact I made sure I put one in his front door.

CHAPTER 10

War Clouds

I listened to Neville Chamberlain's speech in the office of the PPU, under Dick Sheppard's photo. Dick was dead then of course, I remember standing there with tears flowing down my face . . . because we'd failed, a total feeling of failure, thinking 'My God, we've tried, and we've tried and we've failed'.

David Spreckley

Britain entered the Second World War on 3 September 1939, only twenty years after the Treaty of Versailles which had concluded the First World War. John Marshall, who was to become a communist, voices the feelings of many of his generation, not just those who were conscientious objectors.

I heard that broadcast not in my own home but with a couple of fellow pacifists. I remember the drama of it very well. The girlfriend of my pacifist male friend – after a dreadful pause – said, 'I just want to live to learn to live'. She didn't mean just survive, she meant to learn to live. She felt we were so young we would never have a chance to learn to live and they had brought us into another war. And we all had that colossally betrayed feeling, if you like, which we felt a lot of people in our generation must have had.

Dennis Waters remembered his feelings.

Very depressed, because we'd had the false dawn of Chamberlain coming back and saying 'peace in our time' and all the rest of it. You see from my point of view one of the most traumatic things about all this was the ostracism, the pressure that was exerted upon one because one found one was out of step with what all one's contemporaries were thinking and saying and I had a lot of friends who dropped me like a hot potato, they just didn't want to know and they couldn't understand how a person like me could possibly not be thinking and doing all the things that they were doing. That, I think, was the hardest thing that I had to come to terms with.

Young men had been registered for military purposes in 1938, as Len Richardson, a Christadelphian, remembered.

I found myself lining up at the local Labour Exchange, with other young men of my own age to register. I cannot claim ever to have enjoyed being a conscientious objector, being by nature one who prefers to be thought well of, and to go with the crowd. But my conviction was strong, and still is, that Christians have no right to be involved in the conflicts of the nations, and that Jesus Christ's teaching requires them to refuse to take arms. This was certainly the conviction of the early church, and is still held not only by Christadelphians, but by some other communities besides. So on the morning in 1938 when I had to declare my conscience before men, I was far from feeling cocky about it all and I recall that I hardly dared glance round for fear of seeing any of my old friends from the local grammar school, with whom I had previously been one of the boys on the Rugby football field. When my turn came to present myself at the little grille, I told him that I wished to be registered as a Christadelphian conscientious objector.

Edward Blishen had similar feelings when he lined up at High Barnet Post Office.

I didn't ever think of it at that time, but looking back I have decided it did take a lot of courage. You had to declare yourself in the local post office and everybody was declaring themselves at a certain counter, and there was this forlorn counter over here in order to declare that you were not going to join in. I actually felt terrible about it because it felt as though you were separating yourself from the rest of the world really. It wasn't a pleasant thing. If I look back now and say did it require courage, the courage it required was the courage of separating yourself from your friends really, as much as anything. And a feeling that the whole flood of general emotion was opposed to what you intended to do. But nevertheless I was absolutely determined not to be drawn in because I had resolved that the temptation to be drawn in would be very very strong – the natural temptation is to share in the fate of your friends – and I must resist that, but the actual experience is jolly hard. I never look back on it and think 'Oh what a courageous moment,' I think 'What a trembling, haggard woebegone moment it was', very sad.

Tom Carlile was an anarchist living in London brought up with suffragette aunts in George Lansbury's Poplar.

Prior to registering I attended a Labour Exchange handing out leaflets letting people who were registering know that if they wished they could in fact register as COs and that there was an advice service, the Central Board for Conscientious Objectors. In the main people didn't react, there was no adverse reaction as they do now. On occasions people stopped, chaps going in, 'Well what's this about then?' One or two said, 'I might want to use this.' At the same time I was selling *Peace News* on the streets in Bow, in the market place. There was not an adverse reaction, you know, this is before the war actually started, up to when the bombing started. Then most activities ceased when bombing started in the London area.

Tom Carlile worked in the local library.

As far as the chaps at work were concerned most of them were sympathetic, that is to say, 'I suppose you know what you're doing, good on you if you've got the courage of your convictions'.

Cecil Davies was a nineteen-year-old student at London University who was dubbed 'Conchie No. 1' by the *Daily Express*.

I can't really remember ever not having regarded myself as a pacifist (I'm not sure if I would use the word now).

When conscription was introduced and the first lot of conscripts were to register, a reporter of the *Daily Express* went to a meeting at University College in order to buttonhole a potential CO, and they got a friend of mine called Harold Thomson. And then they discovered that he was a year older and wouldn't be in the first wave as it were, so they said, 'Haven't you a friend?' So he rang me up and said this had happened, would I take it on, so I said yes, to publicize the cause. They came to see me, took me out, took that appalling photo – I didn't realize it was appalling at the time – they'd really stood me up in order that people would say I was a lounge lizard and all the rest of it.

The photograph showed a debonair young man, cigarette in hand, posed in front of a grand mantelpiece.

It was taken in Fleet Street somewhere, in their offices. They took me out to a pub, gave me some drinks and I suppose I was a bit naive and I think all the things I said were things I meant at that period. It came out the next day and they ran it a second day as well, as an inside page story.

Then I think I had a day or two when nothing much happened. Occasionally people recognized me on a bus or in the street, and said, 'Hey, weren't you the chap in the *Daily Express*?' And then I had a 'phone call from a freelance journalist, who said, 'This story's gone dead and needs pepping up, and I want you to walk down Oxford Street and I will get a society lady to put a white feather on you.' I said, 'No, I'm not playing that game with you.' And he, foolishly really from his point of view, said, 'Well I can do it whether you want me to or not.'

Wearing a hat and dark glasses Cecil paid his rent and left his lodgings for a friend's Kensington flat – only five minutes before the journalist arrived on his doorstep.

I had a terrible post bag, a few supporters, but on the whole pretty awful shit – literally in some cases. Somebody had taken the photograph and wiped their bottom on it and put it in an envelope. It wasn't very pleasant. However, I didn't regret it, I suppose if I regretted anything it was how I had been conned over the photo.

Cecil Davies could achieve anonymity in London, but for his parents at home in Penzance it was an entirely different matter.

> My parents had a rotten time with neighbours and people at the church they went to. They were Methodists and I was a Methodist in those days, after I became known as a CO they had a much harder time than I did. My best friend at this time was a man called Maurice Frost, we were both Methodists, he was a jobbing printer, and we both shared these views. He was much older than me, he used to do a lot of work for the Masons, jobbing printer work but when he registered as a CO the Masons ruined his business and he had to give up. And he was told when he registered by the Methodists that he could no longer teach in the Sunday school any more, virtually thrown out. Anyway, after his tribunal he had to go and work on the land. My parents were very good to him at that time.

Bernard Hicken, son of an agnostic father and Methodist mother, was quite definite in his decision to register but had no idea what his fate would be.

> My only understanding of what had happened to COs was from the previous war when the treatment was pretty horrific, some of them were put into jail and let out as what was part of the 'cat and mouse' procedure, others were taken to the front line and I had heard that some were actually crucified, or put to death by being fastened to the wheels of a gun carriage; I just didn't know whether I'd be put into prison or what would happen.

Civil servant Walter Wright had spent years searching his soul and his conscience by the time registration came around in early 1940.

> During the week before I had to register, I had serious doubts whether I would be doing the right thing if I registered as a CO, so many of my friends were being called up and I felt – was I letting them down, was I letting my country down? There was of course extreme pressure all around you to conform to the rest of the country – so I registered for military service.

But for a week or two after that registration I was absolutely tormented with doubts whether I had done the right thing or not. It wasn't long before I decided that I had given in to weakness and to pressure and that I really must re-register as a CO. During that week I had a long conversation one evening with one of my office friends, who like me had been influenced by Donald Soper on Tower Hill and he was about the same age; I think he had already registered as a CO. We discussed at great lengths and the upshot of that was that he decided to register for military service – he'd changed his registration and I decided to change mine.

Older men, like Len Richardson, were out earning a living facing public opprobrium and pressure to conform.

My occupation at this time was that of an insurance agent for one of the greatest life assurance companies in the world. The imminence of war, however, and the prospect of appearing before the CO tribunal, made everything else seem rather pointless and life ticked on. War broke out in September, and the pressures built up inside as well as outside. 'When are you going?' became almost a password among the public. And needless to say my weekly round of calls, collecting insurance premiums, became an increasingly traumatic experience; explaining why I was NOT going, to people whose sons and husbands had already, in many cases, gone. The sense of being an outcast, disliked and ridiculed, is undoubtedly one of the greatest crosses that the CO has to endure, depending on its intensity. There are people (I have known some) to whom opprobrium seems almost welcome, and public disfavour an honour. I daresay it was these types that were fed to the lions in early Christian times. It is the stuff of which martyrs are made. In my own case, however, I confess to being a very poor martyr, and I squirmed uncomfortably throughout the entire wartime experiences. I well recall seeing notices outside public houses in those days, reading 'No Coaches', yet it was some time before I realized the true import of these signs, my tortured imagination having translated it as 'No Conchies'.

David Spreckley was still working for the PPU in the early
part of the war.

> The PPU kept very quiet for a while but there was a group
> of 'activists' – if you like – who wanted to do something,
> and we started speaking every week in Hyde Park. In
> those days the police used to send in *agents provocateurs*
> who would shout at us from the back of the crowd. And
> then the police would be standing round and instead of
> arresting him they would then arrest us for insulting words
> and behaviour – because of the *provocateur* who said he
> was being upset. So they used to arrest us, and it was sort
> of routine and we'd come up to Malborough Street Police
> Station on the Monday and be given a £5 fine or seven
> days, and we always refused to pay the fine so we always
> went in for seven days, because we knew for one thing if
> we went in on Monday you'd come out on Saturday, so we
> never did seven days we only did five. So that went on for
> a little while.

The PPU embraced men and women of diverse beliefs which
were reflected in their public speaking. The Methodist minister,
Donald Soper, influenced many COs like Dennis Waters.

> The thing about Donald Soper was that he expounded a
> view of Christianity with which I identified. There's no
> question about it from my point of view looking at the
> scriptures that Christ's example is a non-violent one. Now
> non-violence doesn't necessarily mean appeasement, but
> at the time when I was making my decisions there were
> people like Gandhi and his non-violent protests, that is the
> kind of way forward that I saw and I identified with, and
> people like Donald Soper expressed that very cogently. He
> had to stand up to a hell of a lot of barracking in his Tower
> Hill speeches and I admired him very much. He also used
> to write in *Peace News*.

David Spreckley expressed a different anti-war stance
embraced by the PPU.

> Donald and the Christians talked about the religious aspect
> all the time, I wouldn't go anywhere near the religious

aspect. What I talked about was the fact that there were good Germans and our job now was to find the good Germans to try to overthrow Hitler. And I remember saying quite clearly there were thousands of good Germans, and of course I was wrong, evidence now tells us there were hundreds of thousands of good Germans who didn't want Hitler. And we tried, there was a wonderful bishop called Bishop Bell, the Bishop of Chichester I think, and he used to go off to Sweden and try and make contact with the underground Germans and I did some office work for him for a while.

To many conscientious objectors the Church of England failed in its duty to uphold the true Christian message. Bernard Hicken registered as a CO on Christian grounds.

I was amazed at the attitude of the churches because I couldn't reconcile that attitude of support for the war effort with the description which we get in the Bible of Jesus Christ as the Prince of Peace. The two things just don't seem to reconcile.

Ken Shaw was also astonished at the attitude of the established church.

At the time I was a member of a Church of England group which was called the Brotherhood which used to meet on Sunday afternoon and I actually took the Brotherhood message of the church seriously and I was horrified to find that in the war it was no longer taken seriously and this still bothers me a great deal.

Welshman Meredith Edwards was brought up in a strongly Christian household.

It was taken for granted that the Christian religion was pacifist. Sunday after Sunday we had sermons on pacifism, based mainly on the new testament 'God is Love'. And what disappointed me, when I decided to take some sort of stand, I went to see my minister who had inspired me really and I got no help at all, and this was a disappointment in the early years, that the people who had advocated this and talked about this, when it came, as my father used to say, 'when it comes to the push, they will not stand up'. One wanted help from these different people who had advocated all this pacifism, and it was difficult to get.

Dennis Waters had found guidance in the words of Donald Soper and Dick Sheppard, but found it hard to reconcile the attitude of the established church.

One reacted vigorously against such things as National Days of Prayer, one felt this was the great hypocrisy, whereby God is sort of debased to a tribal deity, and all the time that people are praying to God on this side one knows that perhaps they're doing it on the other side as well.

Although the Quakers were the group most widely recognized as pacifists thanks to their historical witness for peace, conscientious objectors came from many other religious groups – Plymouth Brethren, Jehovah's Witnesses, Christadelphians to name but a few. But while the Quakers and these other groups often provided a support network for pacifists, COs coming from a more conventional Church of England background, like Dennis Waters, were more exposed.

I'm not a sectarian, the people I was mixing with had very much more profound religious views in that sense. I found much more in common with the people who rejected conscription on philosophical grounds, much more difficult to argue their case, they had a lot of trouble when they came up before the tribunals but nevertheless I admire them very much, but my case was religious, I was a believer, I still am, and from a Christian standpoint there is absolutely no question from my point of view, war is wrong.

My elder brother, an army officer, couldn't understand my views but then we very often didn't think similarly in any case, but then as far as he was concerned if that was how I felt then fair enough. But obviously he didn't share my views.

Another religious objector, Ken Shaw, was living at the family home in Southgate, North London when he had to register.

Much to my family's horror I decided to register as a conscientious objector. My father strongly disapproved and my mother didn't know which way to turn because she didn't want me to go, like all mothers. But I'd had a longstanding association with peace groups and I'd signed the Dick Sheppard Peace Pledge – which I'd remind people says that wars will cease when men refuse to fight, which is a statement of the obvious, but nevertheless is a fact. So when war eventually came I felt that my feelings about violence and killing my fellows were such that I decided to register as a conscientious objector.

Just as there was a myriad of religious beliefs among COs, so there were different shades of political objectors. Ernest Lenderyou was an Independent Labour Party activist.

I was not at first, when war came, attracted to the idea of registering as a conscientious objector. It seemed a straightforward course for a pacifist, but I had never been a pure pacifist, and had supported the right of the Spanish workers and the Spanish government forces to resist the rebellion of Franco and his Fascists. And conscientious objection, as such, seemed a bit too like opting out of the political process. By the time my age group was due for call up, however, I had come to look more favourably upon the option of conscientious objection.

Michael Rendel Harris was born into a family of well-known Devon Quakers. When war broke out he was on a Quaker trip to Germany and had first-hand experience of Nazism.

I remember there was a German girl who I was friendly with, and we went into a shop one day and the man behind the counter said, 'Heil Hitler', and gave the salute. And she of course being Quaker and so on just said 'Good morning.' And he shouted at her. And he called another assistant over and they bundled her out of the door and threw her on the ground. And that quite obviously I thought was really terrible. Because here was this nice

and very inoffensive and very pretty girl being treated like
that. And she was ashamed. And she said, 'All my people,
Germans, are not all like that'. And I suppose we all have
a turning point. That was something I saw of obvious
violence which was very distressing to me.

Tom Carlile was also an ardent political opponent of
Fascism. Had he been a little older he feels he would have
gone to fight with the International Brigade.

I was opposed to Hitler from 1932, not from 1939 when
war was declared, but there was this dilemma for most
pacifists, of course, who were opposed in principle to all
that Nazism stood for but could not accept that the only
way to get rid of Nazism was to kill fellow human beings.

I refused to register, because my opposition was to
conscription in so far as I was denying the state the right
to tell me who or where I should kill. I wasn't shall we
say objecting to it as a political member of a political
party but my opposition was then to the state. I suppose
philosophically, I became an anarchist – having gone
through a very short space of time as, shall we say, the
democratic socialist, I came to the conclusion that the
state was the greater evil, the denial of freedom, the
denial of liberty, the denial of the right of a man to make
up his own mind or not, and I was denying the state the
right to tell me that I must kill at their behest. This is
the decision which I maintained which was for me and
me alone.

Of course there was no point in not registering without
me telling them that I was not registering. The object
of the exercise was to make known my opposition. So
I wrote to say that in no way was I going on the due
date to register and stating reasons for it. Well I knew
perfectly well what would happen, it meant that I would
be registered as a CO, because I stated an objection to
registering. So I was duly registered and in the fullness
of time sent a notice saying that I would appear before
a tribunal. The tribunal was held and in my absence it
was decided that I had not got an authentic conscientious
objection to registering or performing military or
national service.

Dorset-born Sidney Renow had come into the world three months after his father was lost at sea in the First World War.

I just realized that I couldn't fire a gun at another human being, or kill him. I'm not religious so my position as a CO before the tribunal was rather more difficult than the religious ones, who really they couldn't argue against. They had this religious conviction and that was that. So when you're an atheist, as I am, you can't put a very convincing case in a way, but nevertheless I managed to convince them and I was given non-combatant military duties.

I realized that some of my friends were of the same persuasion and so I joined the PPU but after a while I realized that it was silly, their chief idea was to stop the war at all cost, and that was fatuous – you couldn't stop the war once it began so I left it. And just went my own way, and I registered as a CO.

I went into the office and said to the officer behind the desk I wanted to register as a CO and he said, 'What a pity' he said, 'In my opinion you would have made a first class fighting man.' Anyway it all went through and I went through a tribunal and eventually was called up.

Some conscientious objectors were in 'reserved occupations' but felt their aversion to the war machine so deeply that they could not accept what they termed a 'cushy option'. Ernest Lenderyou was one of them.

Working in a pharmaceutical research laboratory meant that I was in a 'reserved occupation' and would not have been called up – indeed, I would have found difficulty in being accepted for service in the armed forces even as a volunteer. But in view of my firm opposition to the war, and the war machine, that in turn had come to seem like a 'cop-out'.

As an engineer Aubrey Brocklehurst was also exempt from military service.

I was very opposed to conscription and like everybody else I was required to register for military service even though I was in a reserved occupation. I decided that the registration business was all part of the conscription process so I decided that I would refuse to register. I wrote to the Ministry of Labour and told them that I was opposed to military service and conscription and told them that I was refusing to register. At any rate they had my letter and my details so in a sort of way I registered, anyway they knew about me and they put me provisionally on the COs' register.

CHAPTER 11

A New Generation

*It was such a new thing, such a terrifying thing, to stand up
against the state.*

Meredith Edwards

Once conscientious objectors had registered they waited to
appear before tribunals. First World War COs had regarded
these as something of a farce but the climate had changed
somewhat and there was now more tolerance for the pacifist
viewpoint. To the young men who were to appear before
them they were no less daunting, so mock tribunals were
organized to put COs like Aubrey Brocklehurst through
their paces.

> In Manchester there was one, they introduced you to the
> procedure, so that when you had to face it you were not
> completely tongue-tied or terrified of it all. The tribunal
> was a bit like a magistrates' court and the man in charge
> was called Judge Burgis. They asked me on what grounds
> I was opposed to military service and I said, 'On Christian
> grounds,' and they said, what religious body did I belong
> to, but by that time I had left the Methodist church and
> joined the Quakers, and as soon as you said you were a
> Quaker you automatically became exempt, well more or
> less automatically, and I didn't like this because there were
> other quite sincere people who belonged to other religious
> bodies or none, who couldn't get exemption and had rather
> a rough ride. So I said I didn't want that to come into it.

Meredith Edwards didn't even want to use his Christianity as
grounds for exemption.

I don't think that I registered as a Christian pacifist, because in a quirky sort of way, I didn't feel it was right to do so. I thought it was an understood thing that Christianity meant pacifism, but I wasn't going to take advantage of it. 'I'm registering,' I said, 'because war is wrong. That's why. I've always believed everything I've read in the Bible, George Bernard Shaw and people like that, Tolstoy, it's wrong.' And I remember one chap coming, he was an architect, and one of the tribunal people said to him, 'Do you think that building a bridge is more important than mending a man's arm?' I thought, oh dear we've got a right lot here. Neither did I register as a nationalist. In Plaid Cymru many nationalists stood because they wanted the freedom of their own country first, they weren't going to join the British military state.

Len Richardson didn't have the luxury of a mock tribunal.

I waited for my tribunal with the mixture of apprehension and excitement with which a convicted criminal might await his sentence, and at last in May 1940 the call came. It was customary for a High Court judge to preside over the conscientious objectors' tribunal and to be flanked by two or three imposing gentlemen of public repute who were often more biased and less sympathetic than the judge. One of these had a habit of demanding of each appellant the names of the twelve apostles, and deriding the seriousness of his objection to war if he could not recall all the names.

David Jones was helping victims of the Blitz in Bristol and he regularly attended the tribunals to monitor their decisions.

We had a system of attending all the tribunals and making notes of the decisions, offering help to anybody that was in trouble and monitoring how the tribunal members behaved. Professor Field I think was on the panel – they had an academic and a trade unionist.

David found the Bristol tribunal fairly consistent in its judgements.

Above: Eric Dott during the First World War.

Left: Harold Bing as a schoolboy, 1915.

Above: Harold Blake's wife, Amy.

Right: Harold Blake shortly before the outbreak of the First World War.

Stone-breaking sheds at Dartmoor during the First World War with two unidentified COs.

The spartan contents of a prison cell.

Porridge being served to a prisoner.

At exercise at Wormwood Scrubbs. A deadly monotonous walk under strict guard. Note the warders standing on little platforms.

BANISHED!

On exercise at Wormwood Scrubs Prison with the warders on the alert for talking.

The prisoner's desk with a panel of glass in the wall just above it to let in light.

'Hard labour' on the railways for Sidney Renow (right) and comrades during the Second World War.

H. M. Prison, *Wandsworth*

21 - 12 -191*6*

Dear *Wife*

I am now in this Prison; and am in *Usual* health.

If I behave well, I shall be allowed to write another letter about

_____ *2 months* and to receive a reply, but no reply is

allowed to this. *I have got 2 years will u*

you as soon as allowed

Signature— *H.Blake*

Register No *1718*

Harold Blake's first 'letter' home from prison at the beginning of his second sentence.

Tony White digging out a UXB.

Tony White (second left) and his bomb disposal team.

Creating a smokescreen. Canisters were placed around the reservoir and connected by wires to the plunger-charges in the operations room in the Nissen hut. Dick Lindup was responsible for lighting them.

The Mis Tor work party at Dartmoor in 1917. Eric Dott is in the centre of the front row and is wearing glasses.

Four conscientious objectors at Dyce Work Camp in 1916; they are standing in front of one of the derelict buildings they were forced to sleep in as conditions worsened.

A souvenir photograph of many of the COs at Dyce Camp in October 1916, posed in the quarry where they laboured.

Walter Wright (first row of three, far right) on parade with the fire service.

Non-Combatant Corps men building Nissen huts near the Howden Reservoir. Dick Lindup is second on the left.

Right: News and propaganda circulated among COs on the Home Office Scheme and their sympathizers via news sheets such as this from November 1916.

Below: 'Conchies' on parade. Members of the NCC at Codford Camp, c. 1941.

The Granite Echo

Organ of The Dyce C.O.'s

Edited and Published on behalf of the Men's Committee, by Guy A. Aldred, at Quarry Camp, Dyce, near Aberdeen, and 17 Richmond Gardens, Shepherd's Bush, London, W. Annual Subscription, 1s. 6d. All unsigned communications are written by the Editor, but are not endorsed necessarily by the Committee or Members of the Camp in their entirety.

No 2, Vol. I.] NOVEMBER, 1916. [ONE PENNY.

The Philosophy of Alternative Service.

(By HERBERT F. RONACRES.)

Our Ideals.

(By RUSSELL EVERETT.)

Edith Peet with her third child, John.

Hubert Peet's children, Mary, John and Joan.

Iris Radford, one of the few women COs who went to prison for their beliefs in the Second World War.

Corder Catchpool and his wife, Gwen, 1920.

Maidwen Davies (fifth from right) in Florence with ENSA, June 1945.

Breakfast at one of the Bagwell family peace camps, 1935.

Maidwen Davies went with ENSA to entertain troops in India. The banana in her hand was a rare sight in wartime.

Rosalind Rusbridge, 1941.

Canon Dick Sheppard, founder of the Peace Pledge Union.

I renounce war, and I will never support or sanction another.

Signed
Please write clearly

Address
(Block Capitals)

Only the name of one MAN on each card, please.
(Membership is confined to those of 18 years of age or over.)

PRINTED MATTER

½d

To THE PEACE PLEDGE UNION,
" DICK SHEPPARD " HOUSE,
6, ENDSLEIGH STREET,
LONDON,
W.C.1.

A hundred thousand men and women signed the peace pledge.

Donald Soper speaking to crowds at Tower Hill during the Second World War.

Bernard Hicken, 1938.

Top: Sidney Renow listening to music in his billet.

Above right: Stanley Rickman, 1943.

Left: Ken Shaw, 1941.

James Hanmer (centre right) and other CPFLU members having Sunday tea. Each has his own cake tin, butter, jam and sugar tin.

Sidney Renow (first left) and other NCC men take a break during harvesting.

James Hanmer doing forestry work.

James Hanmer (second left) and fellow members of the Christian Pacifist Forestry and Land Unit.

Tom Carlile on bean duty at the Gloucester land scheme.

Stephen Peet in the uniform of the Friends Ambulance Unit.

The children's room at a centre for bombed-out civilians in Hackney, 1942.

Stanley Rickman and other medical orderlies who served with the paratroopers in Holland, 1944. Only the NCOs (left and right) are armed.

Tim Miles was appalled by the policy of unconditional surrender.

Leslie White, the model soldier turned conscientious objector.

David Spreckley, cavalry officer turned anarchist.

Bill Nightingale, for whom Dunkirk was a turning point.

Roger Wilson, sacked by the BBC.

Actor Meredith Edwards, who questioned his conscience when asked to portray a soldier.

'Conchies' put on Cinderella *to entertain the troops.*

The only kind of criticism really of the tribunals was that they seemed to operate the system of registration as though it was related to your degree of sincerity. So that if you were a terribly sincere person and had all kinds of priests speaking for you you'd get absolute exemption. But then the next down was conditional exemption where you had to do certain things like land work or hospital work, or some other work of national importance. Otherwise you'd get non-combatant registration which meant you had to go into the Non-Combatant Corps. To some extent they seemed to relate this to their assumption about your degree of sincerity and consistency and how convincing they found you rather than to what your actual position was. Some people were quite prepared to accept conditions, but some people were standing out, the absolutists – from a pacifist's point of view that was the desirable stance to be – to have unconditional exemption.

Ken Shaw remembers his tribunal in London.

The tribunals were certainly intimidating, the whole set up was as though you were on trial, and in fact you were on trial there were no two ways about that. But the logic is topsy-turvy, it should have been the people who were fighting the war who were explaining their attitude to me, because to me war is not an option – everything else must be tried first – and therefore it seemed to me that this question of mass destruction and slaughter is so wrongheaded and so destructive of even their own ends. As Alfred Whitehead said, 'The resort to violence is self defeating.' And so I felt I should be sitting up there and the chairman of the panel should be in my place defending his stance. But I also knew I was on losing ground. There was no way I could win that argument because once the war starts rationality and rational behaviour and argument go out of the window.

David Spreckley, who started life as a member of the landed gentry, joined a cavalry regiment before he discovered pacifism. He worked for the Peace Pledge Union at their London headquarters and then did voluntary work with victims of the Blitz.

Then of course eventually I got my call up papers. I personally wouldn't call myself a CO – I didn't like the phrase at all, so I had no intention of doing anything they told me to do, but I went along to my tribunal, and the first thing when my turn came was take your hands out of your pockets. And then I said, 'Look I don't envy you your job of trying to judge my conscience because it's virtually impossible, but if you want to try wouldn't it be more helpful – you're sitting there and I'm standing there, wouldn't it be more helpful if I drew up a chair and sat down round the table with you?' And there was an awful sort of guffawing behind with the audience and that didn't go down at all well. So I just made my statement and got thrown out. I knew I would.

Ernest Lenderyou was a political objector.

I had no wish to pretend to religious beliefs which I did not hold in order to obtain recognition, and although I expressed a moral aversion to war (as would, I imagine, most conscripts), my objection was expressed primarily in political terms. Briefly, and perhaps simplistically, that this was an imperialist war, waged by rival ruling classes in their own interests, and that I identified politically and morally with the German workers rather than with my own ruling class.

The tribunal to whose hearing I was called was that for south-east London. Such tribunals consisted of a chairman, usually a judge, and members from both sides of the political establishment, typically a businessman and a trade union officer or representative. Although there were so far as I know, no binding rules for such tribunal hearings, and different tribunals were well known to vary somewhat in their use of the discretion allowed them, a code of practice or of expectations soon became established with a Christian Pacifist belonging to an officially recognized church, his application supported by a minister, standing a good chance of securing either unconditional registration or one with conditions that he could easily accept; whilst at the other end of the scale an applicant whose objection was expressed in purely political terms, with no religious overtones, was likely to be judged more harshly, even though his hearing might have been formally polite.

Cecil Davies, the young student who had achieved a degree of notoriety as 'Conchie No. 1', fared better in the hands of the tribunal than he had in the hands of the press.

Luckily I had to appear before Judge Wethered – I was told that he was a former Quaker who had resigned from the Society of Friends because he couldn't agree with the Peace Testimony. Now I've never seen it in writing but it would certainly account for his attitude. Anyway you had to write a statement and my statement was really, I'd been reading Clive Bell's *Civilisation* published as a Pelican; Clive Bell was a bit of an aesthete, art critic, but I was much impressed at that time with what he'd been saying and he was talking about beauty, truth and goodness, sounds horrible now, and I sent a very intellectual, although it was meant to be passionate, statement, saying that the individual human was the only repository of these values of beauty, truth and goodness, and therefore if you destroyed that you were destroying these ultimate values, etc., etc. I thought this was the right sort of thing to write, when it actually appeared Wethered had said this is a purely intellectual objection. Now I thought at the time and I've often thought since I ought to have had the guts to say, it bloody isn't. It's not an intellectual objection, I feel it passionately, this is just the way it's worded. Anyway, he went on immediately to say, 'But I don't see why an intellectual objection can't be a genuine one', so I left it alone. Maybe it was a bit craven to do so. I knew it wasn't purely intellectual. I'd made it very clear in my statement that I would only accept unconditional exemption, I was quite sure of that, I was quite sure I would rather go to prison than do alternative service as many of my friends did. One of his assessors suggested alternative service. So Wethered said, 'It's no use saying that because if we give him that he would refuse'. He saw my point. He gave me unconditional exemption.

Tribunals rarely gave unconditional exemption from military service, and the number of men granted this status dropped at periods when the war was going badly. Across the country tribunal decisions were not consistent, for instance in London there were two tribunals – the London Local Tribunal gave 1 per cent of COs unconditional exemption in the first nine months of the war, the South Eastern Tribunal granted 10 per cent of men unconditional exemption. Ronald Rice appeared before his tribunal three years after he had given up a promising career as an aeronautical engineer to become a chiropractor – changing from 'bombs to bodies'.

The result of having made this decision three years before war broke out, was that my path was made relatively easy when it came to the tribunal. I had this record of having changed my work three years before; I had a letter from America where I used to work with a blind student and help him to study by making plasticine models on a board; my own father who disagreed with me wrote a letter to the tribunal. I did have a slight physical defect. At thirteen I very nearly had my left leg amputated, and that's what made me go to the chiropractor who saved it, this meant that I wouldn't be fit for full military service. But the reason I went to my tribunal, rather than just pleading my medical deficiency, was that I could very well have been directed to work in an aircraft factory again and I wanted to make sure that I was not directed to do something which would have been against my conscience.

These things obviously weighed much and the tribunal, which was the kinder of the two tribunals sitting in London at the time, gave me unconditional exemption, which meant I was free to do anything I liked. I remember the wording of my statement which was that I saw there were many possibilities to do all sorts of idealistic things and I would like the freedom to do them. I did work for a few months as a hospital porter at Oxford, moving patients about, and oxyacetylene cylinders and even dead bodies down to the mortuary in the night.

Meredith Edwards had looked to his local chapel for support and guidance before going to his tribunal, but without success, so he wrote to George Lansbury. The reply came on the back of an envelope.

He wrote 'Dear comrade, excuse haste and paper, I am over-rushed with letters. I would do life saving work apart from the military or work on the land. I am not an absolutist. It is very difficult in life to be positively consistent, but we can say this far, no further, and this is my position about war. I may be forced to die for the right – I won't kill.' The amazing thing when I went to the tribunal, I said to them, 'Can you please let me go and join the Friends Ambulance Unit'. And they said, 'No, your condition is to go back to your work as a lab assistant!' What sort of a system is this? I was prepared to take some sort of risk which would have helped me salve my conscience in a way, and yet these people kept the letter of the law, and said no you can't, you do as you're told. There were these people, they wanted to give me conditional exemption to go back to the laboratory. I was a laboratory assistant which was a cushy job. But I said, 'I can't do that I have a conscience. While I'm there my friends are dying'. This is the point about this – how can you prove you've got a conscience? You can't put into words – anybody who's good with words can put on an act, might get absolute exemption, but this is not the point, those people there are trying to get at your conscience but how can they, how can you explain this conscience. And this is the great dilemma I was in.

Donald Soper and other members of the Peace Pledge Union acted as advocates for COs, helping those who were less articulate. This role was also played by elders from the various religious groups, in Len Richardson's case a fellow member of the Christadelphians.

It was also usual for the young man making his appeal to be accompanied by an elder brother of the church to which he belonged. In my case I did a fair amount of preaching for the Christadelphians, both indoors and out. My sponsor requested that permission be given to continue in my normal occupation, to enable my work to continue. The hearing did not last long and was not as terrifying as I had expected.

Len was registered as a CO on condition he worked in agriculture.

> I think I was relieved by this decision, because although I had no idea of what farm work would be like, it seemed if anything, preferable to having to face the continual embarrassment of following my normal occupation. At last one was doing something, making some sacrifice.

Edward Blishen had his tribunal in London in 1940.

> I gave more or less these grounds, that I couldn't summon up in myself any case for destroying other human beings so I didn't believe that destroying other human beings was something that a human being ought to engage in. They I think regarded it as humanitarian, semi-political, I think they had the crudest divisions. I mean on the whole those who were in the best position were those who had religious grounds, these by tribunals were regarded as absurd but nevertheless with some recognizable basis; political objectors were in the worst plight; and objectors like myself who seemed to them to be philosophical objectors were not very well thought of, not regarded as very important – well we probably weren't – sort of adolescent philosophers.
>
> It wasn't sympathetic. No, I must be fair they didn't bully me or anything like that but they certainly were not sympathetic and they certainly made no bones about not particularly liking you. I remember they spent quite a lot of time over my name because they thought perhaps I was a German. Well I have a German sounding name you see, 'Where did the name come from?' and when I said, 'I don't know where the name came from really, I'd always believed that our family came from the Low Countries somewhere', they conversed among themselves quite a bit after that. Anyway I was registered as a CO providing I worked on the land.

Not everyone managed to obtain exemption from their tribunal. Ken Shaw was among those who had to go to appeal to have their claim accepted.

I took what might be called a logical political-cum-spiritual stance that war was so obviously wrong and foolish and idiotic and self destructive that no sensible person could support it, and those are the grounds that I put before the tribunal and I got very short shrift from them actually because I didn't base it entirely on religious objection, but also on political and social grounds which they didn't really think carried much weight. So I was turned down by my first tribunal, and consequently appealed against their decision and at the appeal tribunal they did at least listen to me and were much more reasonable. My offer of service in the medical corps was turned down because the RAMC wouldn't have anything to do with us, and so we were drafted into what was called the Non-Combatant Corps which I hadn't heard of and nor had anybody else and it turned out to be a sort of labour corps working in labour camps.

Bernard Hicken was another who had to go to appeal. His first tribunal was in Leeds.

I went as a Christian, I was a member of the scout movement and I couldn't see that was conducive to taking the life of probably another scout, if there had been any German scouts at that time, but my whole experience of growing up had been peace, goodwill and not just at certain times of the year, but all the time. That was my philosophy and I envisaged a world government, I was involved in an organization for world government subsequently.

Of course it was a wee bit like being in court for having committed a crime, you felt straightaway that there was no rapport or real sympathy from the judge who was in charge of the proceedings. I was told the verdict – I immediately said I would appeal against it and I did and I went to London, to the appeal tribunal, and that was a different kettle of fish. It was held in Church House in London, and the chairman was H.A.L. Fisher and you felt you were talking to somebody who had an understanding and was prepared to recognize your inner feelings, because that was in fact what happened because I was given work in horticulture, agriculture, or forestry and I accepted.

Walter Wright had first registered for military service then changed his mind two weeks later. This must have gone against him at the tribunal where he made this statement:

> 'I believe that participation in war in any circumstances is contrary to the teaching of Jesus Christ, in accordance with which I attempt to live. The grounds for this belief are: 1. That war involves a breach of the unity of mankind, making one man the enemy of another merely because he belongs to a different nation. 2. That where Christians of one nation are at war with Christians of another nation the unity of the world-wide church is broken. 3. That as a method of combating evil, war is inconsistent with the method of overcoming evil with good which was taught and practised by Christ. 4. That if the Christian outlook on life is a true one, nothing which war can achieve can in my opinion justify infliction of bodily suffering and death on the scale which is inevitable in warfare. I recognize that this belief is not shared by the majority of Christian people and of the leaders of the churches and it was only after giving full consideration to this fact that I decided to adopt the course which I have taken.'

The tribunal registered Walter for non-combatant duties.

> In other words I was liable for military service, so I appealed against that. You see during the tribunal they would question you as to whether you objected to the taking of life and such things and what else you objected to. If they could pin you down to saying that all you objected to was taking life, then they would bring you as far as they could into the military machine, they would register you for military service but for non-combatant duties only. I had tried to make plain in the evidence that I gave at the tribunal that it wasn't just the physical act of killing that I objected to, but I objected to being a part of the whole process which led to this. It seemed to me that if you were a part of the machinery which led to the killing, whether you were assisting the army in various ways, non-combatant ways or whether you were making munitions, that you were really just as much a part of

the killing process as if you were actually fighting. And it seemed to me that you were laying yourself open to the charge of just objecting to the more dangerous and more unpleasant parts of the process and opting for the easier parts. I appealed against that, but I again failed to get them to understand what my real point of view was and I was turned down.

CHAPTER 12

Women

If it hadn't been for the very faithful support I got from my wife particularly, and my mother to some extent, I think I might have found it much more difficult, but I met friends in prison whose marriages had broken up because their wives hadn't agreed with them and severed all connections with them.

Leonard Bird

Leonard Bird, like most conscientious objectors, was lucky to have the full support of his wife. Olive Shaw was also in complete agreement with her husband, Ken.

I felt a terrible compassion that war should make these tragedies and a feeling that if everyone objected throughout the world there couldn't be such disasters and wickedness. I think one felt even more strengthened by the terrible things that were happening.

While conscientious objectors had chosen to make their stand, they might be in prison, working in alternative service away from home, or away with the Non-Combatant Corps – but their wives were not always surrounded by like-minded individuals. Olive Shaw's husband, Ken, was in the Non-Combatant Corps and Olive remembers she was not always favourably received as a result.

The experience I remember most vividly, I think because I was so very shocked by it, was when I went to a local post office with my papers and army book to have the army allowance, which was about 4*d* a day. I handed in all the papers and the middle-aged man behind the counter said to me: 'Is this your husband's regiment?'

'Yes.'

'What does it mean, the NCC?'

'Oh, it's the Non-Combatant Corps.'

'What's that?'

'They're conscientious objectors.' And he picked up the papers, the book, the lot, and threw them in my face. They didn't actually hit me because there was a wire grill, but it would have done. And I was very young and very shocked by this reaction and I've remembered it vividly all these fifty years.

He walked away and another young man came up to attend to me and explained that the first gentleman's son had been killed a week previously so it was quite understandable his reaction in some ways.

She did not find all reactions quite as easy to comprehend.

I think most of our feeling was apprehension that we might meet hostility. It didn't happen with colleagues or friends, it was with strangers.

When we first came to Norwich many, many years ago I met a young airman on the train coming down, and we had a long conversation and got on famously and he invited my husband and I to his home to meet his very attractive red-haired wife for Sunday tea before I returned to London. We did go and she was absolutely charming and we had a lovely tea with them. After tea we were all sitting very happily and she asked what Ken was doing and I explained he was working at the Italian POW camp in Norwich and she said, 'How is that then?' and I said, 'Well he is a conscientious objector,' at which she stood up and left the room and never returned. We had to bid our farewells to him and slink out.

The four children of conscientious objector John Bell watched the impact their father's stand had on their mother. His daughter, Dorothy (not her real name), remembered how the experience scarred them all.

Before the war he'd had a very good job in the City in a bank earning a very reasonable salary and then along had come the war and he had decided he wasn't going to fight, he didn't believe in war. And I can always remember my mother saying the thing which hurt her most was my father was asked whether, if the Germans invaded and actually came to England and his family were threatened would he fight to protect us? And he said, 'No, he wouldn't.' And I don't think my mother could ever forgive him for that.

He worked on the land and at the beginning of the war he earned 30 shillings a week. And our rent was 27 shillings a week so I don't know how my mother managed. I've got an idea that she had to sell various possessions in order to pay the rent and buy us food. And I can remember she sent me down to the butcher's one day with a pound note (20 shillings) and a little list to get whatever he had, because you had to take what the butcher had, it was either sausages – if he had sausages that day – or a tin of corned beef. And I lost the money and I had to go back and tell her I'd lost this pound note and she was so distressed.

I know he had principles and I admire him for that and he obviously had courage, but I think when he had a family of young children, I think he should have put them first. And of course if he'd joined the army and gone away to fight, even if he'd been killed my mother would have had a pension to live on. And in the end because of his political beliefs and because of being a conscientious objector it destroyed their marriage.

Dorothy still finds memories of the war years painful.

There were unpleasant incidents because of my father being a conscientious objector and this had repercussions on the whole family. We were called names and the teachers at school were very frosty. The neighbours in our road, a lot of them wouldn't speak, certainly to my mother. And as a very small child, being very aware of atmosphere I think I noticed a lot of things – words like 'Jerry lovers' being shouted by other children.

I can remember my mother telling us that when a bomb fell close by and we lost all the tiles of our roof and she went to see the landlord (our houses were rented) about getting our roof fixed, because everyone else in the street had theirs fixed and we hadn't, and he said, 'Oh I'm not going to repair your house, your husband's a conscientious objector, he won't fight.' And I'm afraid it always seemed to be my mother who suffered.

Two years into the war, on 18 December 1941, a shortage of manpower prompted the British government to introduce the conscription of women. Women were enrolled for the women's services such as the WAAF, but were not required to use arms unless they volunteered. They were also conscripted into war work such as work in a munitions factory.

The procedure for dealing with women COs varied somewhat from that for men. Most women's cases were considered by an informal committee rather than the more formal tribunal.

Gwen Bagwell, daughter of a First World War absolutist who spent three years in prison, was teaching when conscription was introduced. Her exemption appears to have been arranged in a somewhat casual manner.

I'd moved to a job in the Isle of Wight. At the weekends I could go home and I often used to help in my parents' shop, and it was in the shop that somebody came to Dad and asked where I was and why I hadn't registered. The headmaster of the Quaker school in Cumberland where I had been teaching asked me to go back and teach on his staff. I had to give a couple of months' notice and then, before they'd followed me up for registration in the Isle of Wight, I was away in Cumberland. I know that the head got a policeman to come to the school, and he and I and the head were in his study together and some arrangement was come to whereby the head wanted me at the school, I was doing a useful job and I could stay. I was happy with the arrangement that was made, and it wasn't pursued any more.

Joyce Allen had become a pacifist at the age of thirteen and joined the Peace Pledge Union at the age of fifteen.

I really thought it was idiotic, so stupid for a species to go to war. I also think from a Christian point of view, there's no excuse for it – 'Thou shalt not kill'. Of course as it grew more technological one sees the stupidity of it. But most people accept it's stupid in that way, but of course they think it's one of the things that must be and they don't accept you can do anything about it. I think they feel powerless and I don't think I ever did, over that. I always thought that human beings had it in them to be able to stop it.

After I'd joined the PPU I did find young people who were pacifists, in the church, and so I joined the Anglican Pacifist Fellowship and the Fellowship of Reconciliation, so of course I began to mix with people who were pacifists.

When conscription came in I was teaching in a school in Somerset and I got a form that you had to fill in. As a teacher I could have just asked for exemption on the grounds of being a teacher but I said I wanted to be registered as a CO.

When she'd registered, Joyce got in touch with the Central Board for Conscientious Objectors. Someone told her that as a woman she would merely have an interview, not appear at a tribunal. As a result she was unprepared when on 2 April 1942 she became the first woman to appear at a tribunal. More than a thousand women appeared at tribunals and 427 of those appealed. Joyce appeared in Bristol where the tribunal had won a reputation for dealing fairly with COs.

I sat through a couple of men being seen – with supporters. I could have had supporters but everybody said there's no need, it's only an interview. I didn't concentrate on my preparations, I was getting on with the teaching and it didn't occur to me to get wrought up about it. So I just went up and there was nobody to support me, and I had just one letter from the headmaster saying he did want me as a teacher, but his handwriting was rather unusual and they couldn't read it so it was completely useless.

It wasn't so much of an ordeal as it was for somebody who didn't like a good old argument, and I've always been one that did. They asked me all sorts of questions and I was quite keen to answer back and say all these things and they offered me conditional exemption on condition that I went on teaching.

Now if I'd have been helped by the CBCO chappie, I might have gone for absolute exemption because it was the kind of thing I would have done even if I'd gone to prison, I'd have seen that as part of it.

Joyce went home for the Easter holidays unaware of the impact her appearance at the tribunal was about to have.

I went home straight from Bristol down to Essex where my parents were staying with my father's sister who'd taken a house in the country, it was all because of the bombing, and they hadn't a telephone. After a couple of days there was a desperate telegram from the headmaster saying you must stop all these people, because he was absolutely besieged by reporters asking, 'Was he going to take me back?' And the headlines were 'Girl conchie teaches boys' you see, and 'Girl conchie attacks the British constitution'. So I rang him up and then I rang a few of the papers, 'Are you staying?' they said. 'I don't know,' I said. But of course he didn't get rid of me, it was difficult to get staff then.

The publicity didn't upset me, I don't know whether I enjoyed it much, it was a bit remote, because I was in Essex and the concentration of it was in the West Country. When I got back there was fanmail, I had over forty letters and do you know where the bulk of them came from? Men in the RAF and they were thinking it was good. So I think they were scared out of their wits, these young chaps, who were in the planes, dropping bombs, and they just wished they could get out of it.

I had one antagonistic letter. I was trying to mug up my Latin and I used to go to Taunton to a master from the grammar school there who coached me in Latin, and he wrote that he couldn't teach me any more, he didn't approve, but he was really antagonistic. So a member of the PPU, a woman, offered to give me the Latin lessons and I paid her the same fee and she put it in the PPU funds.

Maidwen Davies was born into a deeply religious Congregational family in Godre'r-graig in south Wales. Her older brother registered as a CO and worked on the land and in the National Fire Service in Swansea during the Blitz. Maidwen was called up in 1943.

I remember being summoned to the Employment Exchange where forms had to be signed yes or no, I signed no – they asked me if I wanted to change my mind but so strong were my religious convictions I signed as a CO.

And the gentleman behind the counter who was giving me the form gave me time to change my mind if I wanted to – I remember that very well, but I knew what I was going to sign, I didn't want to change my mind, but fair play he did give me a chance to change my mind if I really didn't want to. Even if the tribunal in Swansea had told me that it was a jail sentence I was prepared for that.

Maidwen, whose first language is Welsh, went to her tribunal at the Guildhall in Swansea where she had an interpreter. She was given social work to do as a condition of her exemption and they agreed she could fulfil the exemption by cleaning her local Congregational chapel. Before conscription she had been about to embark on a singing career, and auditioned for a Welsh choir being formed by ENSA.

My first ENSA offer came, but I could not accept because it would have involved singing at factories which made guns and bullets. I wasn't against the people who were doing work in the factories, but I felt through singing and being paid in factories that were making guns and bullets, I would have been involved in that practical part of it.

Maidwen got a second chance to sing in an ENSA choir.

The question I was often asked was why had I refused the first ENSA offer and accepted the second? That's a very tricky question to answer – I found it more human to sing to the boys of the forces because they were so far away from home to start with. I remember when we arrived in Bombay there was a Welsh social society there. I was singing solo that night and you could see the sadness in their faces because I was singing in Welsh, and in the middle part of the song I was inviting all the people to join in the chorus, and you could hear the sadness in their voices as well as seeing the sadness in their faces.

Maidwen toured with ENSA for nearly a year, first in Italy, which had been devastated as the armies swept across it, the Middle East, Singapore and India. People she met were not generally antagonistic towards her as a conscientious objector.

> They were very appreciative you know. It was different in the Second World War, the COs in the First World War were very ridiculed, people were calling names, 'conchies', but with me people were very supportive, I must say, because I was singing for the boys in the forces.

Joyce Allen, an active pacifist all her life, also found little antagonism.

> Unlike so many people I don't think I've come across much antagonism. Even when I was mixing with people who weren't pacifists, who disagreed with me very much, I never found them antagonistic, like some people did.

Rosalind Rusbridge and her husband Ewart were conscientious objectors in Swansea. She encountered public and professional hostility.

> We had Fenner Brockway coming to speak and we went on our bikes from Swansea, but the meeting didn't take place because a whole gang of people had assembled to prevent it and to prevent anybody getting to the place. When we got on our bikes to go home all these people lined the road and they shouted 'Back to Swansea you bloody "conchies".'

Rosalind was born in 1915 into a Baptist family. She grew up with an abhorrence of war.

> My father was in the First World War and when he came home he had a distinguished conduct medal and a conviction that war was utterly evil. He said, 'It's not what it does to the body, it's what it does to the soul', and he passed that on to the family; my mother, my brother and I have been pacifists ever since.
>
> There was another big influence and that was the church, the Revd James who was our minister and he was a pacifist and a socialist and an absolutely brilliant preacher, and we

all loved him. I did my degree in Cambridge and I was in the Oxford University Pacifist Society, that would be 1937.

My husband's parents were horrified. The first weekend of the war, we went to a meeting for potential pacifists and his mother took the young brother aside and said, 'I'm very cross that you're going with Ewart and Rosalind but wherever you go don't join anything.' And he came back having joined the Fellowship of Reconciliation and the PPU.

Both Rosalind and her husband were teachers and known pacifists in Swansea.

The education committee didn't want to do anything about it, teachers were scarce, of course people had gone off to the forces. But the Swansea League of Loyalists got up agitations and had demos outside the council and made them say that they would suspend COs employed by the Corporation – this wasn't just teachers because my friend Gilbert Bennett, who was more or less an office boy in the Education Department, got sacked I remember.

This feeling didn't arise until the retreat from France, Dunkirk (May–June 1940), then people really expected Germans to turn up at any minute. And then anybody who wasn't pro-war they thought would be a 'quisling'.

Rosalind and other staff had to sign a statement sent out to them by the council.

'I hereby solemnly and sincerely declare that I'm not a conscientious objector or a member of the PPU, nor do I hold views which are in conflict with the purpose to which the nation's effort is directed in the present war and I further declare that I wholeheartedly support the vigorous prosecution of the war.'

That was sent to all teachers and employees except the men at the power station because they knew that if they went on strike the whole town would be in darkness. I was expecting it really because there had been all this fuss and pressure here.

Ros and her husband both refused to sign and on 1 July 1940 were suspended. They both managed to get other jobs.

But there were other women who fared even worse. More than 200 women went to prison for refusing directions to work. Iris Radford was a naive eighteen-year-old when she was called up. Although she had not been brought up in any particular faith, she and her mother had both joined the Jehovah's Witnesses.

When I took my stand as a Jehovah's Witness my father was fighting out in France, he had been at Dunkirk and had terrible experiences out there.

He was what they called a reservist you know, and they were the first ones really that were called upon to go into the forces.

When the war started I was just about to leave school and plans had been made for me to go up to Birmingham and live with my grandmother, and I was also by now very interested in Jehovah's Witness. So as planned I did go up there and I got a job working in a little post office training to be a post office clerk. Meanwhile we were going regularly to the Jehovah's Witness meeting and I got very friendly with them all there and the main thing was that we were studying the Bible especially in relation to how it fitted into world events. And so I became what's known as a pioneer, I took up full-time work with Jehovah's Witness and got sent to various parts of the country to take part in that preaching work.

At that time I was in a place in Wales called Abercahn, and we were doing our ministry. At that time they had what they called Bevan boys, boys who were sent down from England to work in mines and factories and so of course they had to be accommodated and they were using nice hotels. So they directed me to go into one of these hotels and act as a receptionist to these boys. Well the point was that I didn't want to give up my full-time ministry work.

People like probation officers interviewed me and tried to point out to me that I should be doing something for my country and especially reminded me about my father. I had to explain to them the stand we take is because of the scriptures, the Bible, you see, Jesus taught that we should love one another and war is definitely wrong.

I went seven times to court in Abercahn, and I had the same judge every time and he was so reluctant to sentence me; I was eighteen. So he kept on postponing the court case. The sixth time I went they didn't do as they had done previously and that was tell me when to appear at the next court. So when the day of the seventh time came I didn't turn up. When I got back to my digs, my landlady said, 'Oh a policeman has been here and said if you don't turn up at the court today a warrant will be issued for your arrest.' So I went to the court and the judge said, 'Well, I'm very reluctant to do it but Parliament makes the laws and we have to enforce them.'

Iris was just one of many Jehovah's Witnesses – men and women alike – who were sent to prison. She served her month-long sentence in Cardiff gaol. It was a world she was completely unfamiliar with.

I was eighteen and I hadn't really seen much of the world, I had lived a sort of sheltered life, and to mix in with the types that were in there was pretty awful, that was the worst part of prison. Lots of prostitutes who had been carrying on with American soldiers, found on the camps. It was a shock. Some of them had VD, these things you got to know made you a bit frightened.
    I had these harsh prison clothes, coarse calico underwear and an awful grey woollen dress of some sort and black hard shoes. I remember the time they lined all the prisoners up to be inspected for venereal disease and word went around, and there I was thinking oh this is terrible, and one of the warders came along the queue, 'You can come with me, you don't have to take part in this.' That was a relief.

Although Iris's fellow prisoners may have appeared outwardly intimidating they were generally friendly.

I found that some of the wardresses were more antagonistic because of course they thought you should be doing your part towards the war, but then again you see, Christians, true Christians if you try to follow the life pattern of Jesus as he said, 'They persecuted me and they will persecute you also,' so Christians don't expect to be popular for the stands they make.

Iris was in a cell on her own.

> It just had brick walls and a little hard bed with just a
> pillow and a rough blanket and you had a slop bucket and
> every morning you were called very early in the morning
> and the routine was that you go and empty this slop
> bucket and wash all in a very rough way. And then your
> breakfast would be brought, which was porridge made
> with water and your sugar ration for the day was about
> a tablespoonful if that, and then the dinner was usually
> awful. I can remember particularly having salt bacon and
> beans all tasting very salty and horrible, but you were
> always glad to eat it. I lost a stone in weight when I was
> in prison.

When she was released Iris returned to her work with the
Jehovah's Witnesses. But, like Joyce Allen, her case had been
covered in the local newspaper and she was teased and taunted.

> When I came out of prison and resumed my work, then
> people who had read it in the paper, some commended
> me and others abused me because of it, you're bound to
> get that. We'd cycle everywhere and we'd have people
> calling after us 'conchies' and that sort of thing, but we
> expected it.
>
> An American sailor who had docked in at Cardiff at that
> time had read the paper that had the account of my court
> appearance and how I had been sentenced to prison and
> he wrote me a wonderful letter congratulating me that in a
> world of such debauchery and wickedness it was wonderful
> to think that a young girl could take such a stand.
>
> I never felt isolated – we were just so convinced that
> what we were doing was so worthwhile and that it was
> really giving hope to people

The hostility of strangers was one thing, but Iris also
encountered a similar reaction from some members of
her family.

> My aunty, that is my father's oldest brother's wife, she
> was a great worker for the war effort, said, 'I'm ashamed of
> you, you're letting down our family name.' Because they

were so patriotic they took a dim view of my stand really. I wanted to be polite but I remember having the courage to speak up and explain to her why I did it.

My mother said the proudest day of her life was when I went to prison. All her life she was a very strong Witness and it pleased her greatly to think I made a stand like that.

My father was a really good man and he said you have to have the courage of your convictions and if you really believe that and you want to make a stand well then you do it and I'm proud of you more or less.

CHAPTER 13
Non-Combatant Corps

We were just a large group of men coming to terms with our consciences and the needs of a country at war – we were not compromising.

Dick Lindup

More than six thousand conscientious objectors served in the fourteen companies of the Non-Combatant Corps. Set up in 1940 as a section of the army they gave conscientious objectors the opportunity to help the war effort, but with a guarantee that they wouldn't carry arms. The only other army corps which could not be asked to carry weapons was the Royal Army Chaplain's Department. Sidney Renow was called up in June 1940 shortly after the NCC was formed.

I had to go to Great Yarmouth to No. 2 Company NCC, and we did nothing really, we didn't know what on earth we were going to do, we'd got the idea that we were going to be trained as stretcher bearers but nothing came of that. We did nothing else but marching for several weeks which made me pretty fed up. And then they wanted some volunteers to do clerical work so three of us volunteered and we were sent to Hemsby holiday camp just up the coast from Yarmouth and installed in a holiday chalet, very luxurious, and then we were forgotten, left there with nothing to do. We used to go down to the beach, beautiful summer that year, and while we were there No. 3 company was formed and we were attached to it and after a few days we were all transferred to Scotland to Nitsfield camp south of Glasgow and the marching began again.

Londoner Ken Shaw joined No. 9 NCC Company at
Ilfracombe on 2 January 1941.

It was a bitter cold wintry day with snow heavy on the
ground and bitter wind coming off the sea, and we were
met at the station by a Pioneer Corps corporal and put in
a lorry and taken down to the front where the army had
requisitioned these hotels all along the front. The hotels
had been stripped of everything, carpets, furniture, fittings
so there were just the bare rooms with wooden floors and
naked bulbs. So we were sent down to the basement to
gather straw for our palliasses which we slept on, and
issued with three blankets and that was it for the first
night. Three blankets and a straw palliasse was very hard-
going indeed. Our first impression, all of us, is how bitterly
freezing cold we were. It was a very strange situation
because here are 2–300 people from all over Britain
meeting for the first time.

At Ilfracombe we got basic drill and this consisted of us
being paraded up and down the promenade. The second
day we were actually pleased, despite all our conscientious
objections, to put the army uniform on because it was
warm and we were issued with drawers, woollen, long,
which were pulled on with much gratitude – we actually
felt warm for the first time. We were then marched on to
the parade ground on the front and walked up and down
on the paved part by the railings with the sea roaring in and
the bitter cold wind and they endeavoured in vain to get us
to march in some sort of order.

They did this for four or five days and it was called
basic training and the outstanding feature of this was a
demonstration we had from a very crusty old commanding
officer who I think was a colonel and came down specially,
and he was a cross between Colonel Blimp and C. Aubrey
Smith in the Hollywood movies. He had those sort of
features and red face and he spoke like this, 'Now men I've
come to show you how to handle a pick,' and he proceeded
much to our astonishment and amusement to show us how
to handle a pick, because we were going to do quite a lot of
pick and shovel work in the future and would we pay very
careful attention.

Dick Lindup did his basic training in Liverpool and joined No. 8 Company.

> Commissioned and non-commissioned officers were all from the Pioneer Corps and they were not sure how to deal with us. I remember one Pioneer corporal transferred to our company saying that he had been told to be careful about giving us an order – 'Don't order them, ask them'. At the camp of 5,000 there were just 30 of us NCCs and we told our sergeant that we would, of course, parade with the rest every morning but we wouldn't march. The sergeant was naturally very worried – especially as we walked past the camp commander but his only comment was 'Nice marching boys'.

Ken Shaw found the loss of personal freedom hard to bear.

> In some respects it was a bit like being in an open prison and the NCOs who were usually very old semi-retired members of the Pioneer Corps or members of the Pioneer Corps who had been wounded in the First World War or Second World War even, some of them were all right but most of them shouted and tried to bully us quite a bit but we did manage to rise above that. The feeling of being shut in was remarkably like being in a prison except of course that we were allowed out and occasionally once a month we could have a weekend at home.
>
> The same applied to the men who were going to the front but this was a new experience to us, this loss of personal freedom, but it could have been a lot worse.

Major G.W. Clark came out of retirement to command No. 3 Company of the NCC. While he was at Glasgow waiting to take up his command, he heard stories about the NCC men. He recounts the gossip in typical military manner in his unpublished memoirs.

> Religion, or rather religious beliefs, tortured, twisted, thwarted into some forty-five different sects and sub-divisions of sects, was rearing its head. I had been warned that in the camp at Glasgow many individual tents held prayer meetings nightly before calling it a day. And I had

been further informed that these – shall we say red-hot gospellers – did not by any means believe in hiding their light under a bushel. Rather was the technique based, I was led to understand, on that of Hyde Park Corner, where extra-special-exclusive vied with common-and-garden in a series of open-air meetings.

In this modern age conscience is not motivated by religion alone. The conscientious objector of today may equally be an agnostic or an atheistic (*sic*). In fact quite a number of the company were listed as such. Sociological and political beliefs take the place of religion; communists, syndicalists, anarchists and humanists quote conscience as glibly as any Quaker or Plymouth Brother. We had our share of this spurious crop – there and then I christened them, 'The Secular Branch'.

Sidney Renow was one of those whom his commanding officer Major Clark referred to as 'The Secularists', as he was an atheist.

They were nearly all religious and quite a large number of them were Plymouth Brethren, but we all got on very well. There were a few like me who had no religious beliefs at all. It was a very contented period. I suppose we all worked very hard but in the evenings we were near Oxford so I went to the Oxford art classes there, and worked under quite famous painters, and there were always concerts of course.

Some men who joined the NCC, like Dennis Waters, had asked the tribunal for conditional exemption rather than non-combatant duties but were allocated to the NCC.

Now of course the army has no time for round pegs in square holes and we were exactly that because we didn't drill properly, we didn't do anything properly, we didn't have any weapons to carry, we were a dammed nuisance.

During his time with the NCC at Ilfracombe Dennis Waters was beaten up.

The army mind is most peculiar, at Ilfracombe you had certain regular army officers who didn't understand us at all, you had people who'd been called up, solicitors, professional men and what not, who were quite decent in themselves and were worried by what was happening to us. They had a sense of fair play and they didn't like what was going on and then you had the NCOs who quite frankly were the scum of the earth.

Ken Shaw was to spend five and a half years with the Non-Combatant Corps; after basic training his unit was sent to Bulford on Salisbury Plain.

The thing that struck us first of all was that it was rather odd sending an NCC unit to the very heart of the military establishment, and we were surrounded by all these crack regiments, Coldstream Guards and all the rest, and we thought we'd be in for a pretty cool reception. But it so happened soon after we got there, one or two bombs were dropped quite near us and some of our lads turned out for this air raid and did some very useful rescue work and that did our reputation quite a bit of good among the troops in Bulford, and they said, 'Well they might be "conchies" but they're quite capable of making themselves useful.'

Our reception in the garrison town was at first a mixture of hostility and indifference, hostility from some people who thought we had no right to be conscientious objectors, and why should they do our fighting for us. Most of them were fairly tolerant and some of them even said, 'I wish I'd had the guts to do the same.' Our reputation was also helped by the fact that we did form a football team and played the other units in the garrison and much to their astonishment we did manage to beat most of them. Whether it was proof of our masculinity I don't know, these were in the days when it wasn't done to talk about being macho, but being a man meant you were able to go and do something like win a football match. So that helped a little and we were soon accepted as part of the garrison life.

Dick Lindup and other members of No. 8 Company were on smokescreen duty around reservoirs in the Peak District. He remembers an incident which gives an insight into the way ordinary soldiers regarded conscientious objectors, and, in this case, just how wrong they could be.

> Small canisters of smoke-producing chemicals were placed all round the reservoirs. These were wired together and lit electrically from a small operations room in the Nissen huts where we were billeted. One night when we had put up a smokescreen we were 'attacked' – at the time we didn't know this was just an exercise. All the detachment were strategically placed round the reservoir except for two of us – Sandy, our cook, and myself in the operations room. Without any warning two soldiers burst into the Nissen hut – one made for the kitchen and the other one the operations room. Sandy responded immediately with a full Nelson on his attacker. My task was easier. The noise in the kitchen had warned me. My attacker got as far as his arm in the doorway to the operations room when I was able to grab it, close the door as much as possible and wedge the arm there. This was painful and he was unable to move. Then our sergeant came in and 'shot' them and the umpire arrived to pronounce them 'dead' and their mission a failure. We released the two soldiers who weren't too pleased by our reception of them. One of them said, 'We thought you were bloody "conchies",' to which I replied, 'Oh we are. We wouldn't have killed you.'

No. 8 Company had first done smokescreen duty in Newcastle where they were more exposed to the dangers of air raids than the average member of the civilian population. The smokescreen was intended to hinder visibility over the city so that enemy bomber pilots were unable to pinpoint targets. It was made by burning barrels full of tar.

> Obviously most of our time in Newcastle was spent on night duty though there was a lot of day-time maintenance to be done. We had two types of smoke producers that we had to use – mobile smoke producing machines and small stationary pots the use of which depended on the weather. These pots were used by local people as a source of fuel with which to light their own fires every morning.

The smokescreens were made when there was an air raid or the prospect of one. We were out on the streets exposed to all the dangers of an air raid – sudden flares from the machines or pots had to be dealt with immediately. When the danger of raids on the reservoirs became more apparent, we were sent down to the area round Sheffield, the dams there being considered the most valuable.

Ralph Bateman was also a member of No. 8 Company of the NCC. He was sent to Burgess Hill, 8 miles inland from Brighton shortly after his training.

We went out every day to make blackouts for bomb damaged houses so that they could be used as army billets. I was a section leader and one day was called upon to take three Bedford trucks down to Leatherhead to draw stores for the billets. We later moved to Redhill and London. Our billet was not far from the Odeon State Cinema in Maida Vale. We had a lot of work in the day, and fire watching at night, it was the time of the firebombs. We were called out one day to Willesden, near the big railway station. We found five or six terraced houses ready to fall down. A bomb had been dropped across the road from the houses, and the soil was up to the top of the first-floor windows, in fact that was holding the building up. So we got in at the back, and got out goods belonging to the people who had lived there, and then took the houses down.

NCC men also worked on the land for short periods hedging and ditching, threshing and helping with the harvest, and when the war ended and relief aid was needed some went to pack powdered milk in a Somerset factory.

Sidney Renow and No. 3 Company were posted to Swindon.

It had been decided that we were going to do railway work on military railways because there were big depots being put up in various parts of the country. At Swindon there was the supply reserve depot and we did the feeder lines. Laid the lines, excavated, made the embankments, put sleepers down, bashed in the nails, hard labour that's what it amounted to, six years hard labour always on the railways. Then from there we were transferred to Arncot near Bicester where there was an enormous depot being formed and so we did the feeder lines there. While I was in Swindon I was put on detachment to Bristol in October 1940 when the raids started. We were there while they bombed the docks and we went out at night during the raids to help the fire services, what a spectacle that was, all the tobacco warehouses going up.

His commanding officer, Major Clark, recalled one particular night when they were called to a fire at the convent at Henleaze.

They found the convent school building well ablaze, and had to concentrate on preventing the spread of the fire to the main buildings. Later a party of one officer and ten men relieved a party of police and AFS (Auxiliary Fire Service) who for four hours had been trying to cope with the flames. The fires spread so quickly that eight men of the party, endeavouring to extricate civilians trapped in the burning buildings, were themselves trapped, and were able to extricate themselves only by being pulled up and clambering over the roof of a ruined building, and finding a way through a warehouse to the street.

Ken Shaw and his company did work that may not have been dangerous but was definitely as arduous.

We settled into a very monotonous and back-breaking routine of hard physical work. We used to go out and unload railway trucks. It was mostly unloading of Nissen hut parts, these are very heavy curved wooden sheets and although we used rollers to get them off the trucks once they were on the ground we had to lift them in pairs and it was quite heavy work. We'd come back to a tented camp after working from 8 a.m. to 5 or 6 p.m. in the evening unloading these wretched trucks, and there were fairly primitive showers and ablutions and we slept in tents. We had a very uncomfortable six months, that went up to Christmas and January of the next year when there was snow on the tents, until finally the huts were built for us so it wasn't a very pleasant time at all.

Halfway through the war when the prisoners, German and Italian, began to come into the country from the North African campaign, then there was a huge demand for staff for POW camps, we were asked to volunteer as clerical staff in the POW camps. We were then sent on a course to London, that was in the autumn of 1943, thereafter we were posted out to various POW camps and I finished up in Mildenhall in Suffolk next to the great American bomber base and then I was posted to Norwich.

Curiously enough I was asked in the POW camp in Norwich to take part in the so-called re-education scheme, and I gave lectures to the Germans, the lectures were given in English but I could speak a bit of German. What I was asked to do was to lecture them on the history of the Soviet Union which was very interesting from their point of view because the Germans' attitude towards the Russians has been a very peculiar one, they looked on them as barbarians, so they learnt quite a bit. But I made some very good friends with the German prisoners, although they couldn't understand what a 'conchie' was or a pacifist.

They didn't really understand it – they thought the British were very peculiar to allow such things as 'conchies', because in Germany it wasn't allowed.

As the nature of the war changed so NCC work changed. Dick Lindup and No. 8 Company were moved from smokescreen duty on the dams round Sheffield.

When the danger of air raids grew less and the invasion more imminent, we were sent down to Rugby to large food depots, there to prepare small sacks of food to be dropped over occupied territory when the invasions began. Working alongside combatant soldiers (Royal engineers and Pioneer Corps mainly) we didn't experience any real objection to our presence. We had a reputation for hard, reliable work.

Ken Shaw, encamped in the heart of the military establishment at Codford on Salisbury Plain, remembers some hostility.

When we used to go down to the NAAFI, which was established in the village in Codford not far from our camp, one or two soldiers did get rather aggressive, it usually stopped short of serious trouble and we just left it and went back to the camp. Sometimes, especially after an event like Dunkirk they did turn on us as though it was in some way our fault. Some of the villagers also then sided with the regular soldiers there, although they'd been fairly sympathetic to us up to then treating us as ordinary customers. They called us 'conchies' and 'yellow bellies' and said we ought to be sent out on the beach at Dunkirk as well and see how we'd like it. Well of course we wouldn't have liked it, nobody would have liked it.

Any qualms we had were really to do with the fact that our position and our approach was entirely different from the rest. We were actually against the war and didn't believe in fighting so we couldn't put ourselves in their position. We just had to hope it would stop so that our contribution could be made, we couldn't make any contribution to the actual situation and we certainly could do nothing to prevent it, and it was this feeling of powerlessness and frustration which I suppose was predominant, and in my case this made me feel angry at times as well as depressed.

There was a lighter side to life. Ken Shaw and fellow non-combatants were an artistic and talented group, putting on pantomime and performing concerts for the troops in the evenings.

That NCC unit was really my university, because I met people I'd never have met, I mean there were university professors and teachers and several university graduates who were very, very different from the rest. Apart from Keith Vaughan, who was a very sensitive and talented artist and became one of our major postwar artists, there were all sorts of people who normally I would never have met. I was introduced to classical music; I knew all about jazz but I didn't know anything about classical music which I thoroughly enjoyed. I remember going from Codford to my first symphony concert in Salisbury Cathedral which was a magic occasion. So it wasn't exactly a picnic by any means, it still was more like a prison I suppose – an open prison I would call it.

The thing that kept me going was partly that we were all together in one group and we did reinforce each other although we all had widely differing views. Interestingly enough, the only ones we did not or could not communicate with, were the religious objectors. They kept themselves very much to themselves in any case, but for the rest we were talking the whole time, and the kind of discussions which I suppose would be normal at university level were quite new to me because I left school at sixteen and went to work on the stock exchange as a clerk. I remember working in the same groups as people who were talking about all the intellectual pros and cons of the situation and I was quite fascinated by it, and even bold enough to join in, so that did help to keep us going.

CHAPTER 14

Bomb Disposal

I was being kept alive by virtue that there was a war on and there were people that were defending my liberty in a sense. In the event, especially when it came to bomb disposal, they were jobs that one could accept.

Tony White

Conscientious objectors are, by nature, modest and would not like to be called heroes, but among them were 465 men who volunteered for bomb disposal teams. Stanley Rickman was one of them. He was born in August 1915, one of four brothers; the other three joined the army and air force on call-up.

I was converted in my late teens and joined the Baptist Church. I felt a definite calling and devoted my spare time to youth work. As a Christian I could not contemplate killing people – perhaps memories from the First World War played a part. But our pastor turned out to be militaristic. At school I had been a member of the Officer Training Corps and a little bayonet practice and use of firearms played a part in OTC training – one took part with one's companions without a thought.

Another volunteer for bomb disposal was Tony White. A lifelong Methodist, he had a religious experience at the age of fourteen. He also did youth work. When he appeared at his tribunal he was given exemption on condition he joined the RAMC but shortly afterwards the corps had to carry weapons and so instead he joined the Non-Combatant Corps.

The first chap I met was the chap in the clothes depot – the first thing you did was to hand over your personal clothes and be dished out with a uniform – and during the course of conversation we were chatting away quite happily and he said, 'It's strange, you don't seem like one of them.' Now that hurt but at the same time I appreciated it because I do regard myself as normal even though the views I hold are not acceptable to the mass of the people.

I suppose by nature I'm a gregarious sort of chap, I mix in with the crowd, I like people, therefore it was very hurtful for me, in one sense, to have to take the stand I did because it had the immediate effect of separating me from most, not all – I had some superb friends who stood by me. But nevertheless it was hurtful to join up with a group who, although I accepted our reasons for conscientious objection vary enormously, I still preferred to do the thing the gang does really, to be one of the boys. There were times when people made their hostility clear by being offensive. The people who were anti were always civilians – my next door neighbour had no prospect of being called up, he was ten years older than me; people over the road were roughly the same age, no prospect of being called up; the people who criticized at church including the minister, no likelihood of being called up. But the people who supported us were the people in the forces, people we met. I remember when we went on the bomb disposal course that there were chaps there that said, 'We wish we had your guts. We hate this, we don't want to do it but we're forced into it.' This was said to me by a number of my close friends who went into the services who chose things like the groundstaff of the RAF in order, as far as possible, that they didn't fight, didn't have to use firearms, but weren't prepared to take the stand. I always honoured their decision, this had to be a totally personal thing, no doubt about that.

It was not long after Tony's basic training with the NCC that a call went out for volunteers to join bomb disposal. They were attached to the Royal Engineers, but still remained members of the NCC.

We became a section of twenty men in a detachment serving various places around Sussex and Surrey which were areas of attack. The highest officer was a captain, but the rest of us were NCC, and the relationship with the other staff was marvellous, we were just pals together, on Christian name terms.

The NCC chaps who volunteered for bomb disposal – there must be something about us that made us volunteer as a crowd. These were people who became great friends, whom one admired for a whole lot of reasons, who displayed a range of talents. Many of them academically were very bright, we had professors, etc., and we did have a very special bond of friendship. Now I don't know whether that was anything to do with the fact that we were of like mind in one sense to choose to go into bomb disposal with all that that implied, I think it bred between us bonds of friendship that were very deep and very real.

Tony's wife Kathleen was heavily pregnant when he volunteered. She had been encountering marked hostility from neighbours and the minister of their local church until her husband chose this dangerous option. His choice of bomb disposal duties changed their attitude but was not his reason for volunteering.

The reason was that it was doing something constructive in the sense that you were digging out bombs which were meant to harm, immunizing them, and you could see it as a direct service for the community. But the major thing was my own proving something to myself that I wasn't 'dodging the column.'

I think it relates to my original feelings that I didn't want to be different, I didn't want therefore to escape the risk and here was a chance to prove my sincerity, not the front line but relatively dangerous – I didn't know how dangerous at that point. I just thought this is everything to do with my own dignity, wanting to prove something to myself. But bomb disposal certainly gave me that chance, and there's no doubt that there's a lot of those who didn't volunteer for bomb disposal – again I'm not going to judge their reasons. If I hadn't volunteered it would have been because I was scared, and I wasn't prepared to take that risk.

Initially bomb disposal teams had to locate bombs after a raid and then dig them out before defusing them. Tony White remembers the procedure vividly.

There was a hole, you could always see where the bomb had gone in. The fin which did the guiding came adrift, we always found that about 18 inches 2 feet down, then you dug on until you found the bomb. We'd lay a sort of template, rather like when you see people working in the streets when they're digging a big hole, they have to build a frame into the hole to keep the earth from falling back. So it was really a manual job, digging out earth, fixing the frame, the supports, until eventually you got to the bomb and then generally speaking the sensible thing was to be careful. We had a corporal from a company, this chap was a nutter, I think we were fairly new to him, and he to us, therefore on this particular site I think he was determined to prove that he would tire us out. I remember being down a hole with him, he was just mad – we used picks – if you'd clouted one of these bombs with a pick you could have set off the fuse, but nothing ever happened. But I remember thinking, you're not going to beat me, I'll keep going as long as you do. I remember being absolutely exhausted.

You felt your way as you were going down, obviously breaking earth all the time until you came to the bomb, but the drill was to be careful and you had an idea from the size of the hole what the size of the bomb was, and what sort of area we were likely to discover metal.

There were several 1,000 pounders that we got, about 4 or 5 feet long, they were a pretty good size. They were heavy of course, and you got them out by winching them out, with a tripod type of rig to haul them out. We'd take them away and then there was a mechanism for screwing into the bomb, into the powder side, which neutralized the powder with steam, a steam injection. They still use the steam injection method. So you'd screw in and make a hole in the casing, still not disturbing the fuse hopefully, that's the job that had to be done very carefully, and then inject steam which would neutralize the powder or the explosive and then one could remove the fuse safely. And then, the officer would retreat to what was theoretically a safe distance and then explode it with an electrical device. This is where the thing could explode before the officer had got far enough away, he was always the one in greatest risk and we did suffer casualties.

You were never sure when you moved it out of its hole you wouldn't always know immediately if you'd disturbed the mechanism and therefore there was always the risk that the thing might go up. There were all sorts of things like sensible safe distances and safe times and so on that used to minimize the risk or the danger, but it was always there. Without glamorizing the situation, the bomb had fallen and had not exploded for some reason, maybe it was just about ready to go and it hadn't gone, the impact hadn't exploded it as it should have done. In theory, the thing was meant to be as safe as possible.

There was tension, you were never, never sure. It had been known for bombs to go off in a hole or when they were lifted out, but to the best of my recollection nothing like this ever happened.

Having dug out UXBs, Stanley Rickman was one of 162 men who went on to volunteer as medical orderlies with the parachute regiment for the D-Day landings.

Our fellow paratroopers regarded us as abnormal but we were accepted as comrades. Our losses were not great, largely I guess by people being shot down in the air or by landing. Conscientious objectors made up about a quarter of the unit and the losses were in proportion. I can say honestly we took part gladly and well. I never had any wish to be armed. I do not know of any CO comrade being armed, though it was possible that could have happened in action. I had no regrets.

CHAPTER 15

On the Land

*It was terribly boring but I'm so glad since that I did it,
first that I had the experience of manual labour. I haven't
spent the rest of my life being a manual labourer and it
seems to me to be a useful thing for anyone to know what
labour is like, the tedium of it and also the pleasure of it,
the pleasure of being out in the open. I look back on it with
enormous pleasure.*

Edward Blishen

Thousands of conscientious objectors won exemption from
the tribunals to take up work in agriculture. Len Richardson
was one of them.

I came away a little stunned, not knowing how I would
fare in farm work, which at that time was very lowly
rated and grossly underpaid. On reporting the decision
to the district manager of the insurance company for
whom I worked, I was left in no doubt that they would
not keep my job open for me, since I was a conscientious
objector – they had finished with me. But I still had
to face my customers for a few more weeks, and recall
one dear lady with whom I had discussed religion more
than once on the doorstep, who now upbraided me loud
and clear, 'You coward,' she kept saying, 'You coward!
And I thought you were a nice young man! There is my
son out there fighting for you and you a conscientious
objector.' All my suggestions that if he were fighting for
me she should send for him to come back, were to no
avail. 'You coward' – the words stung me and sting me
still. Another result of the tribunal's decision was the

appearance in the local paper, headed 'Ministerial Work for the Christadelphians', and giving a brief account of my appeal before the tribunal. This paper was widely read and led to more unpleasantness. Some of the neighbours were distinctly cold, and one whose husband was a policeman refused to allow me to collect her insurance money, preferring to take it to the downtown office herself.

Agricultural work was regarded as part of the war effort by many COs. Edward Blishen was among them.

I wasn't really happy to do it. If I had been a really courageous CO I would have refused, but logically there is no other position a CO could adopt, whatever he agreed to do was a contribution clearly but I was ready to work on the land and I did work on the land.

James Hanmer, who worked in forestry, contended that useful work on the land does not contribute to the war machine.

It does in one way in so far as if you smile at a soldier you're contributing to the war effort, in that way we're all one. I met people, who argue – 'How dare you have food that's come from abroad, only got here because we have destroyers sinking U-boats' and so on, I mean those are the silly arguments.

Once men had been registered for land work, finding it was the next hurdle. Particularly in the early part of the war, men had to make their own arrangements. Len Richardson was well known as a Christadelphian preacher.

It happened that an elderly Christadelphian owned a fruit and vegetable business in the town, and bought supplies from a local grower about 3 miles away. Through his good offices, I eventually got work in these market gardens, which were fairly extensive, comprising several hundred acres of cultivated land, and three large mixed orchards. So the day came when I set off for my first morning at the new job. We started work at 7.30 a.m. and worked until 5.30 p.m. (longer in the summer) and my starting wage was 32*s* 6*d* per week – very poor pay for a married man. As I cycled out of town that first morning, I had very serious misgivings. I had heard tales of what happened to COs working on the land, some had been beaten up (a friend of mine had been) and others had been thrown into the village pond. Fear of the unknown is always worse, and I felt myself to be riding, rather ingloriously, into the jaws of certain persecution.

Len Richardson's apprehension turned out to be largely unfounded, but many COs encountered hostility and there was often an underlying atmosphere of tension. Edward Blishen remembers being taunted.

There was some unpleasantness on occasions, some people detested us deeply and made that perfectly clear, largely verbally, not physically, there was very little physical, but they made their dislike of us immensely clear.

I can remember a horseman, as we set to work with scythes on the field, terribly badly I'm sure, saying, 'I hope the buggers make tripods of themselves'. That's one thing I can remember in particular, and I can remember the man who used to stand simply and blow a slow, solemn and very large raspberry as any one of us went by. It was all very much at that level, and much of the time with most of the people we worked with it was largely forgotten, or at least they chose to forget it really, we were very busy working. And COs arriving in the country among taciturn labourers were regarded with scorn, quite rightly too; we talked you see, we stood in ditches and talked and talked and talked. Nobody had ever done that on the land, people don't talk on the land, people haven't got breath to waste and there's nothing to talk about anyway. Also we took a long time to pick up the rhythm of the land. If you worked all your life on the land, especially in those days much of the work on the land was labour intensive, you settled down to a plod, and you plodded for the rest of your life otherwise you would have worn yourself out very quickly. But the townie or the intellectual, or whatever he was, the weird person, the CO arriving on the land didn't know this, so his sense of rhythm was all over the place and he worked in spurts and dashes and then didn't work at all.

Each county had a War Agricultural Executive Committee in charge of labour. Until labour became in short supply, many of these committees refused to employ COs. Edward Blishen began his labours with the Essex committee.

> They were curious bodies, largely, we always thought, officered by failed farmers, dispossessed and failed farmers. They were grotesque in many ways, grotesquely inadequate bodies but they were in charge of us and they organized gangs and so on, appointed foremen for us. I moved around, for example I spent a year or so threshing and I moved around Hertfordshire, from farm to farm. Threshing is an appalling job which is usually done once a year in the farm where you work but they appointed permanent gangs who went around doing threshing. I was a lorry driver's mate for some time with the War Agricultural Committee and that required a great deal of moving around too. But then we also moved all over the counties from one field to another digging ditches and so on.

Most of the COs had no idea of the sort of work they'd be doing. It was certainly a revelation for men like insurance agent Len Richardson.

> There seems to be a feeling that work in industry, or the white-collar jobs, calls for special skills, whereas anybody can do jobs on the land. I was to learn, however, that this is far from the truth, and the simple skills of hoeing, planting, picking, hedging, ditching take a long time and much practice, before the raw recruit from an urban background can begin to compete with his rural counterpart. And the 'conchie' put to work on the land as a condition of exemption from military service, was naturally anxious to prove his ability in the shortest possible time. My first summer, and the severe winter that followed, were certainly the worst. I used to think of the bitter complaint of Jacob against his Uncle Laban – 'In the day time drought consumed me and the frost by night'. The endless rows of hoeing to be undertaken, under a hot summer sun, would probably have proved too much for a soft townie.

One white-collar worker, John Bell, left his office job in the City to take up work on the land in Surrey. He was 37 when war was declared – one of the older men. His father had been poisoned by mustard gas in the First World War.

> Since I came out of an office in 1941 I have worked as a labourer with Surrey Agricultural Committee doing every kind of job and somehow getting on with horses until I finished up as carter at Epsom for a man with a large smallholding who had to give up using horses himself owing to a breakdown in health – he is seventy-six years of age and still going strong in many respects. From about 15 acres of cultivated land, orchard, poultry etc. and pigs – a dozen or so breeding sows – we manage to keep three people going.
>
> Going on the land had quite a deal of glamour for most of us until the first winter and a good spell of threshing put a different complexion on the subject (especially for us over-forties), as well as finding out our weak spots. However, after becoming proficient in those jobs required of a farm labourer and overcoming the strangeness of working alone to a great extent, I soon grew to enjoy the life and to feel fit and healthy except for occasional instances of physical strain.

Physique was certainly a factor for Edward Blishen.

> I was unfitted for the work, quite a weedy intellectual type, but, at the end of five and a half years, I could lift. I could unload a 5-ton lorry of wheat in about five minutes, and I could carry a 2¼ hundred-weight sack of wheat on my back and carry it from here to the gate over there (about 100 metres), you learn these things you see, there are knacks for doing these things. I must have become extremely wiry in the course of that time.

John Marshall had been heavily influenced by the writings of Aldous Huxley, and had joined a pacifist commune whose members worked on the land.

> The work on the land was quite a hardening process. We'd never done it before. The winter of 1939–40 was a

hideous one, it was very frozen. We were working in most unpleasant conditions and I continued to do that sort of work for a considerable time afterwards until I did actually join the army. It was harder than quite a lot I encountered in the forces afterwards, living and working in very unpleasant conditions on the land.

The men on the land were a cross-section of the many groups who had chosen to obey their conscience. John Marshall became a communist during the war, John Bell was a member of the Church of England. Edward Blishen was an humanitarian objector.

We were mixed, there were all sorts of strange religious – there were Plymouth Brethren, Christadelphians – and peculiar people – Elimites, the Pentecostal Church of Elim, one or two Jehovah's Witnesses, some political 'conchies' and one or two members of the ILP – remember the Independent Labour Party was pacifist – and one or two highly eccentric individuals like myself, because I didn't have any backing of any kind.

The one thing, and often the only thing, Edward Blishen felt they had in common was their status as conscientious objectors.

We had many of us that unity that comes of having to do work together, which is very important. But many of us disagreed with each other very violently. I didn't believe actually that the future of the world was to be deduced from measuring the pyramids and that sort of thing, so we did have some problems of that nature. But on the whole, our common plight was what in the end loomed more important than differences.

James Hanmer had been a teacher when war broke out, but was given conditional exemption provided he worked on the land. He joined a Christian Pacifist Forestry and Land Unit at the village of Bardney in Lincolnshire.

There were twelve people, managing themselves, feeding themselves, one would be a cook for three months and then somebody else would take a turn if he wanted to be a cook for three months, self governing. Now this man who organized this was very wise – he'd have half Methodists to provide a kind of basis, this was the normal pattern, and then there'd be Quakers, Salvation Army, Plymouth Brethren, one Anglo–Catholic. It was open to anyone.

Christian Pacifist Forestry and Land Units had been set up by a Methodist minister Henry Carter in early 1940 to answer the needs of conscientious objectors looking for work on the land. Eventually nearly 1,400 men joined the units which also found them accommodation – sometimes in old railway carriages – as well as work. James Hanmer was one of a group of COs who worked for the Forestry Commission.

It was interesting work. Planting, weeding in the summer, slashing and burning, preparing the ground for new planting, various odd jobs, dyking, and then of course suddenly we were told that the money's stopped you can't do any more on that dyke you see. We were paid £3 a week. It was the average agricultural labourer's wage. Out of that we fed ourselves.

We had rotas for making sandwiches for the next day, we had a rota for washing up, the person who made the sandwiches at night usually had a short prayer after breakfast before we went to work at 7 a.m. to be at the wood where we were working at 7.30 a.m. and of course we all had cycles – that was the only way to get around.

Once a week, there'd be a kind of get together, a kind of Bible study. Because I was a geographer I gave a talk on the landscape and how it was formed. We made friends with a unit that was running an anti–aircraft gun. Three or four of us were Methodist local preachers. I must say I was happy there, probably happier than I should have been.

The CPFLU was really a religious movement. Units had Bible study groups, some even had their own magazines, and they lived a communal lifestyle.

Anarchist Tom Carlile also joined a community working on the land. Born in the East End he was an active member of the Labour movement. In the early days of the Blitz he had worked as a volunteer, but he was not prepared to have his movements dictated by the state.

I decided to have a good look round and find something I ought to be doing. And there were land work communities being set up to provide the alternative service that was given by the tribunals to COs, one was in Gloucester. I wrote saying that while I didn't claim to be a CO in the technical sense of the word and I had not been given land work as an alternative to military or national service, but I would like to come and work for their community.

I was painfully aware that I was not an agriculturalist. I didn't know what a cow looked like before I left London in 1940, let alone a cabbage. We grew nothing in our gardens, despite burying seeds for years in Bow. Anyway, so I thought if I'm really going to do agricultural work, if I'm really going to be into community movement, I ought to try and learn something and I wasn't learning from fellow COs, who, with one exception knew little or nothing about agriculture.

So far Tom Carlile had not appeared before a tribunal, although he had registered. He started to move from one pacifist agricultural community to another, spending a few weeks at each. First he went to Standish Hospital, near Stroud in Gloucestershire.

There were about three or four perhaps even half a dozen COs employed to do all the work – ward orderlies, working on the gardens, even working in the boiler house, helping to run the hospital. And I got to know some of them, because they came to visit us because there was this interchange amongst COs locally and in organizations like the PPU, and other pacifist or religious organizations, Quakers in particular. I wrote to Standish and said I was prepared to do land work, I understood they did employ COs. Anyway I got a job there working in the gardens, and whilst I was there a summons was received by the Gloucester Land Scheme.

Each time he moved Tom had to change his address with the National Registration in order to keep up his ration card.

I was a most law-abiding anarchist. There was no point in not telling them where I was. I wanted them to know what I was doing.

The next thing I knew two detectives came to the Standish Hospital office and said they understood that I was staying there or working there. I was called to the office and they merely wanted to make certain that I was the person that the summons had applied to. And they did question me a little, and they advised me to stay where I was and I would receive a summons in due course.

At that stage there was no real planning. I realized that what I had done so far was not an arrestable offence and that the only way I could be put in prison was the result of attending a police court who then found me guilty and awarded some sentence to pick me up. So, I thought what am I going to do, am I going to wait here until they make the summons or not? I didn't because of the contacts I had arranged. I decided what I'll do now is I'll now move from here so that they're at least one stage behind me and then I'll systematically visit other communities other establishments, I even went to a war agricultural hostel and worked there for a month.

I went to Stanford le Hope, Moore Place I think it was called, my elder brother was one of the original call-ups. He got land work, and he went to one of the first started by John Middleton Murry, the Oaks, Langham, Essex, which was disastrous apparently mainly because of Middleton Murry. A sort of community movement grew up with a directory so names and addresses were available.

Labour was in demand and Tom found a welcome and even a degree of connivance at the places he visited.

In most of the places I got the tip from them that the summons had arrived, they knew where I was at that point, without necessarily disclosing it, they allowed me to move so I was one jump ahead.

Tom Carlile managed to stay on the run for two years, until finally his companion Maisie was expecting their child and he decided to stay put and face arrest.

Later in the war when the government needed more men to work down the mines, he had just finished his six months in prison.

The authorities got in touch with me saying I was a person liable to national service and they would therefore direct me to land work. I said, 'No way, I was doing land work when you came and arrested me, I'm not going to do land work'. I was interviewed and told them I wanted to work in the pits because I thought that it was work that was worthwhile, it was socially necessary and it was what I wanted to do. They said, 'If you do go in the pits, we'll withdraw the order for you to work on the land, you can please yourself about what you want to do'. That's what they did. It must have been January 1944 I started work at Pensford Colliery, Somerset. So I worked underground and did about seventeen years altogether.

Bernard Hicken was living near Halifax at the outbreak of war. He won agricultural exemption on appeal. But although agricultural work was physically demanding Bernard felt he should be making more of a sacrifice to help a country which was at war.

I felt a wee bit guilty that I was living a life as a civilian in this country whilst other people of my age were facing death abroad, and I suppose being human I wasn't quite satisfied. I wanted to be able to do my little bit, not for the war effort but by helping to feed people, so I accepted that I should do horticulture, then moved into farming because I felt that was more useful, producing food for people who were in this country. It was after I'd been there for some time that I read in the *Reynolds News* about the CO who was actually acting as a human guinea pig in Sheffield for the Medical Research Council experiment and I thought this is something I would like to do because it's humanitarian, it's helping people and also there is a certain amount of risk. This was an opportunity to do my little bit in a more positive way.

I think I was very blessed to actually read that account in the paper otherwise I shouldn't have known about the possibility of doing that sort of work. It was quite a little-known activity on the part of COs who felt that they wanted to contribute something, who felt that they had opted out from the accepted way of serving their country and humanity, this was a small way in which we could play our part.

Bernard went to the Sorby Institute in Sheffield. Still under an agricultural exemption, he tended the kitchen garden for the community of objectors, most of whom lived on site. He was among thirty conscientious objectors who acted as human guinea pigs for medical experiments under the leadership of Dr Kenneth Mellanby.

The first experiment in which I was engaged, was investigating the efficient treatment of scabies, because up to then a sulphur treatment had been used and Dr Mellanby had devised this method where a patient was treated with benzyl benzoate.

We had scabies mites introduced into our bodies and then allowed to multiply and that was unpleasant, not too bad in the day time, but when you got into bed at night and became warm then the mites became active and you'd spend a lot of the night scratching and you had to be careful that you didn't scratch too hard because you broke the skin and probably set up secondary infection.

One of our members of the community, there were four or five in the room, and he was sitting on his bed with nothing on the top of his body and with a hairbrush and he was gently stroking his body with this hairbrush and the look of ecstasy on his face as he got rid of all the itching – it was really marvellous to rid himself of the itching.

Apart from the treatment with benzyl benzoate emulsion, Dr Mellanby was also interested in the movement of the mites. If you see a picture it's not a very engaging looking creature, but the idea was that, we who were on the scabies experiment, a certain number of mites were introduced on to our body usually on the wrist and then every week the doctor or his assistant would count the number of mites and the location of them and see how they'd increased in number and moved around to different parts of the body. Also we were able to use that knowledge by going round to some of the schools and examining the children to see if they had scabies. As you can imagine these wee creatures crawling around under the epidermis where you can't feel the actual movement but you can feel the itching which is caused by them, which keeps you awake at night, that itself is unpleasant but by no means dangerous. . .

The volunteers were also subjected to a shipwreck diet to see the minimum amount of water needed to keep a person in normal health. The guinea pigs were fed on the dried stores commonly found in lifeboats with no water from Tuesday afternoon till Saturday morning. Bernard Hicken was stoical about these privations.

> The shipwreck experiment was connected with the diet that sailors would have to put up with in the case of being shipwrecked. I can't say it made us particularly ill, it was more a case of headaches and that sort of thing. But the lice experiments, they were interesting, because the idea was to introduce head lice to the body and body lice to the head and see if they migrated to their proper place. I had an interesting experience when I went to the Methodist church one Sunday morning; the minister was pacifist. During the service I was aware of something at the back of my neck and removed it and it was one of the lice that were migrating, and I don't know if the person behind saw it or not but they must have thought what kind of person would come to church with lice crawling around.

The Sorby Institute had been researching vitamins A and D for many years and wanted to take the research one step further. The human guinea pigs took part in experiments on Vitamin A deficiency. Bernard Hicken was put on a diet deficient in Vitamin A.

> There was a great deal of uncertainty about that, because I'm pretty sure no one had done that experiment before so there was a certain amount of apprehension because Vitamin A is pretty important throughout the body. But you have this feeling that it's the right thing to do, so you carry on. I think probably parents and friends were a wee bit more concerned about what effect it may have on you. For example if you went out for a meal someone would say it won't matter just have a little bit of this it won't have much Vitamin A in, but you just had to be firm about that and say 'No, no, that's not the point this is an experiment'. Some of the volunteers were on a normal diet, so they were the control group then others were on the diet which excluded Vitamin A. The idea was that

after the war there was going to be a shortage of food and a great deal of hunger throughout the world and the use of the food was going to be vital, so that there's no wastage. You don't want to be giving too much Vitamin A so that what is available can be spread over a bigger number of the population.

Bernard spent eighteen months on the diet.

During the experiment I didn't feel ill. The only noticeable effect, it must have been due to this because Vitamin A is connected with night blindness, in the blackout I used to find I was pretty well at a loss, I couldn't see very well – my eyesight at that time was pretty good normally. We did have very regular checks from the experts, we used to have audiometer checks, visual checks, every week we had blood samples taken and we had to collect our faeces once a week and grind them up into a powder and they were sent off to Cambridge to be analyzed – I suppose that was a check to see that no Vitamin A was being taken in.

After eighteen months of this diet without Vitamin A I suppose nature caught up with me and I had to be taken into hospital and given massive doses of Vitamin A and I was six weeks in hospital with a pleural effusion and that was the end of my experience of experiments because I wasn't able to do any more. When I came out of hospital I was just like an old man, I really did feel shall I ever feel anything else but this, I was about twenty-five or twenty-six.

CHAPTER 16

In the Hands of the Army

It was a move to break the spirit and make us conform and become soldiers. I was beaten up and other people had water thrown over them and they were beaten up as well.

Frank Chadwick

Unlike the men of the First World War only a handful of conscientious objectors in the Second World War experienced army brutality. But there was an undercurrent of hostility among some soldiers, a feeling that COs were 'cowards and shirkers' and should be taking up arms to defeat the common enemy. This underlying discontent spilled over into violence in two main incidents – Dingle Vale and Ilfracombe.

At his first tribunal Dennis Waters was given exemption on condition that he went into the Non-Combatant Corps.

I was not prepared to join the armed forces under any guise because you would be in uniform attached to the Pioneer Corps. When I was arrested and taken down to my unit it was the Pioneer Corps based at Ilfracombe. And there was an NCC detachment who felt somewhat like me but as I refused to obey orders as soon as I got there I was court martialled. I was given twenty-eight days in a military glasshouse, which was in fact Hull Prison which had been taken over by the military, but before I went up there I had this business of being beaten up.

The situation at Ilfracombe was that there was a certain number of COs who wouldn't toe the line, who didn't agree to do non-combatant duties. A certain amount of pressure was exercised on them to make them change their minds and toe the line and the pressure showed itself in the guise of this Sergeant Maloney, who was an ex-wrestler from the dock area of London with a broken nose, and he exerted every kind of pressure including physical violence to make us change our minds.

It all happened one morning. This sergeant was in charge of us and he'd been bawling us out of course as he always did, but whether he was getting impatient with the fact that we hadn't toed the line I don't know but he decided that he would rough us up to make us toe the line. And he went into the room next door where young Ashley Morris was and I heard him bawling and shouting and then I heard the sound of blows – because I was listening through the little hole in the wall, and this sickened me. When it had finished I heard Ashley's voice coming through the wall, explaining what had happened and saying we ought to complain about this and then he appeared in my room and went through the same routine with me.

When you're hit, one has a sort of red mist in front of one. My instinctive reaction was one of rage. Here was this man brutalizing one and getting away with it. But I knew of course that had I lifted a finger against him I would have been in real trouble and he would have had *carte blanche*. So I didn't do anything. I accepted his blows. Then he went stomping off and I heard him doing the same in the next door room.

Dennis Waters was one of four conscientious objectors who were beaten up by the sergeant.

By a merciful providence very shortly afterwards we had a visit from the orderly officer of the day. Now he was one of these who joined up quite recently because of the war, I don't know what his profession was but he was a decent kindly man and I let it all rip. He comes in and says, 'Have you got any complaints?' and I said, 'Yes, we've been beaten up,' and I explained what had happened and he obviously realized what had been going on and he went and got corroboration from the others and then he had us examined by a doctor.

Frank Chadwick, a French polisher from Leeds, had been removed from the register of conscientious objectors at his first tribunal but on appeal had been put in the Non-Combatant Corps. He was called up in 1940 but refused to go and was arrested by police and taken under escort to Dingle Vale in Liverpool – a school which had been requisitioned as a training camp for the NCC. It was here that the only organized brutality against COs took place.

> I went there Friday night towards dusk, it was dark by the time we got there and I was immediately put in a sort of a cubby hole, which presumably was used for the books and it was just the size of a toilet without any cistern or basin in. I was put in there for the night. They came every hour or two to make sure you didn't get any sleep or were on your feet, that was part of the treatment. We were kept in there for about three days altogether.

Frank was one of a small group of COs who underwent this sort of treatment at Dingle Vale.

> There was a history of this sort of thing happening in the beginning. It would go on for maybe two or three weeks in total for different people, for me it only happened over a period of three or four days.
> We were issued with battledress, boots and what have you, and the other stuff we were wearing was taken away from us and parcelled up. Then after we were taken for the haircuts, which was rather amusing, because we went in the hairdressers and we sat in this chair, but he just took two bits down the sides and then came over the top of the head and we ended up with no hair and we were shorn. Everybody got this treatment, all the 'conchies'.

Marked out by their shorn hair, Frank and the other COs were now subjected to an organized attempt to make them join the army.

> We lost track of time and chronological order of events but at sometime over the weekend or in the first three or four days I was taken out, I was in the uniform at this particular stage. I was taken outside with other soldiers,

and I was the only CO in the midst of the platoon of soldiers, and they were drilling. They tried to get some sort of order and semblance of acquiescence. We were non-conformist, we weren't going to accept orders and we weren't going to be soldiers. But we were taken out in this pack of squaddies, drilled and marched about and given orders, right turn, left turn and at ease and attenshun and all this. Actually the first time I was taken out I was in the school playground and all round the outside was the railings and people were walking and I suspect that there were one or two that were sympathizers, people in Liverpool that had heard about us being there and had come to see what was going off, and one woman shouted out, 'Leave him alone.' I shouted back to her, 'Yes, you interfere Mrs'. Then I was taken inside with Sergeant McPhail, the sergeant that was ultimately charged with beating up COs, a Scottish sergeant, member of the Black Watch. He beat me up and thumped me in the stomach a couple of times and that's when I learned the words, 'Knock the piss out of you.' That's about it. I said 'I'll sign, I'll sign.' I thought I had to sign to agree to a pay book. I'll sign anything to stop the punishment but in fact I never did sign and I never was issued with a pay book.

I was knocked up and then taken outside, beaten about a bit by both the sergeant and the corporal. Then I was taken outside again but I wasn't co-operative. I didn't do the drill, I was very weak so I was taken back to the cubby hole again. I think they brought food once during this period and I sent it back I didn't want it.

You were kept in the dark all the time. You were deprived of your sleep, that was part of the treatment. After three days in the dark my complexion which had been sunburnt turned sallow and I looked as if I'd yellow jaundice. I was a bit dispirited and not making a great effort to move, I was conserving my energies I suppose. I wouldn't say I was discouraged. It was what I had actually expected. They gave up on me.

While the men at Dingle Vale were being beaten up, they were largely segregated from those who might be able to bring it to a halt. Frank Chadwick found out what had happened later.

In fact I got to know afterwards that somebody had smuggled a letter out and that this had caused questions to be asked in Parliament about what was happening in Dingle Vale and as a consequence inquiries were made. There was a bit of a public furore and description in the newspapers.

Dennis Waters managed to get a letter out from Ilfracombe to the Central Board for Conscientious Objectors in London.

One of the difficulties was letting our own people know what was going on. I mean when you're being beaten up it's difficult to smuggle the news out. We used to have food and what not sent in and people used to send stamps in with the food and then we had the difficulty of getting letters out to send home. But fortunately some of the people who were our guards were members of the Non-Combatant Corps and favourably disposed towards us, and if we slipped letters to them they used to post them for us, that was the way we got our news out. They raised the matter with various people in the House of Commons and that is why this bloke was taken off.

Sergeant Maloney was court martialled on thirteen offences relating to the ill-treatment of COs at Ilfracombe, but was acquitted on all charges. Denis Waters still remembers the outcome with disbelief.

I mean the man was out on a charge and court martialled, he got off. A fine example of army justice. The guard said, when they were asked if they'd witnessed what was going on, they'd been looking elsewhere! There was a sort of cover up as there always is on these kind of things and I remember marching away from his court martial thinking, well my goodness if this is army justice they can stuff it. But in point of fact what happened was having had questions asked in Parliament about it they took the man off us – quite obviously they didn't want any more trouble. But when ever we saw him in the town afterwards he was always bawling and shouting.

Dennis Waters and his fellow COs were also court martialled – for disobeying orders.

Whilst waiting for court martial they had to find things for us to do and they used to find the dirtiest and most humiliating jobs that they could find. I spent a lot of my time on my knees scrubbing floors because they'd taken over hotels, and when I was in glasshouses (military prisons) on two occasions, all they could find for us to do was to scrub the spots of whitewash that had dripped down on to the coal beneath.

Dennis Waters was court martialled three times. He received sentences of twenty-eight days and fifty-six days which he served in Hull and Shepton Mallett Military Prisons. Finally he was sentenced to three months in Wandsworth, a civilian prison and was therefore allowed to go before an appeal tribunal where he was exempted on condition that he worked on the land.

After his beating, Frank Chadwick was in such a bad way that he spent three weeks in the sick bay.

At the beginning I wouldn't eat anything, I was on hunger strike, it was the natural thing to do, the only thing you could do but while I was in sick bay I was visited by the CO (Commanding Officer) and the RSM (Regimental Sergeant Major), this chap named Terry, he was sort of apologetic for what he had done. He referred to his own experiences in the war bayonetting people which had sort of sickened him.

After a period of days in there the Church of England padre came to see me two or three times and finally tempted me with an apple. I ate the apple and from then on started eating.

Frank was discharged into the guardroom – the old school cloakroom.

There I met quite a number of COs, we were all in there together maybe a dozen to twenty of us. I met these Scots that had been to Barlinnie and a lot of them were Plymouth Brethren. They'd been in Barlinnie for twenty-eight days and then shipped down to Dingle Vale, maybe half a dozen of them altogether. They were all shorn and so we knew each other by that small fact. That was sort of a treatment to get at you and an attack on your dignity I suppose and a sort of softening-up process.

A court of inquiry was held and in March 1941 one officer and five NCOs appeared before General Court Martial. Three of the NCOs were acquitted but the others were convicted on some of the charges. Sergeant McPhail was found guilty of two assaults and was later reduced to the rank of corporal, but Frank Chadwick refused to give evidence against him.

> I'd forgiven this chap, he'd beaten me up and been fairly nasty and he was a sadist so possibly he enjoyed doing what he did, but I'd forgiven him for doing that, so I couldn't redeem that attitude of forgiving him with giving evidence against him and the case was adjourned where I was concerned and I was court martialled.

This was Frank Chadwick's third court martial. He had already served two sentences of sixty-three days and twenty-eight days. This time he was sentenced to two years in prison for refusing to give evidence and refusing to obey orders.

> It was the worst part of the war for COs, it was the worst scenario where COs were knocked about. They had a hard time in Barlinnie Prison, a hard time in Chorley Wood and a hard time in the glasshouse in Aldershot, wherever they went in military prisons they were given a hard time. But that was the ordinary military scenario. Everybody that went in those camps was given a hard time. Everything was at the double. Ordinary soldiers had heavy packs put on their backs and were drilled up and down the parade ground for four hours may be. If they didn't obey the orders they were put in detention cells, they gave them a hell of a time so that they might not come back again.
>
> With us COs we were determined we weren't going to have to go back a second time. In fact the CO needed to get eighty-four days detention or imprisonment which allowed him to appeal and go before another tribunal for a reassessment of his case (in fact that was the object of refusing orders) which in nearly every case resulted in them being

discharged from the unit with a condition of agricultural work, hospital work or a more acceptable condition.

I got two years of course, I only served about three months of it, and then I came before the tribunal, was discharged from the army and discharged from the prison as well after three months. I got agricultural or hospital duties as a condition of exemption which I accepted.

There were one or two exceptions to that rule. One of the Jehovah's Witnesses in particular that had 'cat and mouse' treatment for months and months. He was sentenced three or four times without being given the chance of appearing before the appeal tribunal again. He was the exception to the rule, but in nearly every case they were given the first sentence of sixty-three days in the military prison to see if that would break them or give them pause to think. Some COs did think twice and they accepted non-combatant duties, but most of those who refused to accept non-combatant duties got this eighty-four days.

CHAPTER 17

The Absolutists

I remember jocularly saying, 'With a bit of luck I'll get enough white feathers to make a pillowcase.' I did in fact collect three. But there was a lot of criticism. As I often say, there were pals of mine who'd gone in the forces and were fighting away there for something they didn't even believe in, I am at least struggling for something I do believe in.

Leonard Bird

As in the First World War, there were conscientious objectors who took their stand against military service to its logical conclusion. Known as the Absolutists, like the 1,500 most radical men a quarter of a century earlier, they refused to co-operate with the state by taking any form of alternative service.

Ernest Lenderyou refused to attend even a medical examination and received a summons.

My father accompanied me to court and knew, I think, that he would almost certainly be saying goodbye to me for a while. It was soon apparent that the magistrates clerk who seemed to run the proceedings pretty well as he wished, was out to get the maximum sentence for me. In particular he had read out, with suitable expression of indignation, some of my more 'stroppy' letters and observations, including my request for a stamped addressed envelope for the return of missives from the War Office. If that was really his objective he notched up a victory. I was given a sentence of six months hard labour and was taken down to the cells with just time for a nervous wave to my father.

I was not much more than twenty years old, and felt suddenly very lonely. I knew a little of what I was going to face, but it was in large part a journey into unknown territory. Despite my bravado I had no real idea of how well I would cope with it.

Leonard Bird was an articled clerk in a solicitor's office when he was called up. He was refused exemption at his first tribunal but went to appeal in Manchester. He was granted exemption provided he did alternative work.

I took the view that if we oppose war we oppose all war and we don't do something where we can be exonerated from doing more service. I could have gone into a hospital, but if I'd done that I might very easily have been faced with the situation a friend of mine was. He went into a hospital and one of the porters said, 'You've come here and now you've made me liable to go into the forces.' I think that if you're doing some useful work in civilian life, then the fact that a war's broken out, not at your behest, then that's no reason for changing the work you're doing. If you're not doing something useful then you ought to change it anyway, not simply because there's a war service attached to it.

Leonard had already had several opportunities for exemption through the firm where he was articled.

I could have got exemption on the grounds that I was a student for some time; my firm could have applied on the grounds that I was required because several members of the staff had been called up into the forces; or alternatively I could have gone to work in a hospital because one of the partners in the firm was the chairman of the board and would have been delighted if I'd gone to work in the hospital and worked in the office part-time. I also had a rather unusual opportunity to be exempted for no trouble because another partner was a brigadier in the army and was in charge of all the air-raid defence in the south Midlands, and on one occasion when he came on leave and came into my room he said to me, 'When you get all this nonsense of conscientious objection out of your head you come and work for me.' Now I could have gone and had a very easy number working for him, as two lads in the office did. We should have been under no risk of going into the army and getting called up for military service in any case, and getting home every weekend and being the blue-eyed boys, but I was not prepared to do that so instead of doing that I went to prison.

Aubrey Brocklehurst was in a reserved occupation but had insisted on being placed on the register of conscientious objectors.

The Ministry of Labour provisionally or temporarily put me on the CO register and after that I was taken off that and put on the military register, but of course I was in a reserved occupation and it didn't really affect me at the time. I continued like this until the autumn of 1942, and by that time I really had felt not just disquieted but very, very unhappy that I was being sheltered from military service and all the challenges that faced other people, simply because I was in this reserved occupation so I left it. And because I was opposed to conscription I didn't seek permission of the National Service Officer, as he was called. I simply wrote him a letter, a copy of my notice to my employers that I was leaving – and of course that was against the law, I was supposed to seek permission first.

Aubrey was summonsed for leaving work without permission and appeared at Salford Magistrates Court. He was fined £3 with a guinea costs.

On principle I refused to pay. A few weeks later I was summonsed in front of the court again and I got a month's imprisonment. After that of course I was no longer in a reserved occupation, I was properly on the military register, and I was not in any work, so I was called up for a medical.

I wrote and said I was unwilling to go because I was a CO and was opposed to war and opposed to conscription. Then I got summonsed for not going for the medical, and ordered by the court to be taken by the police to the medical examination centre. There was another young man appearing before the magistrates on the same charge on the same morning, so we were both taken along to the medical examination centre. I said to this young chap, 'Now I'm going to refuse the medical examination'. He was a bit confused and not sure what to do. I had already been in prison for a month and felt that I knew the ropes and was not going to be intimidated too easily. So we both refused to be medically examined and we were taken back to the police court and the cells, had to stay overnight. Next morning we appeared before the magistrate again, this time on a more serious charge, this time we had disobeyed the court's order so we got nine months imprisonment each for that.

Aubrey and his fellow CO were to serve their sentence in Strangeways Prison.

I said to this young chap, 'When we are in prison it is much better than police cells, we'll have proper pillows put under our heads instead of a telegraph pole.' I was quite cheery about it all and rather blasé. We got into prison, in my case for the second time and the time dragged a little bit, but I was fortunate, one reason was that I was in because I had chosen that particular course. I hadn't any bad conscience about it all, I hadn't committed any offence against society as say someone who had stolen property or injured somebody.

David Spreckley had asked for complete exemption at his tribunal on humanitarian grounds.

They gave me either land work or full time ambulance work. And I said, 'No to ambulance work, if there was another Blitz I'd be there, I'm not going to support the war effort when there's nothing going on and I'm certainly not going to a cushy job on the land.'

David and a group of friends set up a small anarchist community in London. A hat hung by the door and anyone who had money threw some in.

We were getting a bit short so I got a job as a film extra, a pound a day, somebody gave me a couple of lines to speak and somebody said, 'Why don't you try and be an actor,' and I said, 'Well they're going to catch up with me – they're going to send me to prison in a few months, I've just got to fill up time'. So they said, 'I know an agent,' so I went to see this agent and he got me a job on the stage within a week. I'd done some amateur work, but I'd never been on the stage in my life and I went off to a rep in Leicester and became leading man in the first week, it was incredible, and it was taking much longer than I thought for them to arrest me.

David went on tour with a production of *Private Lives*.

And at that time they'd got my warrant and they were always a week behind me, and apparently they must have gone to about four or five theatres with this warrant in their hands and I'd always just moved on. Somebody told me it was happening and I knew they would be round soon. But it went on very much longer and I was a leading man for a bit over a year, before they did catch up with me.

Another anarchist, Tom Carlile, also went 'on the run'. Like David Spreckley, it had not been a conscious decision, he was merely keeping one step ahead of the authorities.

I wasn't shall we say objecting to it as a political member of a political party but my opposition was then to the state. I suppose philosophically, I became an anarchist. Having gone through in a very short space of time the democratic socialist ideas, I came to the conclusion that the state was the greater evil, the denial of freedom, the denial of liberty, the denial of the right of a man to make up his own mind or not – and I was denying the state the right to tell me that I must kill at their behest. This is the decision which I maintained which was for me and me alone.

Tom Carlile was eventually arrested and sent to Gloucester Prison.

Leonard Bird was imprisoned for not complying with his conditions of exemption.

I was I believe the third person in Britain to be so prosecuted and sent to prison. We had a very hard-faced stipendiary magistrate who himself was an old sweat, as we termed them, and had decorations, and he promptly gave me twelve months which was the maximum sentence for someone who was liable for not complying with the conditions. It was unfortunate in the sense that if you were sent to prison you had no right of appeal again. The lads who were in the army had a right of appeal and often when they went to a tribunal then their exemption was altered. We had no right of appeal so strictly when I came out of prison about eight and a half months later I was informed by the Labour Exchange that I'd got to go into alternative service. And I remember going down once with my wife who was very irate at this and she said to the clerk down there, 'What do you think he's just done twelve months in prison for if he's going to do the alternative service now?' It never bothered me.

After that I was contacted a few times but I resolutely refused to do any alternative service and was left alone until I fell foul of the regulations regarding firewatching. I did voluntary firewatching when I was working in the firm of solicitors but when it was a compulsory requirement and I'd not obtained exemption from that, although I had applied, I refused to do compulsory firewatching and got prosecuted four times and got sent to prison two more times.

A lot of the absolutists refused to do firewatching, including some of the First World War COs. Alan Litherland was born just before the beginning of the First World War. While he was studying organic chemistry at Cambridge he joined the Methodist Peace Fellowship. He emerged on to the labour market in 1939 after getting his Ph.D., and with war looming, he was offered a job with ICI.

They were largely concerned with fertilizers and that kind of thing and they offered me a job but it was fairly obvious that there might well be war and I was concerned about this and I said, 'If war breaks out your work will largely be moved over to war work won't it, explosives and that kind of thing.' And they said, 'Yes,' so I said, 'Well, if that happens, I'm not coming.' They still offered me the job. When war did come I wrote to say I wasn't coming so I was without a job at the beginning of the war. I was a very obstinate blighter.

Unemployed Alan returned home to Knutsford in Cheshire where he did a first aid course, grew vegetables and did voluntary firewatching at a babies' hospital.

I applied to be a CO – my attitude was that I was not willing to do any alternative service of any kind, in other words I was what was called an Absolutist. So I went to a tribunal, this was an occasion when Judge Burgis was the normal chairman of the tribunal in Manchester and he was a very reasonable chap. Unfortunately one of the alleged pacifists stabbed him in the back so he was off duty for a period of months – I imagine that particular CO was not registered. Anyway so it was a different chap, not nearly so tolerant when I went. I applied for absolute exemption. I was registered as a CO on condition that I did non-combatant work in the forces. So I said, 'No I'm not doing that.'

The result was in due course I received a call-up paper. They left it for a long time and then I got a note from the Ministry of Labour instructing me to attend for a medical examination on such and such a date, and I wrote back politely saying that I wasn't coming; nothing happened. Then I got another one some months later and again I wrote saying I wasn't coming and then it happened a third time and that must have been March or February 1941. And I received it again so I was duly arrested and taken to the Magistrates' Court in Stockport and instructed to attend for a medical examination. And I duly went to this place and they said, 'Are you willing to be examined?' and I said no and that was that.

I was taken back to the Magistrates' Court in Stockport and tried and duly condemned to twelve months' imprisonment. My crime at the second attendance at court was disobeying the instruction of the court and it was that which carried a maximum sentence of twelve months. It was a particularly severe magistrate at the time, some got no more than three months, and I got twelve months so off I went to prison.

Alan Litherland served his sentence in Strangeways Prison.

And I was there actually for two months because you had the right after three months' imprisonment to appeal to another tribunal who could vary the condition of your exemption. I appealed but as a prison sentence was automatically reduced by 30 per cent after two months I went off to the appellate tribunal and I applied for, in effect, exemption on condition that I would work as a chemist. . .

Alan's reasoning was on similar lines to many COs.

My attitude was I'm not going to help the war effort in any way but I'm willing to do what is my proper job. The logic of these reasonings may be quite difficult but it's mainly you've made your decision and you've got to stick to it, it's obstinacy right through. And I was quite certain I was not going to do anything which I regarded as assisting the war effort. I realized that I was in a little minority among COs, there were not many that took the line but quite a lot did alternative service but that was what they felt was the right thing for them to do. Whatever line you took as a CO was not easy and so we had that bond. I don't sit in judgement on other people, I didn't at that time either, that was what they felt was the right thing to do and that was up to them.

Leonard Bird served three sentences in Armley Gaol, Leeds.

Prison is a terrible experience, anyone that says it's a holiday camp and a home from home and all that sort of nonsense doesn't know what they're talking about. It's terrible to be away from your home and terrible to be away from your work or your friends and everything that you know. Incarceration in prison is such a horrible experience you tend to make light of it of course, otherwise you'd die a quick death if you didn't. So you look back and you think of some of the amusing occasions but in fact it really is a horrible situation. I remember the first day I came out I was terrified at the pace at which the buses were going.

During his time in prison Leonard Bird discovered the work
he'd been given was war work and went on a work strike –
following an example set by First World War COs.

> I knew there was a regulation from the Home Office saying
> that conscientious objectors were not to be given war
> work. Despite that the governor, quite wrongfully in my
> opinion, sent my pal and I to five of the six punishments
> for refusing work – bread and water, solitary confinement
> and seven days loss of remission which meant another
> week to serve. I petitioned the Home Office, but of course
> somebody up there just threw it in the waste paper basket
> and said it was not applicable.
>
> When we were in prison we had different experiences,
> some of the officers were terribly antagonistic, one or
> two others were understanding, and I made friends with
> one or two. The senior officer in the engineers' or work
> department where I was sent after refusing work was very
> good. I refused to work on the gallows when somebody
> was going to be hanged for a murder and he understood,
> and took me off that and put me on other work. One of the
> other officers was very antagonistic and gradually got to
> know a little bit about us when we argued with him and he
> treated us quite reasonably. It did vary enormously from
> one day to the next.

Most prisoners were held in solitary confinement but the
silence rule had generally been lifted since the days when
conscientious objectors had been imprisoned in the First
World War. Ernest Lenderyou, a political objector, had been
sentenced to six months' hard labour.

> The hard labour part of my sentence, which had worried
> me at first, amounted, it soon emerged, simply to sleeping
> for the first two weeks without a mattress on a bed, the
> base of which was made from heavy canvas similar to that
> from which mailbags were sewn, and with hard seams in
> inconvenient places.
>
> There was at that time no common association or
> recreation during the evenings; so apart from work periods,
> the shuffle in single file round the yard known as exercise,
> the weekly bath and the Sunday service (attended by

most agnostics and atheists as a break from the general monotony), it was the locked cell and solitude.

Prison work varied. Some conscientious objectors like Alan Litherland worked in the library – a sought after job – others in the kitchens, and of course there was always that old standby, sewing mailbags. Aubrey Brocklehurst had been an engineer before he was sent to Strangeways.

A hobby of mine used to be repairing watches, and when the war came along a lot of people asked me if I could repair their watches and I did this in my spare time. When I was in prison they asked me what I was doing and I said well I had been an engineer and was now repairing watches and clocks, so on my second nine-month sentence the prison people said would I like to repair the clocks in the prison because a lot of the clocks weren't working. This was nice for me because normally prisoners had to do what was called cell tasks in the evening in their cells and in the daytime of course you'd be out, in my case sewing mailbags in the daytime, and you sewed mailbags in your cells in the evenings. Anyway they said instead of my sewing mailbags it would be more worthwhile if I repaired clocks in my cell. The only slight snag was the cell was rather cold at night-times, and when I was doing mail bags in my cell I used to put the mailbags on top of myself to keep myself warm. But when eventually I started doing watch and clock repairs of course no mailbags came and then I felt cold. I had to ask for an extra blanket which wasn't very forthcoming – the prison doctor didn't think that I merited it. But eventually one of the officers arranged for me to have an extra blanket.

Alan Litherland hated prison although he enjoyed its solitary nature.

In the first week before we had been allocated to our departments, the new boys were put into what was called K wing where we sat on benches all day long picking fibre used for mattresses and it required kind of dispersing, pulling apart. We weren't allowed to talk.

If you wanted to leave the room you had to put your hand up, that kind of thing. This was not a room, it was a gallery with a walkway around the sides like all the old-fashioned prisons, with a central space. This walkway was not very wide and we had a bench which we sat on going obliquely across this walkway all facing the same direction with the prison officer at the end keeping order, but he didn't have much to do, he would shout if somebody talked. After a week we were allocated to the library. We had the job of taking books around to the prison cells, we must have had an officer with us to open the doors. When we were not circulating with books we were repairing books in the library. For the most part the officer was not there so we were completely free to talk as much as we liked. There were two or three others, they were all Jehovah's Witnesses, so there were lots of arguments.

Another inmate of Strangeways was Aubrey Brocklehurst.

Prison life hardly had its pleasant sides but it had its less oppressive sides at any rate. Weekends would drag a bit, especially Saturday afternoons and I could hear Manchester Town Hall clock striking and I could faintly hear the noise of the traffic through my cell window, but quite often the sun would come streaming in. One just had to accept it and I always thought there were men far worse off than me, men who were out in the front somewhere fighting, facing real danger and I wasn't in that situation.

There was plenty of work at Maidstone Prison, where Ernest Lenderyou served his sentence.

I was lucky enough to be allocated to the garden party, which was fairly high on the list of desirable jobs after the cookhouse and the library. There was fresh air, exercise, companionship and the chance to supplement the standard food ration. The food at Maidstone was of reasonable quality but deficient in quantity, so that I used often to wake up at night from vivid dreams of unlimited eating. The additional food from which we of the garden party benefited consisted mostly of raw carrots and parsnips, which we cleaned of as much dirt as possible and ate squatting behind the potting shed. We even tried raw potatoes, but most of us found them quite inedible, even in our ravenous condition. An extra bonus sometimes came on assizes day, when breakfast was taken across to the remand prisoners whose cases were to be heard. Perhaps because of their nervous loss of appetite, a good deal of uneaten porridge came back, which we intercepted when we could and ate from flower pots, using bits of broken pot as spoons. The porridge was cold, congealed, lumpy, unsweetened and generally pretty awful. But it filled a gap.

But worse was to come when Ernest was transferred to Wormwood Scrubs prior to appearing at the appellate tribunal.

The Scrubs was large, utterly impersonal, dirty – in fact it could I think be fairly described as filthy. The food was foul. Rotten potatoes were a common occurrence at dinner.

Leonard Bird recalls occasional antagonism from other prisoners, but there was some feeling of comradeship with fellow inmates.

It was interesting to find quite a number of ex-soldiers in prison for such things as committing a small theft or hitting a policemen on the nose and we knew that they'd done it so that they could avoid getting sent abroad into active service. We'd very little argument and very little trouble. We'd more trouble really with the officers and the chaplain who didn't understand when we inquired about praying for our enemies, and where did that fit in with the Christian gospel and so forth.

Although Leonard Bird was among those COs who were imprisoned several times, the authorities had learnt from their experiences with First World War Absolutists that this did not achieve a transformation from 'conchie' to willing conscript. Ernest Lenderyou found the Absolutist stance desirable but difficult to maintain.

The authorities must, I think, have realized that to go on imprisoning conscientious objectors, especially those of a political motivation, presented an unnecessary burden upon the system as well as risking the odium generated by the harsh provision for COs during the 1914–18 war. So they introduced a provision for COs who had been imprisoned to be able to be referred back to an appeal tribunal, with the object of finding an acceptable form of service. My first inclination was to continue to take an Absolutist line and to reject such measures of co-operation with the system. As time went on, however, I began to have second thoughts. I found the prison regime increasingly irksome, not so much because of physical or mental hardship or deprivation, but rather as a consequence of the isolation from the social and political life of the world outside, upon which one could have no effect except any slight impact as from an individual act of opposition or rejection; an impact which, one suspected, must decrease steadily the longer one remained inside. It began to seem like a rather pointless waste of any personal resources one had. In addition there came the recognition that what measure of hardship was involved was suffered not so much by me as by my mother and father, who had lost my small, but probably significant contribution to the family income, and any physical and moral support I might otherwise have afforded; and in addition had to worry about how I was coping and the financial and other strains of visiting me in prison. So I decided, finally, to take a more conciliatory line when my appeal was heard.

David Spreckley's experience was like that of many others. He served his six months in gaol and when he came out the authorities seemed to ignore him and he went back into the theatre. He maintains prison was an unpleasant, but positive experience.

Not pleasant, but I'm very glad I had it. It did me a power of good actually. I learnt a lot about the wrong way to treat prisoners. Many years later I was asked to go for jury service and if you're picked for jury service, that's it, you're not supposed to have any exemptions and I said I wouldn't go, and they said why, and I said, 'Well, I've spent six months in prison and until they alter prison conditions I'm not going to send anyone to prison, so what's the point of putting me on the jury?' And the magistrates were completely, absolutely upset, you can imagine, huff, huffing away, what can we do with him?

CHAPTER 18

Service in the Blitz

I was worried about people's views about not going into the forces, obviously that was the sort of thing that was shameful, not to one personally but in a sense people were highly critical. One advantage of being in something like the Pacifist Service Unit was that there was a group of people, a network, so that made it easier really.

David Jones

During the Blitz 60,000 Britons were killed and 86,000 injured. Thousands of homes were destroyed and as the population struggled to carry on their lives under these dreadful circumstances many conscientious objectors felt there were roles to play which did not compromise their pacifism. Many, like David Spreckley, found constructive voluntary work helping people affected by the war.

The Blitz started, and we'd got this awful feeling of failure, so a group of us got together and we said now what do we do? We discovered that the only preparation the authorities had made at that time for civilians if there was a Blitz was to produce 500,000 papier mâché coffins. It hadn't occurred to them that people would just be homeless, perhaps be without electricity, without gas, or without a home, and nothing was done about that at all.

Somebody gave us a PDSA (People's Dispensary for Sick Animals) wagon which they'd used – we never had to use it as the ambulances were all right – and a food kitchen. And right through the Blitz we'd go down to the East End every night with a vast quantity of bread, things to put in the sandwiches and tea and sugar, which we got simply by walking up to the local government offices in the East End of London and saying, 'Can we have some off the ration', and they used to give us all the tea and sugar we could possibly use, because nobody was doing it.

People were coming out of the tube stations in the morning, having slept in absolute squalor down there, and if they did get home they would find perhaps their homes had been bombed or they had no gas or electricity. They couldn't eat before going to work, so we used to be there as soon as daylight came. We never ever went into a shelter ourselves, we used to use schools. We had this great urn thing, I suppose 25 gallons of water or something, which we put over a big gas burner and I think we lit it at about 6 o' clock in the evening and it was just about burning at about 4 o' clock the next morning, and we'd take this and dish out the tea and the sandwiches.

There was really a sort of kamikaze feel about it, we deliberately refused to go down a shelter, because we felt we'd lost this battle (for peace). Then I also volunteered for the LAAS, the London Auxiliary Ambulance Service, and I used to do three nights a week on the ambulance and three nights a week with this unit in the East End, right through the Blitz.

In 1940 the Fellowship of Reconciliation and the Peace Pledge Union set up Pacifist Service Units in major cities. David Jones was a volunteer at first and then gave up his job to become a full-time worker.

PSU at the time was quite clearly an attempt to enable COs, who were only men at that stage, to find avenues of service which were not part of the war effort. It was a secular version of the FAU and the Friends Relief Service which was sponsored by the Society of Friends.

David worked in Cardiff, Bristol and Liverpool.

I was in Bristol for two or three years and it was a very big group. It had the whole range of people there; Plymouth Brothers, who in a sense had a quite clear position, right outside things; Jehovah's Witnesses, who might fight in a kind of Armageddon; Friends; religious people – a whole range of people from the main churches, particularly Anglican; there were Roman Catholic members; all sorts of non-conformists. Friends House in Bristol was a kind of centre for everybody. Also, there was a strong group of left-wing people, doing volunteer service, their stand was essentially on political grounds and they were kind of fighting the revolution, and they weren't prepared to fight the capitalist war. Some of them were members of the ILP, but there were also anarchists who in fact even had connections back up to the Whiteway Anarchists' community in Gloucestershire. A whole range. There were quite a lot of people in the pacifist unit in Bristol who weren't going to be called up, they were beyond military age but they came in and helped on the firewatching and whatever had to be done if there was a raid.

Ted Parrish had already got unconditional exemption when he and others in the Herne Hill branch of the Fellowship of Reconciliation set up a Pacifist Service Unit.

It was agreed that we set up a Pacifist Service Unit to undertake . . . we didn't know yet what, but we felt sure there would be things we could do. The unit was to be financed partly from a capital sum we would all contribute to, plus regular giving from the women members and members too old for war conscription. My own contribution, most of my PO savings account, was I think £50, which represented something like ten weeks' earnings.

They were given the use of a house in Eltham, kept as a home for missionaries home on leave, and moved in at the time of the Battle of Britain raids as Ted recalled in his memoirs.

We soon found our services in demand for firewatching duties at hospitals, various community centres where bombed-out people were being looked after whilst homes were being repaired, etc. We attended special first aid courses teaching us how to apply tourniquets, after finding the artery pressure points, bandaging and stretcher work though I don't remember any of us actually needing to use the knowledge.

Soon we were working with a Care Committee at Woolwich, using a small van loaned to us through the Courtauld family. This was used to collect emergency food, clothing, household cooking utensils to take to families whose homes had been bomb damaged and who were living in empty houses and flats taken over by the local authority.

We also helped to man a mobile canteen which Len Turner and I took it in turns to tow behind a 14 h.p. Wolseley, round to various underground air-raid shelters in the Deptford and Lewisham districts. Other members brewed up and served the tea, cocoa and coffee provided by the local authority and Red Cross. This driving in the blackout with very dim headlights, and not infrequent bomb craters across roads, was quite new to us, but people in the shelters seemed very grateful to us.

Welshman Meredith Edwards was told by his tribunal he could have exemption provided he remained in his job as a lab assistant. But he wanted to do something more useful, so while he was waiting to appear at the tribunal again he took up acting.

I heard about the Pilgrim Players who were a religious company and we went all over Britain. We played in the crypt in St Paul's, we played in gardens, in shelters. I remember one underground shelter, we were doing this religious play and all these people who were sleeping there were going in and out and really being part of the whole thing, and I remember particularly being in the church which I forget the name of, opposite Waterloo Station and I was blessing the Christ child and saying 'The Lord bless thee and keep thee and make his face to shine upon thee and give thee Peace,' and sitting in front was a lady with twins, very small baby twins, and as soon as I said the word peace, a bomb dropped at the back of there, and blew the altar down, and I looked up and they looked quite peaceful, nobody turned. It was an amazing moment, really. So I went with them, I asked if I could get exemption to go with them, in order to do a religious drama when it was needed, and they refused.

Cecil Davies was given unconditional exemption and, after working with evacuated children in Devon, he also took up acting to keep up the spirits of the hard-pressed civilian population.

The first part I played was St Francis in five of Laurence Housman's plays of St Francis and then I played a couple of small parts in Richard Ward's brilliantly abridged version of Marlowe's *Dr Faustus* and at first we were in London and we did some extraordinary things, we played in St Peter's Windmill Street and we played under Smithfield Market. I suppose the most remarkable London bit of the story is Christmas 1941. In the morning, we did the Marlowe at the United Services Club, more or less under the shadow of Big Ben, and in the afternoon Richard had written a play called *Holy Family*, which was a modern nativity play. We all went on in ordinary modern clothes and it was written in verse and we were doing this as our Christmas thing. In the evening we did *Holy Family* in Bethnal Green tube station. Later in the war there was a terrible tragedy at Bethnal Green tube station – it had never been used as a station – it was a huge shelter – and the tragedy was when everybody crowded down the steps into it, the doors at the bottom were shut and there was a sort of Hillsborough-type disaster with many, many people killed. But at this time it was all right. It had got a little auditorium in it with a stage and lights, it was vast, and we did *Holy Family* – that is memorable.

Later on we did other things. The government introduced a thing called 'Holidays at Home', and we went to all sorts of northern towns doing plays for 'Holidays at Home' and we played in Royal Ordnance Factory hostels and places of this sort.

Life for many city dwellers, particularly in London, meant prolonged periods in the shelters. Ted Parrish and others in the Pacifist Service Unit were trained in setting up de-lousing centres.

This was to teach us how to ensure people were stripped of all clothing, the clothing then being passed through steam boilers, then dried and collected by their owners after they had been compulsorily bathed – rather like the sheep dip idea. This was because of the fear of the typhus break out, should conditions get that bad. Body lice were the carriers expected to be the danger – and a great many people in poorer areas were getting lice, infected from the close quarters and poor hygiene of prolonged shelter life. In these shelters, there were just hundreds of bunks, and very primitive washing and lavatory equipment. But the training fortunately was never put into practice.

One of the least pleasant tasks, across the Woolwich ferry or via Blackwall tunnel, was in the shelters at Stepney. Part of our task, there being some sort of breakdown in arrangements, was to manhandle up to the surface metal dustbins, full to overflowing with human excrement and urine, and empty them down sewer manholes. We were actually supplied with rubber gloves – and I believe even the non–smokers began to take to a pipe or cigarettes on these occasions. Fortunately that episode was fairly short-lived and some sort of less primitive emergency toilets were installed there.

Although London endured more sustained bombing than other cities, Pacifist Service Units also operated elsewhere. David Jones, born into a Welsh non–conformist family was working as a civil servant in Newport. He volunteered for the PSU and spent his weekends working there.

When the time came for me to register for military service I did register as a CO and also resigned from my job and joined the Bristol pacifist unit. They were doing relief work during the bombing, taking round food in the shelters, helping the shelter population with refreshments and so on. They were based in Bristol Children's Hospital, and they both acted as the firewatching for the hospital and for the Friends Meeting House. Most of them were volunteer people, but there were four full-time people and I was one of them. So I was a full-time worker, on a pocket money basis, I think we got half a crown a week, plus keep.

The full-time people actually lived in the Children's Hospital, on the top floor of it, and did portering in the hospital but we also did outside work in youth clubs and going round the shelters, etc. These weren't set up, they were youth clubs that existed, and with the war they tended to be disrupted so the people in charge, the youth services, were very welcoming of volunteers. The club I worked with was in east Bristol and the vicar was Mervyn Stockwood, who later became Bishop of Southwark and also there was another church with a High Anglican vicar who was also a pacifist.

When the raids became a thing of the past, the units lost their war relief purpose, so they tended to develop other kinds of activity, particularly things like working in youth clubs and with the homeless. There was a unit in London which was actually an Anglican based unit, and they had a unit under Hungerford Bridge which accommodated homeless men, drunks and so on.

Ted Parrish was one of those who set up a youth club in the crypt of the Congregational church in Deptford High Street.

Many families had returned from evacuation into the country areas, and there were no youth clubs in such areas. The youth-club members were very tough youngsters up to fifteen/sixteen years old, as big as some of us and not very pleased, at first, to find we were a bunch of 'conchies'. However, even when they occasionally put out all the lights and had a bit of a barny it was mainly only furniture that got hurt. Eventually a sub-group of about four members of the unit went to live at the church, so as to save travel, and also to carry on daytime social work among the very poor families there.

Vandalism and crime had begun to thrive during the blackout hours. Cinemas had closed, as had many youth clubs when congregations had gone away, or premises been bombed to bits. Help was given with cooking and cleaning for mums with large and young families, taking people to hospital treatment, redecorating damaged rooms.

In 1948 the Pacifist Service Unit became the Family Service Unit, one of the organizations which developed the ethos of modern social work. The foundations were laid by the Pacifist Service Units in Manchester and Liverpool, the city where David Jones moved to in 1943.

The work I was doing in Bristol was becoming increasingly diffuse and lacking in point and some of the people involved were moving off to other things like the FAU or Friends Relief Service. So I visited Liverpool and was so enormously struck with what they were doing there that I applied to join the Liverpool unit. Although the work there came very much from the relief situation – the Liverpool people had a very severe type of bombing, and PSU did a lot of work in the shelters, helping people – but then as the raids stopped, there was the problem of what to do with all the people made homeless by the bombing. Now most of the people could make their own thing, had family and so on, and were able to get re-established with their lives, but some people weren't able to cope, particularly people from the poorer neighbourhoods. So the authority kind of accumulated quite a lot of families living in these big old houses in Liverpool which they requisitioned. The unit was asked to supervise them in these houses which they went round, visiting them, but then helping them to get established in their own homes when they got rehoused. They developed this kind of work that the Family Service Unit finally became. It was really invented in Liverpool and it was based on the idea of providing very close personal help on a very active basis.

Each family had a key worker who was supposed to do whatever they could for them, not only within the home itself but also by working with all the agencies that might be relevant to them, arranging money, liaising with authorities, going to the courts with them, taking their children to school and so on, lots of practical help.

It was all done on bikes, we used to move the furniture around on handcarts.

In Liverpool David met Margaret Britten, a twenty-one-year-old from Buxton, who had got conditional exemption to do social work and joined PSU.

The unit was a bit like being at university or boarding school at first. I was the first woman resident and I had to have a chaperone every night to sleep with me, because they were all men on the committee. It was vital so that the PSU could not be criticized.

It was family case work and the poverty was absolutely dreadful, there were children in the streets with no shoes on when we started. They wouldn't go to school because they had no shoes. And the houses! You'd go into a family of five children, mother and father, and father was working, and there was no furniture except a chair and a huge mattress on the floor which they all slept on and the smell was . . . outside loos, it was terrible. That's when we used to go in and help decorate and get the home together. Then there was a lot of prostitution, girls who were one parent families, which would be nothing now, but then it was very difficult for them and they'd have their children taken away very easily but we used to help there.

They loved us and we loved them. Very few people were aggressive to us. They were so pitiful really, and they were only so thankful to have anybody go who would go in to talk to them in this squalor. And in a way, they were a bit like us, they were ignored by the community.

We helped them budget and use their money – a lot of them would be in debt and we would collect the money for them so they wouldn't spend it and pay it in to where it had to go.

Margaret and David Jones both remained in social work, and David was awarded the OBE in 1960 for his work with the Family Service Unit. They both continued to work for pocket money and it wasn't until 1948 that they received a 'pay packet'.

Many conscientious objectors worked elsewhere during the Blitz. Men in non-combatant units stepped in to help firefighters during bombing raids, but there were also conscientious objectors in the fire service itself. Walter Wright was a civil servant working for Customs and Excise. His office was evacuated to Blackpool.

In the spring of 1940 I had decided I would volunteer for training for first-aid work and they had all the first-aid workers they needed but they were wanting more volunteers for the Auxiliary Fire Service, was I willing to do that. I said, 'Yes, certainly,' and I joined that and I was still a member of the Auxiliary Fire Service, which by that time had become the National Fire Service, when I went before my first tribunal.

I had decided that the only satisfactory thing to do in deciding how far you were willing to go in war work or anything else was to make up your own mind what you would be prepared to do and stick to that, because if I was diverted from that to do anything else then I felt I was becoming a party to the war. So I made up my mind that I was willing to go into the fire service as a full timer if required but that was as far as I was willing to go.

Walter was registered for non-combatant duties only.

There was quite a chance that I would be put in the fire service, but there was no guarantee – I might easily have been called up for other service in the actual army.

He appealed. The tribunal rejected the appeal but recommended that his non-combatant duties be served in the fire service. While tribunals could give people exemption on condition that they found certain types of work, the tribunal could not be sure that form of service was open to them. But Walter was fortunate and he joined the fire service, in a small town near Blackpool, Poulton-le-Fylde. He was the only conscientious objector.

While I was a member of the service the worst raids on Liverpool and Manchester took place and some of the members of the fire service in this place were among those who were sent over to Liverpool or Manchester for assistance and this happened one night when I was not on duty so I was not among those sent.

Every alternate night you were on duty, you attended at the fire station and you did drills and that sort of thing. One night a raider that had been over Liverpool dropped a whole lot of incendiary bombs across fields nearby. Although I wasn't on duty I had gone to the fire station because this is what you were expected to do if there was an actual air-raid alert, and I remember going out to pick up the burnt stubs of these incendiary bombs because they were wanted for research purposes.

Later in the war Walter moved to Dumfries, where he was once again the only conscientious objector on the staff.

All the people from the Northwest region who were being called into the fire service were being sent to Scotland soon after the Clydeside raids. They'd found great difficulties with a shortage of water in fighting fires and they decided they needed to lay a lot of pipelines and install static water tanks and so forth, and so they wanted to more or less double the size of the fire service in that part of Scotland. I travelled up there with two or three other people who were being called up to the same place and got quite friendly in the train with another fireman and remained very friendly with him for a few days. Then there came a time when he stopped talking to me and I was told by other members of the fire service there that he had heard that I was a CO and he said, 'This gives us all a bad name, people think that if you're in fire service uniform you are a conchie'.

I can remember the officer in charge of the fire station at Dumfries was giving us a lecture one day and it was the sort of morale-building lecture, and it seemed to me he made a special point of saying that in the fire service you're in one of the most important of the services and you're doing a very positive job, you're defending lives and property and not destroying them. I felt at the time that he had probably heard how this other man was treating me, I couldn't help feeling that he was making a special point of this for my sake.

I think they were on the whole quite sympathetic, I never had any further opposition or hostility as far as I can remember from anyone in the fire service.

There was no blitz in Dumfries, but there were still moments of danger.

I was on duty overnight in Dumfries. A bomber that was taking off from Dumfries airport crashed on take off and caught fire. We were called out to that but by the time we got there the flames had almost died down, There was nothing much we could do but the man who was in charge of the fire service, not the one I've already referred to, but actually his superior, who was much less a man to be respected I felt, had taken charge of things and ordered us on to the remains of the plane to recover the bodies of the crew. Of course they had all been burnt and they were just charred flesh which was quite unrecognizable. He had no right to order us to do that, it was the job of the RAF staff. But anyway we started complying with his order, and very soon we found belts of machine-gun ammunition were going off all around us. There were some small bombs on board which this wretched fire service officer ordered us to remove. He told us that they weren't live bombs, they were only practice bombs. So we formed a chain and started tossing these small bombs to each other and one of the RAF officers who had been standing by came up to us, 'I shouldn't do that if I were you, they are live bombs!' So much for the fire service officer.

Actor Meredith Edwards joined the National Fire Service after a struggle to be released from his condition of exemption, which stated that he return to his job as a lab assistant.

I went to the National Fire Service and went to Chester and Liverpool, and I had twinges – how do you define conscience? And I thought I'm giving into them, I should have gone to jail. By this time, I had a family and you see, you're making an excuse, you're not making the supreme sacrifice if you like. So, as Shakespeare says 'conscience doth make cowards of us all, here he comes', he was a great man your Shakespeare. He understood it.

I was in Chester first which wasn't too bad, but we had to go to Ellesmere Port on standbys in case the bombs were dropped over Liverpool, because there they were unloading the octane which was driving the planes. I went once and my cousin who was very much like a brother to me, he didn't want to go to war and he was lost, killed. And I thought well here I am going there, trying to protect this oil and keep the war going. And I said, 'I'm not going'. I decided to go in front of the section leader and he kept on saying, 'Why are you not doing this?'

Eventually I had to say to him, 'Look, I'm a CO, don't you know?'

He said, 'Christ, what is a bloody CO? If they came to rape your mother or your sister, then what would you do?'

I said, 'The fact is, if I was called up, I wouldn't be there to protect them.'

Meredith was sent before the divisional officer.

> This man was a very understanding man. I told him
> about my cousin, and he understood and I did more work,
> ordinary work, in order to make up for it. But it was
> conscience pricking me again.

Walter Wright's conscience pricked when he was stationed
at Crewe.

> It was decided that they ought to introduce something for
> the firemen to do in their duller moments. There were
> railway works there and for about two hours each afternoon
> we were given the job of helping to produce grease boxes
> for railway trucks, some fairly innocent sort of job which I
> didn't mind doing. But soon after that when they thought
> we had done enough of that, they said we should help make
> some aircraft parts for the local Rolls-Royce aircraft factory
> – of course these were for military aircraft. I thought that
> was going a bit too far, I wasn't going to do that. So I
> told the officer in charge of my objection to it and he was
> quite all right about it, and he gave me another job to do
> while the rest of the station were involved in this. And I
> remember one day while I was doing this one of the other
> men came up to me and said, 'I admire you for standing
> out like that, I wish more of us had the courage to do so.'
> That was another indication of the friendly attitude.

Other acquaintances were not always friendly as Walter
found out on several occasions.

> It was at the end of 1941 that I had my first tribunal and of
> course this was announced in the Blackpool evening paper
> which had a very anti-CO attitude, and on the evening, or
> maybe the day after my appearance before the tribunal,
> they came out with a great headline 'Why so many civil
> service conchies?', because there were quite a few of us in
> the various civil service departments in Blackpool. I think
> the local paper suspected some sort of conspiracy in the
> civil service. Anyway they came out with this headline and
> it so happened that the son of the family with whom I had
> lodgings at Poulton-le-Fylde was in the Lancashire Police

Force and one day shortly after this when I got back to my lodgings in the evening the landlady said to me, obviously most regretfully, that her son Jim (he was about to be called up for military service) had said if I was still there when he was due to come home on leave he wouldn't come home. So she was very sorry but she had to consider her son and asked me to leave.

So I had to try and find some more lodgings and wherever I went to ask if they would have me, I made it clear why I was having to leave those lodgings. Of course a number of people turned me down right away, and there was one house where the man said that he didn't agree with me, but so long as I wasn't going to try to preach pacifism to them he was quite willing to have me stay there. I went there and a few days after I went there the son of the family came home on leave, he was in the army, and we were sitting round the table having supper, and suddenly this chap sprung up from his chair, flung out of the room saying, 'I can't sit here any longer while he's sitting at the table.' So then of course his parents said to me, 'Sorry, but I'm afraid we must ask you to find somewhere else.' There were lots of people like that who had prejudices, but on the whole I found people in the forces were more sympathetic than the general public.

CHAPTER 19
Friends

If there were six soldiers fully armed, waiting to go to the front, no one would give them a lift. We regarded that as a positive step towards aiding the army, which we were not prepared to do.

Michael Rendel Harris, Friends Ambulance Unit

During the Second World War, Quakers gave active service in many ways. The best known was the Friends Ambulance Unit revived in 1939 by Paul Cadbury who had served in the FAU in the First World War. Stephen Peet, youngest son of First World War Absolutist Hubert Peet, had volunteered for the unit before he appeared at his tribunal in the spring of 1940.

I attended the tribunal in Birmingham near the FAU training camp. Two or three of us went, I remember, accompanied by the redoubtable Paul Cadbury. He came with us to speak for us. I was very conscious that it was all too easy. I was accepted on condition that I continued work in the FAU. If I'd had to stand up for myself and produce strong arguments as to why I was doing what I was doing I don't know whether I would have convinced any tribunal. I have a guilt feeling about this. I feel I got away with it too easily. It was easy to join an ambulance organization which was accepted officially instead of fighting for my rights or fighting for my conscience. I did what I felt was right in the same way that somebody brought up in a strongly traditional militaristic family would have no question about volunteering for the army right away at the beginning of the war.

Michael Rendel Harris was the scion of an old Quaker family. Right at the beginning of the war he was rung up by an old school friend, a Cadbury, who told him the FAU was being reformed, and asked whether he intended to join it.

About a year previously, I had a very great friend who'd put himself down for the Naval Reserve. And I thought right, well I'll do the same. And then my mother heard about it and she said, 'You can't do that'. And we had a long sort of argument. And I said, 'Okay, I'll put it off. I won't do it straightaway.'

It was while walking on Plymouth Hoe that Michael discovered his latent pacifism.

I realized then that there was a simple way of looking at it – it should not be for one human being to take the life of another one. As simple as that. And I've always adhered to that right the way through. And I still have got that today. And it was quite a simple thing. But I felt very strongly that we'd been given life. And we had the opportunities to make our own choices. And it was basically a religious decision. But beyond that it was the ethos, the philosophy, that we weren't sent into this world just to kill each other off.

Michael also registered at Birmingham and was accompanied to his tribunal by a great friend of his mother's who was not only a Cadbury but a Justice of the Peace. He was given exemption to work with the FAU. Like Stephen Peet, he felt a certain guilt that as a Quaker he could get exemption with apparent ease.

One felt a bit of a fraud. Was it really too easy? Because later you heard that some people had a very, very difficult time.

Although members of the unit wore khaki in the field as they had done in the 1914–18 war, the FAU was careful to stress it was a civilian organization. Its 1,300 members worked for pocket money, like many of the units in which COs served. Stephen Peet and other FAU staff were trained in first aid and driving.

Although it was called the Friends Ambulance Unit in the First World War that's what it had been, mainly driving ambulances in France; in the Second World War when it set up it re-established the same name but the work at first, apart from a band of people who went to Finland, was all sorts of other things in an emergency medical service scattered round England. A few of us worked on an ambulance train for several months – that was one of about fifty ambulance trains that were a whole lot of converted big wagons that had been carrying fish, we found out, with racks for stretchers and a doctor and female nurses and half a dozen male medical orderlies standing by for invasion time to evacuate hospitals on the east coast and take all the patients inland to make hospitals available for casualties from an expected invasion. And this is what happened. The train that we happened to work on was parked at Stevenage or Newmarket. Sometime in September 1940 we had notice to move and evacuated a hospital from down near Felixstowe I think to Bradford, and unloaded all the poor old people, they were mostly geriatric people out of the hospital – but the invasion didn't take place.

The first overseas work was a convoy which went to Finland. In the team was Michael Rendel Harris.

At last we were going to do something. At last here was the great opportunity to show what you could do. And of course one was very keen on this great adventure.

Half the convoy helped in the battle zone where the Finns were fighting the Soviet Union, the others evacuated civilians.

That was quite sad. Because you went into a farm – it was mostly rural areas. And you had to take the families out. And the families had to leave all their possessions, they were only allowed to take what they could carry.

Driving along icy roads between huge banks of snow, Michael had to deliver twins in the back of his ambulance. When the FAU were pulled out they retreated back to Britain via Norway just as the Germans invaded.

The first day over into Norway, we were machine gunned. And the idea of machine gunning people from the air hadn't been heard of before. In the Low Countries the refugees going out of Belgium and so on were very badly machine gunned, and in France later. But there we were, driving happily along with big Red Crosses on top of the ambulances, and we saw planes coming, and somebody shouted. We saw that they had the cross on the wings. We jumped out and took to the ditch. And then we were machine gunned. And several of the ambulances including the one I'd just dropped out of were hit. And I remember with great pride my kit bag full of clothes was full of machine gun bullets so that was really war.

Michael and his half of the convoy got out on the last troop ship from Namsos. The other half of the convoy wasn't so lucky and was interned in Sweden for nine months. Back in Britain he went to a military hospital in Gloucester.

It was just at the time of the fall of Dunkirk, and so it was very full. And one worked very hard and very long hours, emptying bedpans, bathing people. And that I think was the time when one did have a lot of flak. And one could imagine that many of them were very badly wounded. There were quite a lot of deaths.

On the Home Front FAU work was unglamorous, but invaluable. Stephen Peet made a short film of the work of the unit in 1940 and it records the mundane nature of many of the tasks that members carried out – a sharp contrast to the 'heroic' role of Corder Catchpool and fellow members of the FAU who served behind the lines in the First World War.

A whole group of us were in the East End, at one of the unit sections at east London working in hospitals and air-raid shelters. I was working in a geriatric ward in one of the East End hospitals for several months which was a medical training looking after aged old men, working in an operating theatre some of the time. We worked as medical orderlies or male nurses, then worked in special buildings when people were bombed out. We had a little badge on the shoulder and we were treated as male nurses, and in some hospitals

doing all sorts of other things like emptying the pig buckets
of unwanted food, stoking the boilers and all sorts of things.

When the Blitz started at the end of 1940, relief work of this
kind came into its own. Quakers have a long tradition of
helping the victims of war, a tradition established in the last
quarter of the nineteenth century. After his adventures in
Finland, Michael Rendel Harris also worked in the East End.

> They'd taken over old warehouses – particularly
> underground warehouses, some of them these arched,
> huge underground warehouses; with damp and dark, sort
> of electric light bulbs hanging. And sanitation was non-
> existent, the air was very bad and so on. And a lot of the old
> people went down there, and they stayed there for weeks
> because they were afraid to come up, or there was nowhere
> else to go, or their houses had been damaged – this sort of
> thing. That was a very bad period. I had a van, and used to
> go up to the Red Cross Headquarters in Belgrave Square,
> and I used to go up every afternoon and collect large
> quantities of cough mixture and all that sort of common
> drug and take them back.

Michael also worked in a big evacuation centre in Essex
for elderly people from the East End. With the end of the
Blitz opportunities came for work abroad and he spent three
months on a troop ship travelling to China where the FAU
was transporting supplies of drugs to hospitals, tending
wounded soldiers and civilians. The conditions under which
FAU truck drivers worked were often dreadful.

> It was a filthy, dirty job, banging on those terrible roads,
> and the mud and the filth and the trucks wearing out;
> the lack of spare parts; the whole thing held together
> with bits of string and old bits of wire; and the charcoal
> burners which were filthy dirty; and living in Chinese
> inns and the bed bugs and the lice; and never a bath until
> you got back to base. They had a very difficult job. In a
> way I think that you felt you were making up for having
> refused to live as a soldier.
>   I think there was some feeling of, say, justification, but
> at least a sort of balance in people's minds. That I'm living

in these filthy conditions that no soldier would ever live in, and therefore in a way it made up for what you had refused to accept before. I wouldn't say that happened to everybody, but I think it was fairly strong.

And I know I felt it when I was working in a hospital for a year down on the Burma front, then going out as we did behind the lines. And you were facing a very considerable amount of danger, let's face it. And you were doing all sorts of things like operating and saving people's lives and this sort of thing. Which again was a justification for this step that you'd originally taken. And so, therefore, I wouldn't say you challenged danger, but you put on a good face.

With the Blitz over, Stephen Peet and other members of the Friends Ambulance Unit also had opportunities for work abroad. Some FAU teams went to Ethiopia and the Middle East. Stephen Peet sailed in 1942.

Thirty-six of us went out on a huge convoy around the Cape of Good Hope and up to the south end of Suez and became a large part of the male staff of a mobile hospital and for the next year or so right after the Battle of Alamein we were belonging to No. 1 or No. 6 mobile military hospital and we went up to Tunis and back by slow degrees and set up camp in various places.

There were big 3-ton trucks and enormous tents and folding beds, there were hospital wards and a mobile operating theatre, an entire mobile hospital run by the army and we were the medical orderly and drivers, I drove a 3-ton truck.

They were sent to Palestine and from there a small team went to the island of Kos.

Somebody found a building somewhere down the coast in what had been an Italian agricultural college, in some empty buildings and it was my job to boil up the instruments and sweep out a room and make an operating theatre for whatever might happen.

And indeed right away there were people who were sick and people who had a car smash and that kind of thing. Then one morning I remember being woken by my colleague Dennis Westbrook. I was sleeping out on a roof, it was rather hot, and he woke me up. I'd been a bit disturbed by the fact that there seemed to be a lot of aeroplanes flying around and guns going off and things, and he shouted out of the window, 'Enemy friends have arrived', as a little strange joke. So, I popped my head over the side of the roof and it looked like an extraordinary Hollywood widescreen film – there was a great invasion fleet on the coast 2 miles away of dozens of little ships and landing craft and a lot of little figures. There was a battle in progress in fact, and there was a great German invasion. So all this firing was for real and very quickly there were German soldiers at this temporary hospital and we were prisoners because they were there in a large quantity.

Casualties were coming in, we had a Red Cross flag up, everybody was very hungry, the English soldiers and the Germans. The English cooks were cooking great piles of baked beans, and then we began work in this operating room, for quite a number of hours with quite a number of casualties, Germans and English and one or two Greek civilians who'd got injured and there we were, prisoners, full stop.

As it happened the Germans were very short of medical staff, because I think a ship had been sunk, either a hospital ship or a ship with a medical contingent but there was one doctor, and one or two German medical orderlies. There were eight, nine or ten army medical corps orderlies, us two from FAU, and the two officers operating the operating theatre.

On that first day of the invasion of the island of Kos there's a memory I have, a very strong memory of coming out of the little operating theatre for a breath of fresh air – I suppose I had a white apron, my work was mainly cleaning operating tools and holding people while they were being amputated and so on – and in the passage way under an archway outside this room various Germans were around. And we saw an English soldier going along in a crouching position, rifle in hand, near a wall, 100 yards away and a German soldier near me picked up his rifle and shot at him. The English soldier fell over wounded. Then the German soldier put his rifle over his shoulder, and at the run, with battle going on around him, ran out to fetch the English soldier, put him over his shoulder, came running back with him, carrying him and brought him to the door of the operating theatre. It was uncanny. It was like one unnaturally long scene in a film which seemed to me to sum up the whole horrible business of war – to do what he was instructed to do in a battle, to shoot the other side and then risk his life to save the man. It was extraordinary. As a matter of fact he wasn't badly hurt, he was shot in the leg and we got him into the operating theatre and he had his leg attended to and he recovered perfectly all right.

We weren't taken prisoner in the normal sense, there were a lot of prisoners being rounded up on the island; I don't remember seeing them. There was only about a day of sporadic fighting and then it was all over. Quite a lot of people got over the top of the island and down the other side and were picked up by submarines and all this kind of thing, but these were only rumours at the time.

Life continued as before, officially we were prisoners but we were surrounded by sea and we were busy. Other military people there tried to escape – there was one South-African pilot who tried to swim, it was about 6 miles across to the coast of Turkey, but very strong currents, and he was brought in by a German air-force boat which picked him up. He was brought in with exhaustion, and then the men who'd picked him up came back that evening with some bottles of wine or champagne or something. The Germans all had a party round his bed to congratulate him on his attempt to escape, it was all crazy.

At their makeshift hospital, Stephen Peet and the other members of the medical team also received casualties from a ferocious battle on the nearby island of Leros.

There were an awful lot of casualties on the other island, German and British, and they were lying out in the sun untended for quite some time before it was possible for them to be brought across. And they were lined up, rows of stretchers outside the hospital, and I think it was something like thirty-six hours almost non-stop work helping patch up those people – that was a grisly time. The doctors went up and down the lines and had to make

the decision not to treat that person because it would be a
two- or three-hour operation, and to save instead three or
four others who were fairly simple operations. Having to
make these life or death decisions was a frightful thing to
see, and it was done with no attention to the nationality of
the sick person.

During their captivity on Kos, Stephen and the rest of the
medical team were given the opportunity to escape, but with
the help of the military.

I was out getting water from the well nearby, when a
Greek thrust a note into my hand and it turned out to be
a message from a submarine officer giving instructions for
the staff of the hospital to go to a certain house that night
at 7 o'clock, where they would be given civilian clothes
and taken across the mountains and away. I gave it to
the doctor in charge and they made plans to leave. I said
that myself and the other FAU man would stay, because
as civilians perhaps we'd be OK; we volunteered to know
nothing more about it. It worried me because here was,
in effect, a military operation, that I didn't exactly feel we
could take part in.
   We said we would busy ourselves like mad, being
everywhere at once in the hospital and wouldn't know
anything else. But just before the deadline when people
were supposed to leave, the German doctor came into the
English doctors' room with two bottles of wine and said,
'We're going to have a bit of a party this evening'. And he
stayed there for two hours and then went away, obviously
with knowledge of what was going to happen. That was his
way of stopping it without actually taking any decisions.

The prisoners were taken to a POW transit camp in Athens,
and from there Stephen Peet recalls they began a cold and
uncomfortable journey to a German prisoner of war camp.

One day, a few days into the journey I'd been saving up
in my bag of things an army emergency block of chocolate
in a tin. It was in six squares and there were half a dozen
of us who were in this group. I remember one day very
surreptitiously getting out this block breaking it carefully

into six pieces. The first person took one piece, the second person took one piece and the third chap grabbed the whole remaining bit and crammed it in his mouth because he couldn't stop himself and none of us did anything. We did nothing because we all understood he couldn't stop himself. Ordinary morality had broken down, but not broken down so far. Another few days and he would have been leapt upon and walloped, or some-body would have tried to put their hand in his mouth, or probably I would have been myself secretly eating it. But at that moment there was a silence, he had to do it and couldn't help it.

By 1946 the FAU had served alongside the forces in China, India, Burma, Africa and finally in Europe as the Allied forces swept to victory. Several lost their lives and a few decided they would join the combatant forces they had been serving alongside.

Back in Britain other Quakers, and non-Quakers, joined organizations like the Friends War Victims Relief Service which was renamed the Friends Relief Service. Roger Wilson, who had been sacked from his job at the BBC because he was a conscientious objector, became its General Secretary and spent the war years tirelessly travelling the country coordinating work in hostels for those evacuated from major cities. In May 1942 he wrote to his wife Marjorie.

Tomorrow at crack of dawn I set off for Norwich with a car load of reinforcements for a couple of rest centres full of old crocks. The mobile squad went up on Thursday and late last night rang up to say that the problem was beyond them and they needed some girls; so I spent a good bit of the night thinking of complicated chess moves and this morning with the aid of most of the modern forms of telecommunication we assembled a team from the ends of the country. So now we can but hope that tomorrow will be fine, that there won't be any more raids but that the seventy-year olds won't melt away before we arrive.

The bombing of these small places is pretty horrible, though one can't help but think that it's a good sign. From our very local point of view, it has given us something to do; four men went to Bath and six to Norwich and we shall probably send six to York if it is raided again. Just

how severe the raids really were it is difficult to say at the
moment. One hears very conflicting reports.

Living for a large part of the war in London's East End
which was heavily bombed, Roger arranged training for
hostel workers, attended tribunals with those trying to get
exemption and sorted out endless staffing problems. The
hostels catered for women and children, and also the elderly;
one was in a village hall near Filey.

> About the pleasantest house we have for old folks. It is
> really a most lovely nineteenth-century village hall, but our
> staffing arrangements have been all wrong and will have to
> be changed from top to bottom. However, we've now got a
> competent young saint as one member of the staff and can
> perhaps build round her. Looking after a lot of sickish old
> folks who don't like one another all that much is a tough
> job and I am much moved by those with the grace to do
> it. While one of the staff is trying to get a memoryless old
> lady to have a bath, and others were trying to see what
> to do with an old lady who had every sort of (perfectly
> real) internal trouble and was now diagnosed to have some
> form of glandular TB, I tackled 4 tons of coal that had
> been dumped in the drive and had to be shifted under
> cover. It was the hardest, simplest job I've done for a long
> time. It was extremely satisfying, too, until I went round
> to the other side of the pile and saw what an incredible
> lot I hadn't shifted. I worked for an hour and a half and
> I suppose moved round about 1½ tons. It's perfectly
> true that administrators don't realize what is involved in
> wardening until you stumble on that sort of thing. Just
> think of having to tackle that when tired, as well as all the
> other jobs that have to be done.

Cecil Davies was not a member of the Society of Friends, but
found himself attracted to their philosophy and beliefs while
he was at university.

> After I'd registered as a CO, or maybe even before that,
> I came to the conclusion that it would be wrong of me
> to become a Quaker at this stage because I knew that
> Quakers always got exemption. People always used to

say, 'Oh well you're a Quaker so it's all right for you to be a pacifist.' So being young and proud and all the rest of it, I didn't want to be sheltering under a Quaker umbrella so I decided as long as the war was on I wouldn't apply for membership.

When my course was over, I had to decide what to do. I knew I wasn't interested in the FAU – it was far too closely associated with the army for my mind, but I was told there was another thing called the Friends War Victims Relief (Committee) and they had a training centre at Spicelands, near Cullompton, so I went there.

Cecil Davies soon found that cases taken on by the Quakers were generally those that the authorities, for one reason or another, were not able to deal with.

They were running a sort of camp, literally a camp, down in a field to give kids in Plymouth who were being bombed a break and they sent me down there, and then they asked me to go and do a job looking after unbilletable evacuees in Wincanton. These evacuees were nearly all unbilletable because they were bedwetters or they'd got impetigo or they'd got scabies. But there was nothing the matter with them in any other sense. I did the gardening when they were in school and my job was to look after them and entertain them when they weren't at school.

Cecil moved to another job with evacuated children, this time in Redruth.

I expect it's still there, an old nineteenth-century hotel called Tabb's Hotel in the middle of Redruth in Cornwall which had been turned into a hostel for unbilletable evacuees. It was a big rambling place, open staircase and it was run primarily, medically if you see what I mean, because of these scabies and impetigo and stuff and only secondarily because people were unbilletable because of behavioural problems.

The head of it was a matron and she was very, very authoritarian in her own way but she didn't back up her staff. She would show up her staff in front of kids and when I went in first and there were the other staff, they said, 'Oh another one, you're about the tenth or twelfth who's tried to do this job.'

On the ground floor were the youngest kids, on the middle floor they were a bit older and the top floor was the eleven plus up to about fourteen and that was where I had a room. Those who were too bad to go to school had a schoolmaster who looked after them and taught them. Now a lot of the rules were really connected to their medical problems: if they had a pillow fight which they did on one occasion, this was terrible because you might catch something from one of these skin conditions.

The authorities had dumped on it all the delinquents they didn't know what to do with, so in addition to these usually rather sensitive types, bedwetters and the like, you had these toughs, some of them were rather nice – but they were jolly hard work, there were a couple of Jamaicans from Cardiff, or Swansea Docks – they were pretty tough, several chaps bigger than I was, the oldest was the son of a bargee, he was very rough.

Joyce Allen, who had been the first woman conscientious objector to appear at a tribunal, also worked with the Friends Relief Service. She went to the Friends Service Centre in Liverpool 5, and the work done there, like that of the Pacifist Service Unit, has been termed as the beginnings of modern social work.

When I started at the Friends Service Centre, the fleas came out to meet me because they always came out to a fresh person, a nice taste or something. These young chaps who'd gone round to these houses in baggy pants, trousers, the fleas of course that they'd bought home settled and colonized in the Friends Service Centre. Somebody who started with me instituted mopping, and we mopped with slightly disinfected water, but that didn't seem to work and after she'd left we had a couple of females who came and thought the best thing to do was polishing and that did beat it in a way, we used to get on our hands and knees and polish all the floors and polish did deter them, but the dreadful thing for me was that my husband – they didn't like him so they didn't bite him, so he would probably be bringing them home and I was bitten to within an inch of my life.

There were lice, they came in, of course they cling to people, but fleas were the real trouble. We used to bring up the furniture and Alun Davies had a blow lamp and he used to go round all the cracks and used to burn them, then we'd take the furniture back. You'd no idea how badly infested the place was and sometimes we'd look at children and the whole of their stomachs would be covered with little pinpricks, they weren't coming up because they'd been bitten so many times they weren't reacting. Very badly infested.

People from Canada and America sent clothes and they sent those to the children and they tried to encourage the children to go to school when they didn't and get grants for people or send women who were not managing at all well to some sort of a home for mothers and children, all sorts of things of that nature, social work.

Similar work was carried on throughout the war by Friends, and eventually teams went out to help on the Continent bringing relief to displaced persons and civilian populations which had borne the brunt of the struggle between the great powers. Roger Wilson was in the vanguard organizing and recording what he saw in his diary.

Cologne June 1946
Met with the burgomeister in charge of food and the woman doctor in charge of school feeding. The former showed us figures indicating a loss of 5 kilos weight in municipal officials since February. The latter said that even supplementary fed children were going down in weight. She herself finds it less exhausting to stay in her office without lunch, than to go down six flights of stairs to get it.

Food shortages weren't the only problem. The sheer number of displaced persons threatened to engulf existing populations, as Roger Wilson noted.

Wilhelmshavn is frightful. The area with a population of 750,000 will have to take 160,000 refugees. But since then I have heard of villages that have had to take up to 200 of their own strength. On Wednesday morning we looked at an army orthopaedic department where they make

limbs but are very short of material. Then to a couple of
barrack camps for refugees. It's rather like Petersfield,
but not nearly so crowded and with the people making a
remarkably good go of it.

In August 1945 Roger went out to Salonika in Greece to
organize relief to civilians affected not only by the war with
Germany, but the Greek Civil War. He recorded the plight of
one village in his diary.

The village, Hortias, was a dreadful sight – a large one
built up a steep hillside; I should judge prosperous before
the war. 2,200 population, now 1,700. ELAS ambushed
the Germans in the neighbourhood just about a year ago.
The population and village president had done what they
could to prevent it because they knew reprisals would
be taken. After the ambush the Germans and the Greek
security battalion turned up. Most of the men cleared out
when they saw them coming. Some of the women and
children stayed (they say encouraged by ELAS who said
they would protect them, but this I doubt, since either
more would have stayed or more would have cleared
out when ELAS went). The Germans surrounded the
village, which the Greeks then proceeded systematically to
burn. Not a house is intact. But they also shot and burnt
(possibly partly alive) two groups of about seventy old
men, women and children, one group in a cottage, the
other group in the village bakery. The names are painted
on crosses at the two spots. This was done by the Greeks.
The Germans helped some of the inhabitants to escape
at this point, and the villagers maintain that no German
actually took part in the killing.

As people tried to pick up the pieces of their pre-war
existence many conscientious objectors wanted to help in the
postwar reconstruction. One was Aubrey Brocklehurst.

I'd always wanted to play some part if I could, in
reconciliation and relief and so I approached the Friends
Relief Service to see if they wanted any help in any of their
work and they asked me to come down to Friends House
in London, I lived in Manchester then, and asked me if I

wanted to work in the offices organizing people's travel, because a lot of people were travelling all the time, and going to Germany and Greece and Poland, all over the place, all over Europe and it was quite a business. People had to get passports, visas and of course travel was not normal then, the military controlled most of the travel so it was the job of somebody to contact the authorities and get places on military trains and get passes on boats because air travel was only in its infancy in those days. It was quite a full-time job and that was the job I did for the next three and half years, actually I found it very interesting and I was sorry to leave at the end of 1949, by that time relief work was scaling down quite rapidly.

The Friends Relief Service spent nearly £500,000 in providing overseas aid, excluding the costs of administration, and a further £150,000 on providing relief at home.

CHAPTER 20

A Change of Heart

*I wasn't prepared to be a minor prophet. I think you have to
have enormous conviction to stand against your fellow man
in a situation which is physically proved and I didn't have
that. I'm enormously grateful to the tolerance of the society
in which I grew up, in a way I wish it had been less tolerant.*
Alan Stephens

Alan Stephens, not his real name, was eighteen years old
when he registered as a conscientious objector. He attended
his tribunal, was even granted exemption on condition that
he did non-combatant duties, and after a year at university
in Oxford he reversed his decision and joined the intelligence
corps. Men who registered their conscientious objection to
war, yet later participated in it, were not uncommon, but
many became reluctant to talk publicly about it. One former
member of the Friends Ambulance Unit who left to join the
forerunner of the CIA in Burma, summed up one possible
reason for this reluctance when he said, 'I felt I was a failed
soldier and a failed conscientious objector.'

Stephen Peet remembers several men who left the FAU
to join the forces, although he doesn't remember any FAU
members who left to become absolutists.

Everybody understood, I remember not feeling any
antagonism at all. They were making a very difficult
decision, probably I rather admired them because they
were leaving. And, this is a very difficult thing to say, the
probability of surviving the war was considerably greater
remaining in a medical unit I'm sure, and statistically quite
obviously so, rather than joining the armed forces. And,

this again is a bit of conscience feeling about it – were we in on a cushy easy job? Were we saving ourselves belonging to this kind of thing? I'm not sure.

Bill Nightingale was born in 1914 and during his teens became what he calls a 'religious fanatic'.

One of my school friends invited me along to a thing called Crusaders which was very evangelical – particularly because it was run by a Plymouth Brother, so it was very strict. So that caused me to have a breakdown when I was at school, so I left school when I was fifteen and a half, because I used to spend hours praying, read the Bible all the time, I became a bit of a religious fanatic. I reverted to being more of a Methodist, and didn't go back to Crusaders after that. I became a local preacher, rather prompted by one of our assistant scoutmasters, and I've still got a talk I wrote on why we should all be pacifists. I was very convinced then, but so were so many people around me, pacifism was a thing a lot of people believed in quite seriously in those days. You'll remember the famous Oxford Union vote that 'On no account does this house believe that we should fight for King and country', which in retrospect was one of the things which encouraged Hitler, who thought that he was free to do whatever he wanted because England was a pacifist country.

However, by the time war was declared Bill's ideas were beginning to change.

Even though I felt strongly against war I didn't think I could stand apart altogether and I joined the Special Constabulary and I registered as a CO, but as I was in a reserved occupation as a works manager, it was not until after the fall of Dunkirk that the call-up came. And I can remember hearing the news of Dunkirk and feeling a bit of a quiver.

It was the imminent threat that this island would eventually be invaded unless we were able to do something about it. So it was a crisis point, it came as such a shock to think that we had got to this point, we were really on our own, therefore we depended on other people who were going to feed us and maintain our liberty, so I think it was perhaps self conscious but it was one of the deciding factors that you couldn't go on being neutral.

From then on I realized that I was not prepared to stand aside, and then I read this article by Dr Maude Royden who was an early congregational minister which said that there will come a day when faith will be able to heal bodily ailments but until that day comes we can't discard the surgeon's knife. And the analogy was that for the moment we hadn't the strength of our faith to make pacifism work. And so it was just that article really that was the deciding point for me so I wrote and said when I'm called up I'm not registering as a CO, and when I got the call-up papers saying did you want to go before a tribunal I wrote back and said, 'No, I've changed my mind'. It really was the pressure of events, the fact that I couldn't let other people fight for me and stand aside, plus on the religious side, somebody whom I could regard as being a mentor saying that we needed to use the surgeon's knife. So there had been a slow softening of my attitudes. I didn't know how I would have to fare if I had to actually shoot at somebody, but I was put into a signal training regiment, and eventually went as a signaller in the Royal Artillery.

Eventually he served with the Fifth Division in Italy.

After a year in Italy, I was wounded during the crossing of the Garigliano river (near Monte Casino) which was again fairly miraculous because I had the picture of my then girlfriend and my army paybook and various things and a bit of shrapnel went through that and just missed my heart by inches but there were sadly a lot of casualties at that point because the Germans were firing at fairly point blank range, and the chap that drove the ambulance that took me back across the pontoon bridge was an American Quaker, so I thought, 'Who's the bravest?'

If you are a CO doing a job like that, you're on your own. One of the things that makes the army possible is that you're with a lot of comrades, and there is a great strength in being with others who have accepted the rigours, that at least have a common purpose. To be like that ambulance driver, doing a job on your own must have been extremely lonely, so I don't know whether I would have had the guts to do that.

Frank Hoare also became a signaller although he too had become a pacifist during his time at Monmouthshire Agricultural College when he had been heavily influenced by a fellow student who was a Welsh nationalist.

Mostly, I was impelled by the fact that I'd come from this family which had broken apart and therefore what I wanted to do more than anything was to find a nice lady, get married, have children, have a nice home, have a job. And therefore by 1939 when Mr Chamberlain was waving his paper about being an utter mug, and saying that he'd got Mr Hitler in his pocket, with being a Socialist, a libertarian, I couldn't think of anything worse than going in to the British Army and being shot at either by Germans or Japanese. For that first year of the war I was in a reserved occupation as an agricultural trader, in Lincolnshire. I was frightened. I'd never had a fight in my life. I'd had boxing lessons, and anytime anyone smacked me in the nose, I bled. I didn't find any of it attractive. But then Russia changed its mind, I was supposed to be a Socialist and I thought oh well, I was fed up with feeling myself to be outside the pale a bit, because I wasn't telling anybody much that I was a CO, so I rescinded it, in that first year.

Frank was called up on 3 September 1940 and found himself in Burma and in the front line.

I felt with marriage and children I had to become the norm. I was in the RAF, I was a signaller. I used to sit on the big transmitter, sending out messages to the bombers.

Derbyshire-born John Marshall had several major pacifist influences, among them an elderly Quaker and the writings of Aldous Huxley. When granted exemption he was one of the conscientious objectors who, in line with Huxley's idea of constructive pacifism, formed communities to work on the land. Also in the community were some Austrian Jews.

When France fell, Hannah, the fiancée [of one of the Jews], was in utter and total horror and panic. I have never seen anybody in such a state of abject terror. I must have been able to understand why because they must have mentioned the nature of the Gestapo to me in passing although I can never remember them dwelling on it. It was then that I was appalled by my apparent helplessness to help her you see. I didn't know what to say to her and this was when the question of 'to be a pacifist or not a total pacifist' came out in all its stark reality you see. And one of the nicest, the most intelligent and hard-working members of our community, said to me in private, 'The country that gives you the liberty that we've got makes you want to fight for it doesn't it'. Incidentally, this was something that never would have been said in the circle itself, it was said in the grounds outside.

Still an anti-militarist he began to find himself in a dilemma. What could he do now?

We couldn't do anything very much you see, we had taken a certain line of action, to backtrack on it was extremely difficult and in any case we didn't know how the war was going to develop – it hadn't resulted in total destruction. And the general feeling among a number of pacifists that I talked to was well they could only help other people in case of crisis, they couldn't kill anybody else but they might be able to help in some kind of way.

I wasn't disposed to take any quick decisions about it but what hit me even worse than these incidents was the defection of a number of those who had helped us build up our philosophies. And that happened at two levels and led to a great deal of bitterness. I think a feeling of abandonment was probably what delayed me in taking all kinds of decisions. I thought I had been abandoned by virtually everybody.

First of all my Quaker friend who it appeared was not a 100 per cent committed pacifist. After Dunkirk a friend, who had got total exemption, went to see him and got the remarkable reception one morning, 'I expected to see you in uniform.' So my friend, and through him me, felt betrayed by our own people as it were.

The second blow to us was some of the arch intellectuals who provided and stoked up the rational intellectual side of the pacifist movement – Bertrand Russell, and C.E.M. Joad, both virtually recanted following Dunkirk and on top of that Aldous Huxley had cleared off to America where they weren't in the war and it was relatively safe. You see he hadn't even stayed to practise his pacifism in London during the Blitz. So one felt completely abandoned and betrayed.

John was deterred by what he knew about the negative nature of army life, instead he left the relatively convivial pacifist land commune and went to work in forestry in the Lake District.

What unquestionably helped me to make my mind up was the entry of the Soviet Union into the war. I found in a curious way this had affected quite a number of people who weren't communists or necessarily communist supporters, they had felt that this was the crunch, if Hitler beat the Soviet Union then this was it.

I became much more pro-Soviet through reading. But even before that I was increasingly unhappy about my own position, but since I already had a job which was regarded as useful to the war effort – I became more and more oppressed by that too because I realized the ridiculousness of the pacifist position when I was actually part of the war machine even if a very insignificant part of it. My job was actually producing pit props for the mines. I wasn't washing my hands of society, morally, I couldn't detach myself from it. I was doing a job in it, a very arduous one as it happened and rather unpleasant, particularly in winter. So I felt that my position was getting more and more eroded anyway from a personal standpoint. I didn't rush into any decisions.

In January 1942 he joined the Royal Signals Corps.

Conscientious objectors had often found sympathizers among the forces so it is hardly surprising that there were soldiers who changed their minds and became conscientious objectors. Among them was David Spreckley, a career soldier, who was born in 1915. Few conscientious objectors share such an extraordinary background.

My father was an officer in a Gurkha regiment. They sent the Gurkhas to fight in France and as you know the Gurkhas are very good fighters but trench warfare is not their cup of tea so they discovered apparently after about six months that they'd sent several battalions and they were completely wasted, so they shipped them all back again. I was about nine months old then and went on board a troop ship to go home, my father, my mother and a sister of three and myself and a nanny. And I got some kind of a bug or snuffles or something at the last minute and they took me off the troop ship to follow in the next one, and that ship that my family was on was torpedoed and all my family were drowned, so I was adopted by a first cousin once removed and was brought up as their son. They were what I'm afraid you have to call landed gentry, so I was brought up in that kind of environment, I was the only son in a very large house in what is now the stockbroker belt 5 miles north of what was Gatwick racecourse when I knew it, but is now Gatwick Airport and I was a totally spoilt brat. And I was brought up with the standard beliefs that not only everything was right for the world but we were on top of it and it was perfectly right that we should have whatever it was – we had 6 indoor servants, 5 gardeners, 2,000 acres of land, all around and that was the sort of life I was brought up in.

David decided to join the navy and was sent to Dartmouth, but was invalided out with bad eyesight as a teenager.

I had eighteen months to kill between Dartmouth and Sandhurst – at sixteen and a half, and so they said you'd better go off and learn a foreign language and this was one of the best things they ever did for me, thank God, and so I went off to Germany to Dresden, and I lived with a family for nine months. And that was one year before Hitler, and Germany had five million unemployed, five million! That's where I got my first mental kick, until then obviously it wasn't a question of believing, it was a certain knowledge that the British Empire was the most marvellous thing that had ever happened in the world – Britain had never lost any battles and all this sort of stuff and I suddenly found I was talking to people who had slightly different ideas about things. I remember, particularly, we had a very interesting conversation, I started talking about Jutland which I knew of course we had won, the British navy won every battle and they said there was no battle at Jutland, and I said of course, and we discovered they call it Skaggarak – I said that's silly you can't call it Skaggarak we call it Jutland, and they said well we won. Then we sat down and thought how do you decide how anybody wins naval battles, is it the number of ships lost, the tonnage lost, the number of men lost or the strategy or the tactics? Five different ways and we just worked it out, I forget which they were exactly now, but I discovered of those five they had won three and we'd won two.

Modern history books do record the Battle of Jutland in 1916, as a 'draw'. It was the only encounter between the British and German fleets in the First World War. Germany destroyed and crippled more ships but Britain retained control of the North Sea. David's German friends were able to fill in more gaps in his historical knowledge.

They were not Nazis or anything like it, they were Christian Democrats, middle of the road people, but for the first time I'd learnt what the Versailles Treaty had done to them and that of course was something I had never been told at all in my history books. So my mind was beginning to query this sort of awful glass bowl that I was living in.

On his return David took the entrance exam for Sandhurst and to his amazement came out top.

When I got to Sandhurst I found they were incredibly stupid. On one end of the scale you've got the chinless aristocratic wonders who were going in the household brigade of guards and the other end of the scale you've got the hard-working grammar school boys who were going to fight like mad to get a commission in the Light Infantry or some lowly regiment down the bottom but they were all thick as two short planks, so again I began to think something is wrong somewhere.

The regiment was posted to India where David found himself beginning to rebel.

As a second lieutenant I was in charge of thirty men, and I found I had twenty-three Indian servants. That, I thought, was a little odd. And my mind just began to tick and tick but I still was very keen on trying to be a good soldier.

David began to break rules purely on humanitarian grounds – lending his men money, visiting them in hospital when they had venereal disease and grooming his own horse. He also refused to play polo because, he felt, the horses did not enjoy it. Meanwhile, he read A.A. Milne's book *Peace With Honour*, which continued the mental questioning begun by his stay in Germany.

We were put off in Egypt because the Italians were in Abyssinia and we were supposed to be defending the frontiers or something but we didn't actually do anything at all. We pitched camp in a desert outside of Cairo and just spent all our time as usual. A circular came round one day when we were in Egypt from the Army Intelligence Corps, I think it was, asking for volunteers to go on a course, and it said French or German speakers required. I must have been one of the most fluent German speakers in the whole army because none of them spoke any languages at all. So I phoned up the adjutant and said this was surely just the sort of thing I ought to be doing because I do speak fluent German. And he said, 'You're not going on a course, I'm not sending you on a course until you learn to play polo.'

And then we came home, and I phoned up the adjutant and said that I'd like to resign my commission and he practically kissed me on both cheeks he was so glad, which I did, and then I went home to these snob parents of mine, and said I'm off and they virtually threw me out. They didn't cut me off without a penny because there was a certain amount of money which my own real father had left with him which produced an income of three hundred a year, which was enough to live on in those days. So he passed that over to me obviously, and they did virtually say no we can't have any more to do with you.

By that time, I would classify myself as a pacifist so I joined the PPU. This was 1937, I think or 1936, went up to the office and volunteered to do some work in the office. I said I don't want any money because I've got this income to live on, I don't want any more. Dick Sheppard actually gave me a job, not as a volunteer but full time so I became a member of the PPU staff and I was assistant group organizer. I was only twenty-one or twenty-two and I was incredibly naive, politically unaware.

Leslie White was hardly in the first flush of youth when he began to reassess his conscience. Born in 1911, he went to work in a clock-making factory in Leatherhead when war broke out.

I was called up and I didn't register as a CO because I didn't think that my objections were the traditional ones and because I had the impression that it was only those who had religious convictions who would be accepted as COs. As most of the British people I knew were utterly for the war, one would have to appear to be a bit of a crank.

Leslie had shown early signs of non-conformity as a teenager.

When I was about sixteen I remember going on the bus past the Cenotaph and everyone raised their hats and I didn't.

Tim Miles was from a conventional middle-class background, brought up near Darlington by unreligious parents.

One of my memories is my mother bursting into tears about the issue of war and saying I hope there won't ever be another war, and this has stuck in my mind. I must have been about eight at the time. I know in about 1938 or so I was swearing black and blue that I wouldn't take part in any war, quite how I came to change my mind I'm not sure but I went up to Oxford in 1941 and there wasn't anyone to guide you as to what you should or shouldn't do. I'd rather got it into my head that you had to join the Officers Training Corps which was quite harmless – you had a play at being soldiers – and it was only when the time at Oxford was due to come to an end in 1942 that I suddenly thought what am I doing, is this really right? With some hesitation I decided that it was, and I went to train as an army officer at the end of 1942. A rather weak compromise was that I was in anti-aircraft which was defending people against things,

which was a rather bad argument I think. Of course a lot of
the things you do you're just playing at soldiers – not doing
any harm to anybody.

In 1940 Leslie White, who was also not a religious man, was
called up into the Royal Army Ordnance Corps. He saw the
training and drill somewhat differently.

The job involved things like getting provisions to
the troops, but in the first couple of months we were
training as ordinary soldiers, how to kill people and do
all sorts of horrible things. After that we went to Derby
to the big camp there and then we were made into the
REME (Royal Electrical and Mechanical Engineers) and
did work in general stores and instruments and what
not. I used to go to the public library and look at the
newspapers and there to my surprise among them was
Peace News and I looked at that and I saw the address
of the Central Board for Conscientious Objectors in
Endsleigh Street.

He was posted to Oswestry and promoted to the rank of
sergeant. But this model soldier was soon to shock his
commanding officer.

Several things were troubling me. It was the most
beautiful summer's evening and I had walked to a field
just outside Oswestry and I was just lying back and
enjoying the peace of it all when aeroplanes started
coming over, coming from around Shrewsbury where
there were large airfields and there were dozens and
dozens, hundreds going out to drop their bombs on
Germany. That was the last straw. When I was on leave
next time I went in to the Central Board for Conscientious
Objectors. I sent a note to my commanding officer and
they were astounded by it because I had been a good
soldier. The thing was, I was prepared to do things which
would help the nation, things of national importance, and
I was not prepared to do the killing, I was trained to do
the killing and I felt that I'd been skulking behind the
uniform long enough. I think I would have felt pretty
awful if I hadn't made the decision.

Many COs had a network of friends who had also registered, but Leslie was the only one among his acquaintances at the time.

> I was expecting to have no end of bother when I said I wouldn't do any more service. The first consequence was that a policeman arrived at the door. The policeman told me to go back to camp and he'd pretend he hadn't seen me and say I hadn't been at home. I would have been AWOL. He didn't realize that I didn't intend to go back. Next thing was two soldiers arrived, a corporal and a private to escort me back to Oswestry and when I got there and I saw the sergeant major they told me to help out in the cookhouse.
>
> A lot of the other soldiers understood and said they'd like to do the same thing. There had been about a dozen others before me who'd done it and I'd read about them in *Peace News*.
>
> I was called in by the captain and asked why I wouldn't carry on because I was in a corps and not in a fighting unit. He gave me the order to go back to my post and carry on with my duties. I refused and he told me I would be court martialled and go to a military prison and he told me it was tough. I said I thought that it was only the Germans who behaved like that.

Lieutenant Tim Miles was posted out to the Middle East where, even in defence, he found he was having qualms at giving men the order to fire.

> On one occasion when I was in the air defence of Alexandria, and I gave the order to fire, as far as I know nothing happened and I don't think the aircraft was ever shot down or anything but certainly I remember that because it's a decisive point. The fact that I do remember it is a measure of my unease, I don't say I was moved to cancel that order to fire, but I did think, well I've committed myself now and I was defending a city. I don't remember thinking I hope to goodness they get away. I remember it as a point that I'd given an order which could result in somebody being killed.

In 1944 Tim was transferred from his defensive anti-aircraft unit to an infantry regiment.

And this, of course, was quite a different story, we got to stick bayonets in people and all the rest. I suppose doubts were mounting, this was towards the end of 1944, and we'd gone over to Italy by then, this was the crunch time. There'd been a thing called the Cairo Parliament, this was a foretaste of the rather left-wing views that were predominant after the war and I had the job of distributing pay to a number of soldiers. And the corporal who was assisting me, we somehow got talking, and it transpired that he was a really rabid communist, he'd been involved with the Cairo Parliament and was horrified that apparently some authorities had closed it down which shows how persecuting they are. Then we got talking and I was talking about my interest in philosophy. I mean you didn't meet many people with any sort of intellectual approach, so I was glad to talk to him. And I'd been talking about philosophy and works of Socrates or someone and he said, 'Well yes, that's all very well but you're just waiting until everybody is just like Socrates and you'll have to wait a jolly long time.' And just as we had finished the job of paying people, he suddenly said to me, 'Tell me, honestly, do you really support the war?' And he didn't. This was 1944, there was a policy of unconditional surrender which was ghastly. I just murmured the cliches about, well you've got to resist when people are evil and we parted and I haven't seen the chap since that day, he doesn't know what he set off, but I knew, at the moment he'd said that, 'There we are, you've got to answer that.'

Within a few weeks his answer to the question was clear and he had decided to resign his commission. But the troops were sent off to intervene in the Greek Civil War – a posting which confirmed his decision, so he went to his commanding officer.

And he was totally baffled by that, he wasn't an unkind man or anything but he was totally baffled and sent me on to the next man in the hierarchy who was a brigadier, and I think he was rather baffled too and sent me on to the next chap above. My thinking was that if it really was necessary at all to resist evil in the form of Hitler, it certainly wasn't necessary to insist on unconditional surrender.

Tim Miles was sent home and allowed to resign his commission. He went through the tribunal system, and eventually on appeal was granted exemption and allowed to return to Oxford. Leslie White had to go through a court martial before he was allowed to leave the army.

My grounds for objection were that war was such a wicked crime against humanity and in particular against the civilian population and it was contrary to my nature and to my understanding and I would not have any part in it. I didn't invoke God or Christ or anybody else. My barrister told me to get them to accept that I was a good natured sort of crank. There were some very belligerent COs who didn't do the cause much good.

He was sentenced to three months imprisonment entitling him to go to a civilian rather than military prison. He appeared before a tribunal and was discharged from the army. The tribunal allowed him to continue as a watch-maker on condition that he did voluntary work as an ARP warden.

I thought the shop window would be smashed in. I put up posters on the wall – one which the PPU had produced, 'Wars will cease when men refuse to fight.' I still had customers, no one commented. The Canadian army was stationed nearby. I think I was extremely frightened, I was prepared for all sorts of brick bats. People used to say, 'I don't know how you can mend watches with bombs falling'. I said, 'I couldn't stop them nor could those who are dead'. People didn't seem to have any qualms about those who had cushy jobs and were making millions out of the war.

CHAPTER 21

Hindsight

*The pain of being a conscientious objector was the increasing
knowledge of the enormity of what the Germans were doing.
So that was really the challenging thing, not the war, so
much as how can one justify not somehow trying to do
something about it.*

David Jones

In 1945 peace was signed six years after it had been shattered.
But as the relieving armies moved through continental Europe
that summer the true extent of the damage became apparent.

Stephen Peet was in a prisoner of war camp in early 1945.
Despite his pedigree of conscientious objection, as the son of a
First World War CO, he had struggled with his conscience for
much of the time he served with the Friends Ambulance Unit.

There were quite a number of people who'd joined the
FAU and others who I met who were COs, who really
had to fight and work out their beliefs and fight for the
right. In my case I felt I'd walked into it too easily. I was so
immature I don't know whether I could have worked out
the moral feelings and been able to state them for a tribunal
in a convincing way.

I do remember in a prisoner of war camp which was
about 30 miles from Dresden being there in February 1945
when planes came over, and in the distance there was an
awful amount of explosions. And it went on hour after
hour after hour and in this camp, when the planes went
over in daylight quite low, there was quite an amount of
excitement and cheering when they saw the markings on
the planes, but as the hours went by and the noise went on,

bombing and bombing and bombing, pretty well everyone went silent with a kind of a shock wondering what on earth was happening and I remember then thinking, this is the moment when I truly feel for the first time that I can honestly say with complete conviction I'm a pacifist.

Even fifty years after the decision to register as conscientious objectors, faith in the rightness of that decision can be shaken. Ken Shaw is one of the many who still question and probe their consciences today.

Three years ago I went for the first time to Amsterdam in Holland, and naturally we went to Anna Frank's house. And when I saw what that child had gone through and what her fate was, I felt that, well maybe I was quite wrong and I did have misgivings, and you're bound to have them because what in the end was the answer to the dreadful things that Hitler did? It's difficult to say. And it was in Anna Frank's house that I, for the very first time, had grave misgivings about whether I'd done the right thing or not and I told my wife and son this. Unknown to me they bought me a copy of her diary, although I'd got the paperback copy they bought the hardback, and they'd inscribed it, 'Dad, we think you were right', and that encouraged me to think that maybe I was right – although it's no satisfaction to even consider whether you're right or not in that situation, you do what you feel you have to do. I did what I felt I had to do then and I feel pretty sure I'd do the same the next time.

David Jones did relief work with victims of the Blitz in Bristol and Liverpool.

I've always had this kind of question in my mind as to if one had been more aware of what had been happening in Germany in the camps, the Jewish extermination, as to what one would have done then. I still don't know what the answer would be, if I'd known.

The knowledge that comes with hindsight also made Yorkshireman Frank Chadwick question his conscience.

Possibly if I'd have known at the beginning of the war all about the Jews, the Holocaust and all about the other things he was doing I might not have been a CO. It was touch and go, but the fact that I didn't know that, and the fact that I didn't know that God was working in my life, was another factor, so by and large when I came to a knowledge of God I then knew that I'd done the right thing.

It is the Holocaust which is the stumbling block for many COs when they examine their consciences, among them Cecil Davies.

Wilfred Owen said he was a conscientious objector with a bad conscience, and I think lots of COs often had a bad conscience, and while I still think I was right to do what I did when I did I suppose if I had known about the Holocaust it might have been different. And there were many times during the war when one asked oneself whether one was doing the right thing. Today I'm a member of the CND, and sometimes when I read about what the Japanese did to prisoners of war or what the Japanese are doing to the Chinese I have this guilty feeling, 'Well when's this atom bomb going to drop?' Life isn't simple.

During the war, Cecil was confirmed in his views by a visit from a friend in the forces, Roland Jones.

Roland Jones, now in the forces, comes to tea and he talks quite a bit about his training and so on, swimming across estuaries in full kit and so on. But Roland came to see us and I think this is something that made an enormous impression on me, made me feel again that I was right. He was obviously trying to shock us. He said, 'Do you know the best way to silence a sentry?' So I said, 'Oh shoot him I suppose.' He said, 'No, put a bayonet in one ear till it comes out the other.' I knew I was right. I couldn't have done otherwise.

John Marshall, who joined the forces after his conversion to communism in 1942, points out that while we now have the benefit of hindsight, before the war little was known about the atrocities which accompanied Hitler's Third Reich.

We had heard of concentration camps, but remember that the British Government itself did not release details of them until the war had started. It was the left-wing elements who drew attention to the concentration camps. The pacifist attitude was – amongst people that I knew – 'yes these things are dreadful and shocking and if we are to be genuine pacifists we are going to probably have to face the fact we may be done over by the Gestapo ourselves'. This was one thing we did face up to morally. We accepted them but maintained that horrible though they were they were less serious than the totally destructive nature of war. . . . And remember the First World War even now creates a horrifying picture to us doesn't it – life in the trenches and so on. Well we assumed it was going to be worse. We assumed it would be Armageddon utterly and completely. Almost as we now think about nuclear warfare. This is the point to remember, it was not that we wanted to capitulate to Nazism, it wasn't that. We thought that even Nazism was the lesser of two evils.

Bill Nightingale had also been a pacifist and registered as a conscientious objector, but was propelled into the forces by the retreat from Dunkirk. While serving in a now defeated Germany at the end of the war he had dinner with German friends.

He said, 'I do hope that you in England have realized that you must never again trust the Germans, if you don't do it for your sake, do it for ours, because we are a stupid people. If somebody comes up and promises us that we can conquer the world we will believe them and we will follow them completely until once again we are defeated, so if you take British soldiers off German soil it will be your own fault if you win another war, and we lose again, but for our sakes I hope you won't'. So that has always been something I've remembered. Then of course with the discovery of the concentration camps . . . .

I had known right from the start that I had made a decision that I could live with as far as my conscience was concerned. Those sort of things only reinforce the fact that sad and unnecessary as war is, one must do everything to try and prevent it, and that does mean keeping your goods and strength. A strong man regards his goods and I think it is true in this world pacifism is a wonderful ideal and I think Christ was a pacifist but I don't think necessarily it is better to take prevention than cure and I think we should always have a strong army.

Alan Litherland had turned down a job as an industrial chemist, because when war came he would have been involved in the manufacture of explosives. He went to prison for his stand.

I don't remember ever feeling guilty, perhaps I ought to have done, I don't think I was. Maybe because I knew that if I hadn't been a CO I wouldn't have been in the war anyway, but I don't think that influenced it. I think I was so determined that I was right that I didn't have those kinds of thoughts.

Aubrey Brocklehurst also went to prison. He had been in a reserved occupation.

Although my religious views have changed a little bit over the years I've never regretted the stand I took, no I've always felt I did the right thing, and this one thing in my life I feel I did right. There's lots of other things I haven't been successful with and I've disappointed myself in things I haven't done and situations I failed to rise to, but this I've always been pleased I did, if I hadn't done it I would have been a miserable man for the rest of my life. So I'm always very pleased that I took this line. I felt it was the right thing and I still feel it was the right thing.

In later life one of Aubrey's sons queried his stand.

I think once one of them said he thought it was an easy way out to be a CO but he didn't know what he was talking about, it wasn't an easy way out at all. I would much rather have faced military service and the front line than face hostile public opinion quite honestly, and this was the big penalty that you paid for taking this stand, people would not understand and say, 'You were a coward, you're just dodging a dangerous, possibly life-threatening situation and that you were just running away from it'. But whether there were any men who took the conscientious objection line who were like that I rather doubt it; there may have been the odd one but most of them were quite sincere. I would say it's much easier to face military service than face hostile public misunderstanding. I mean a few people misunderstood but most people were supportive I found in the Second World War.

Tony White was one of those who put his life in danger by volunteering for bomb disposal. After the war he became a member of Christian CND, and had no doubts about his own decision as a pacifist.

I wouldn't claim, necessarily, that we are right, all I can do is try and understand and interpret what I understand of the Christian Gospel and the nature of God and all we talk about in church about the nature of God and offering the other cheek and so on which is the last thing we do in war, so much of it is a nonsense. But the reality is that love is the greatest force, that war proves nothing, cures nothing, solves nothing and we're seeing that over and over, we keep saying this in every generation.

The fact remains that if we are prepared to try and live out what we believe, what I believe to be a Christian way of life, then we put ourselves at risk. The big dilemma was putting your wife also at risk, or great disadvantage anyway, when you take a particular view like that in war. But we talk about 'hammering our swords into plough shares', singing the hymn with great effect, but we don't believe it, we're not prepared to melt our swords, or our atomic weapons, but it's an act of faith which you can't make anybody have, you can only come to through your own thinking, your own believing.

I love my country, I reckon I've served it in all the various things I do in youth service and so on. I went into teaching, and the police, and the youth and the scouts work – when people came to the war and thought they were being patriotic because they joined up, they'd done sweet f.a. for the community until then, and many of them very little since, that was the one thing, the war situation absolved them not altogether voluntarily.

In 1946 demobilization followed for combatant and non-combatant forces alike. Conscientious objectors in alternative service were also released and resumed normal life. Frank Chadwick went back to work as a French polisher.

> I don't know that I ever felt guilty, but I did occasionally feel out of it. With retrospect you obviously felt out of things when all these people were talking about having brought down Hitler, which was part of the war's object.

Walter Wright, the only conscientious objector at the two fire stations he served in, also felt isolated.

> Yes I did, I think probably that was the hardest part of it, harder than bearing the many insults, and ill feeling that was shown, I think the feeling of isolation was stronger I think and harder to bear than the other things. Then of course there was the fact that at that time I was single and very much liked to have a close girl friend but you felt so limited in that way because nearly all the girls around, or those that you would like to be friendly with, they were all going for the soldiers and the airmen and such like, so there was that as well.

A whole generation of young men and women who lived through both world wars lost their youth and the freedom which accompanies that. Edward Blishen was alone among his close friends in becoming a conscientious objector.

> My best friend wrote me a letter just before the war broke out, and we were discussing what we were going to do when the war broke out and he said, 'I can't tell you at the moment what I shall do but I believe that certain things will prevail with me and among them will be the desire to join in the experience of my generation.' And I think I understand exactly what that man meant. To have excluded yourself from this enormous general experience was painful and did leave a sense of having missed out, a very curious sense of not being there. I mean it's got nothing really to do with whether you would have wanted to fight or not fight, there's a sense in which by your action you excluded yourself from common experience

which is not an easy thing to do and not an easy thing to think about afterwards.

All my combatant friends have all been enormously sympathetic, always were, but I always felt towards them a sense that I ought to have known what was happening, or ought to have been part of what had happened. And I wasn't part of what was happening to them.

I suppose all experiences in war counted as common experiences actually, and of course the pacifists by the nature of things were not excluded from the war at all – I mean I lived mostly near London throughout the war and you were not excluded from the war by any means. Those who lived in London were very much in the war – of course you weren't on a battlefield, you weren't in Africa, you weren't in France, you weren't in Burma, but you were in England which was quite a tough place to be at the time.

Dennis Waters had been beaten up by NCOs during his time with the Non-Combatant Corps.

Being in military hands and being beaten up and so on was very unpleasant, but the long term effect of being despised by ones contemporaries – if you haven't actually been through it yourself – you do not actually realize what a depressing thing this can be. Admittedly, I had help from my family because, although they disassociated themselves from my views, they understood that they were sincere views and of course they stood by and I mean my elder brother who was an army officer himself was absolutely appalled when he heard the treatment that I'd had at Ilfracombe. I would say that the social ostracism was as bad as anything.

I did receive white feathers through the post and I did have the unpleasant shock of several of my friends disowning me more or less, but on the other hand of course I met some splendid sterling characters that I would not otherwise have come across.

One thought so differently one tended to disassociate oneself from all these national movements like the melting down of aluminium and pots and pans. It all seemed a bit hollow in a way and one felt perfectly convinced that it wasn't gong to happen anyway. It's all part and parcel of this syndrome that you are not as other people, and it's a very uncomfortable feeling. One likes to feel one is a member of one's peer group, it's as simple as that and if you are not it is most uncomfortable and you've got to come to terms with it. It's not a pleasant sensation and I wouldn't like to have to do it again. I don't do any tub thumping about that, I don't wish to be a martyr at all, one doesn't like doing this sort of thing, but there are times when one has this categorical imperative, 'No I won't do that'. I had it then and I hope I'll always be able to have it.

Sidney Renow, another member of the Non-Combatant Corps, remembers feeling guilt.

Yes, because a number of the men did transfer to the combatant forces. You did feel that other men were out putting their lives on the line fighting, and here we were relatively comfortable without much danger, except sometimes when we had to go out to repair bombed lines or as in Bristol in the air raids.

Ken Shaw remembers one of the philosophical discussions held in his NCC unit during the war.

When it came to the actual crunch, some of us questioned whether we really had the guts to stand up, as some people in Germany had to – they either joined the army or they would have been shot – whether we would have been strong enough to do that. Many expressed doubts, and that could only have been tested when the moment came, and how I would react to that I don't know. I think the chances are I would have gone (into the army), not being a very brave person, and I think that was fairly common amongst the rest, saying well in that case we'd have to go. But this doesn't mean to say that 'conchies' really are cowards, although there's a fearful streak in all of us of course.

Ex-cavalry officer turned anarchist David Spreckley courted death by remaining on the streets during the Blitz. Would he have been prepared to die for his conscience?

I think the answer is yes I would. I think judging by my mentality at the time, particularly as we had a kamikaze sort of feeling, which was why we went down to the Blitz, refusing to go in an air-raid shelter.

Alan Litherland became Chairman of the Fellowship of Reconciliation and an active member of CND in the years after the Second World War. Would he have been prepared to die for his beliefs?

I don't think I'd worked it out but theoretically I knew what I should have done which is to go all the way, in other words whatever happens to refuse to carry a gun or shoot anybody or take any military act which some people did. Particularly during the First World War, many COs were in fact forced into the armed forces and they had to either shoot or be shot, in some cases, not many. There had been a considerable change in the way COs were treated – they were treated much less brutally in the second than in the first, so we had the example of COs in the First World War to know what it might mean, and we just hoped that if that occasion arose we would be able to stand by our principles – but of course you can never tell in advance what you would be able to stand up to.

I think I would have gone through with whatever was necessary, at least for quite a long way. Whether I could have stuck it out to the end I simply can't say.

Ernest Lenderyou was a political objector who served a prison sentence before joining the fire service.

Let me clear out of the way any charge that my reaction to the war situation was one of cowardice or, less forthrightly, that I retreated from or turned my back on the crisis situation. I was in a reserved occupation, and would, I think, have been rejected had I volunteered for military service of any kind. Both the other three COs working with me, all of whom were given conditional or unconditional exemption from call-up, and the majority of my fellow workers who loyally supported the war effort (including one belligerent patriot who made it his special job to hound the 'conchies' in any way he could devise even at cost, in terms of his and their time, to the war effort), saw out the war years in the relative shelter of the laboratory.

Len Bird, who served three prison sentences, is also unrepentant.

I would do it again. When I was coming out of prison the first time, one of the senior officers was talking to a few of us and he turned to me and said, 'Do you feel any different now to what you felt when you first came in?' And I said, 'Yes, I do.' And he slapped his thigh and said, 'There you are, I knew we altered you. How different do you feel?' And I remember saying, 'When I came in I *thought* I was right, now I *know* I was.' Which of course wasn't exactly the answer he was waiting for. My only feeling now is I wouldn't go to a tribunal again because I think judging someone as a conscientious objector is an impossible task, you can only apply a very rule of thumb method, you can really only judge how bound up a person's been in working for a peace society. Now most young people of eighteen, nineteen, twenty and so on can't be expected to have very much experience in that direction. But it seems to me that people generally have got to realize that war just has no place in modern society. We've given up duelling, at least we have in most countries, we don't hang people here for murder and so on, and I think that people generally the world over have got to recognize there's no place for war. There are other methods of solving your difficulties. We don't go punching our neighbour on the nose because he doesn't do what we think he ought to do.

Ronald Rice is another conscientious objector who is still just as convinced of the rightness of pacifism.

The illogicality of young men, hundreds or millions of young men from different countries slaughtering each other, when if they'd met normally in peacetime they'd have been perfectly good friends. I feel that this problem is still with us. If you ask me now whether in the present circumstances or in the latter part of the last war I had a feeling of guilt that I hadn't joined in with the rest in preventing a despot spreading over Europe, or in the circumstances of the Gulf War, would I feel guilty, I would say, yes, I do have times when that side of it comes up, but I would feel just as guilty if I hadn't made this stand. A Hitler or a Saddam or an Alexander the Great or a Napoleon, they have no power of their own, they could hardly lift a cannon, they certainly couldn't load a bomb under a rack of a plane's wing, they only have their power because people obey them; if they didn't obey them, they could only be an ordinary common little criminal in the police court. It is the power of the military code of obedience which gives these individuals their enormous scope for power and therefore if the species of someone who refused all military ways became an extinct species it would be wrong. That idea must be kept alive even if it's an extreme. Just as people who don't drink at all are a good example to people who just drink a bit, and people who are vegetarians now are quite a good example in the present ecology. I feel now that in between the two we're working towards a position where people could have a conscientious *discretion* as much as objection, a conscientious discretion as to what they will accept orders to fight for and to kill for.

David Spreckley, a full-time worker in the Peace Pledge Union both before and during the war, doubts whether conscientious objectors achieved anything concrete.

From my own personal point of view the most positive thing I ever did was saving the lives of thirty Jews, that was positive, and that was before the war, but during the war, no we didn't have an effect, I'm afraid, that's where I think we, the PPU, failed badly. We should have pushed this business of finding the good Germans much more than we did.

The only thing it did do is maintain a principle. And of course compared with the First World War there were many more of us, so to that extent and for the fact that CND grew out of it and the Fellowship of Reconciliation got stronger and the other organizations like that, and pacifist influence in the churches I think are stronger, perhaps not in the Church of England but the rest of them, yes, it's built up there.

In 1953 actor Meredith Edwards played a Welsh soldier in the film *Dunkirk*. Even taking the part pricked his conscience.

> This bloody conscience has been with me all my life. 'For God's sake don't be so self righteous,' I keep saying to myself. Well, acting was more difficult to get jobs in then than it is now, and I went to the director Charles Friend, I said, 'I can't, it's a war film.' He said, 'I promise you I'll make it as anti-war as I can.' And whether I was salving my conscience again but I did manage to get one sentence in that, which helped salve my conscience, and it was in Welsh, when I'm dying in the orchard, I said, 'Oh mam, this terrible war, why do we?' Now you might think this is silly, and the director said, 'Who the hell can understand that?' I said, 'You'd be surprised.' When I've been on holiday, it's amazing how many people have come to me and said, 'We knew what you said.'
>
> But you see I had a discussion with an old friend of mine, fine actor, Hugh Griffith, he got an Oscar for *Ben Hur*, he and his wife had a discussion about this and I was worried and she said, 'Look if you were playing Danny in *A Night Must Fall*, a murderer, you wouldn't think twice about doing it, your function as an actor is to portray the part that you are given.' I still toy with it. I don't know. But there are facets about things which are not war which you have to decide. We come back to this again, this conscience thing pricking at you all the time.

Most conscientious objectors have remained pacifists and many have continued to work for peace. Every year at the eleventh hour on the eleventh day we remember those who died in both world wars. For Walter Wright, Remembrance Day still arouses some conflicting feelings.

> I can go along with the ceremonies in so far as they consist of mourning the losses of life and the injuries suffered by those who 'fought for their country' – I willingly take part in half-muffled bell-ringing on these occasions – but I jib at the idea of being 'grateful' to those who 'gave their lives that I may be free!' For one thing, I did not ask them to do it, would much have preferred that they didn't, and would have been prepared to take the

consequences of their not doing it; no one can really say what those consequences would have been.

I think that COs should go along with Remembrance Day activities as much as they can, and I deplore anything that separates us unnecessarily from the general populace – for example I very much dislike the white poppy campaign – I feel that red poppies, traditionally associated with Flanders Fields are a perfectly legitimate way of commemorating the evils of war.

I do feel a little isolated at Remembrance time. There is a general expression of honour and respect to those who were in the forces, and I am of course unable to share in this. It is not that I feel any sense of guilt – I still feel that the line I took was right, and I would do the same again if necessary. This is not to say that I have a closed mind on the subject – I think I honestly do my best to appreciate the arguments on the other side (which can be quite strong) but even if I occasionally waver I become more and more convinced, as time goes on, that non-participation in war is the right course.

Cedric Smith became less convinced in the postwar period of the rightness of pacifism. Then he discovered that a fellow Cambridge graduate had worked at Bletchley in decoding Enigma – work that is widely accepted as having turned the tide of war. Even while he was Treasurer of the Friends Peace Committee he found his doubts increased.

I found out that some of the confident assertions made in pacifist literature proved to be wide of the mark. It was said that the deliberate brutalization of conscripts would result after the war in a brutal set of criminals. It did not: the world returned to a reasonably normal peaceful existence. It was said that the fighting during the war would leave an enduring legacy of hatred. On the contrary, whereas the French and the Germans had been very suspicious of each other before the war, and had fought bitterly during the war, afterwards they began to co-operate to build the foundations of a new united Europe. Standard pacifist thought had it that war was the greatest of all possible evils. But there were many other horrors in the world – such as the killing of hundreds of thousands by nasty dictators. If war was the greatest of all possible evils, why was it that ordinary citizens would occasionally be willing to fight for freedom at the risk of their lives?

Whatever the rights or wrongs of their stand Ernest Lenderyou argues that conscientious objectors played an important role in a wartime democracy.

At the very least I would argue that it was valuable to have in time of war dissidents who were prepared to speak out in defence of their principles and in defiance of authority. Every nation or group tends to become to some degree more totalitarian when conducting a war, and most people at such a time find it more difficult to question the official conduct of affairs. I would never suggest that only members of the Independent Labour Party, pacifists or conscientious objectors were prepared during the war to question the conduct of the war by the politico/military machine. To mention but one example, Aneurin Bevan's was a critical voice in Parliament, and a number of churchmen protested against operations such as the mass bombing of the civilian populations. But, although in a sense it was easier for opponents of the war to speak out (though less likely that they would be heeded), I think that in some measure they were able to contribute to the maintenance of sanity and humanity in public life.

Further Reading

Boulton, David, *Objection Overruled*, MacGibbon & Kee Ltd, 1967

Catchpool, Corder, *On Two Fronts*, 1918

Davies, Tegla, *Friends Ambulance Unit A*, George Allen & Unwin Ltd, 1947

Hayes, Denis, *Challenge of Conscience*, George Allen & Unwin, 1949

Moorehead, Caroline, *Troublesome People – Enemies of War 1916–1986*, Hamish Hamilton Ltd, 1987

The grim reality of prison life.